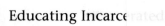 

Educating Incarce

Educating Incarcerated Youth

Exploring the Impact of Relationships, Expectations, Resources and Accountability

Lynette N. Tannis
Education Consultant, USA

First published 2014 by
PALGRAVE MACMILLAN

Palgrave Macmillan in the UK is an imprint of Macmillan Publishers Limited,
registered in England, company number 785998, of Houndmills, Basingstoke,
Hampshire RG21 6XS.

Palgrave Macmillan in the US is a division of St Martin's Press LLC,
175 Fifth Avenue, New York, NY 10010.

Palgrave Macmillan is the global academic imprint of the above companies
and has companies and representatives throughout the world.

Palgrave® and Macmillan® are registered trademarks in the United States,
the United Kingdom, Europe and other countries

ISBN: 978-1-137-45101-9

This book is printed on paper suitable for recycling and made from fully
managed and sustained forest sources. Logging, pulping and manufacturing
processes are expected to conform to the environmental regulations of the
country of origin.

A catalogue record for this book is available from the British Library.

A catalog record for this book is available from the Library of Congress.

Tannis, Lynette.
  Educating incarcerated youth : exploring the impact of relationships, expectations,
resources and accountability / by Lynette Tannis, Education Consultant, USA.
    pages cm
  Summary: "What happens to school age children when they become incarcerated?
Although juvenile justice courts were established in the US more than one hundred
years ago, there has been very little research on the provision and quality of education
programs in juvenile justice facilities. This book is the first to provide an inside look on the
perspectives and practices of juvenile justice principals and teachers. Exploring a range of
educational facilities in the US, Tannis argues that educational programmes characterized
by strong relationships, high expectations, appropriate resources and an effective
accountability system equate to the strongest possible learning environments for
incarcerated youth. The book seeks to identify the support structures in place for juvenile
justice educators and examine the quality of educational and vocational programmes
in confined settings, to reveal the best ways in which to provide for incarcerated young
people and prepare them for their transition back into society"— Provided by publisher.
  ISBN 978-1-137-45101-9 (hardback)
  1. Juvenile delinquents—Education—United States. 2. Juvenile delinquents—
Rehabilitation—United States. I. Title.
  HV9081.T36 2014
  365'.66608350973—dc23
                                                                    2014026277

Transferred to Digital Printing in 2015

This book is dedicated to my mom and dad, who instilled a love for God and a passion for education. Your sacrifices and persistence helped ensure that I received a high-quality education and heightened my desire to ensure that all children—free or incarcerated—are exposed to a high-quality educational program every day.

Contents

List of Tables and Figure

Tables

Figure

Preface

Few people have any sympathy for someone who commits a crime. The laws are clear, so why should we help those who have violated the law? There has long been a debate whether criminals should be punished or rehabilitated. The reality is that most of the world's criminals are not serving life sentences. This means that they will return to one of our many communities. So here's the next question: because the majority of those who are incarcerated will at some point return to society, wouldn't we want them to be better off, better educated, better equipped, and more responsible citizens?

While some work has been done at the adult prisons to ensure inmates are exposed to educational and vocational programs, far less attention has been given to our nation's incarcerated youth. I've seen children as young as 12 years old in some facilities. These youth will be confined for 6 months to 2 years, and some even longer. Within the United States, approximately $241 per day is spent to house and care for an incarcerated youth.[1] With these resources, it's a societal imperative to ensure that these youth are also properly educated and able to learn a vocation so that when they transition out of incarceration, they can make positive contributions to society.

There are so many components that must be addressed. Students worldwide should be exposed to a high-quality education no matter what they look like or where they live. This should be in place for each student, every day. Many of our communities need additional resources and support structures in place to ensure quality schools with school leaders and teachers who are willing and able to provide such education.

I recently had a conversation with a prison officer in Trinidad who respectfully disagreed with my mission of ensuring all incarcerated youth receive a high-quality education. Although he shared that he understood my point, especially since the youth would be returning to their communities, as a prison officer in the maximum-security prison for adult male inmates, he was almost repulsed at the thought that they could be given the opportunity to earn a college degree for free while being locked up. He always wanted to attend college but grew up in a home where it was very difficult to make ends meet, so college was never a part of the equation. I think that is a crime: all those who truly want a college education should be provided with the means and opportunity to receive one. So many things need to change.

We also need to have more opportunities for all children and adults, no matter what they look like or where they live, to be gainfully employed. We need to ensure that laws and biases that currently exist, which have led to the incarceration of a disproportionate amount of people of color, are reviewed and changed. The necessary social services must also be in place so that our facilities are also not overpopulated with students with special needs. All of these are valid, and it is my hope that researchers, practitioners, and policy makers focus on these areas to ensure that every child in the world has an equal and equitable opportunity to be great—to be all that he or she can be, fully challenged and supported to achieve their maximum potential.

In the meantime, my focus for the past five years has been to ensure our nation's incarcerated youth receive the high-quality education they deserve while they are confined. If education truly is the key, we must use this key to open doors to educational opportunities so that our children can improve their own lives and society. Currently only 65 percent of our nation's juvenile facilities offer an educational program for all of their incarcerated youth.[2] This would be a crime if these children were "free." Juvenile justice implies justice, but these statistics reveal an appalling injustice.

While working on my doctor of education degree at the Harvard Graduate School of Education, I began exploring this topic. I realized that many people weren't even aware that schooling was provided for incarcerated youth, and very few studies were done to explore this topic of juvenile justice education. As I learned about these atrocities, I was compelled to make this my charge, my mission.

I realized, however, that it was important for me to look at this issue at a systems level, versus one facility or even a few classrooms. It's easy to draw conclusions when visiting schools. One could walk into a classroom and see students with their heads down and wonder why the lesson lacked engagement. Looking at the bigger picture—the bird's-eye view—allows one to collect other forms of data, like the support or lack thereof from the school district and the unrealistic demands and expectations placed on the principal, which further trickles down and cripples the educators and the students. It is with this lens that I present this book. I started as an elementary classroom teacher in 1995 and served in various capacities since then, including high school athletic coach, literacy coordinator, vice principal, principal, and intern superintendent. Additionally, since graduating with my doctorate in May 2013, I have had the opportunity to spend additional time in facilities throughout the United States and internationally and have witnessed firsthand some of the exact issues addressed within the four case studies presented.

After spending time in four Florida residential facilities, interviewing each principal and two to three teachers at each site, and spending an additional two days at three facilities to observe the classroom instruction, treatment team meetings, and educational staff meetings, I compiled and analyzed my data, which revealed four major themes: educational programs characterized by strong relationships, high expectations, appropriate resources, and an effective accountability system equated to the provision of a higher quality of instruction, more students on task, and fewer disruptions occurring within the incarcerated students' learning environments (see Table 6). While these four themes are familiar in other contexts (particularly in urban education, highlighted in Charles M. Payne's *So Much Reform, So Little Change*[3] and Brian D. Schultz's *Spectacular Things Happen Along the Way: Lessons from an Urban Classroom*[4]), this is the first study within a juvenile justice educational setting where these four themes emerged from the data collected. This context provides unique challenges, including safety and security issues and a significant proportion of disenfranchised youth.

I recently had a conversation with an educator from Illinois who attended a leadership institute at the Harvard Graduate School of Education. After learning about my work, she approached me eagerly. Excited about my work with incarcerated youth, she asked, "What program do you recommend?" While I was delighted to discuss my work, I immediately told her that my work is not about recommending any program, and this is also what I submit to you through this book. It is my hope that policy makers, researchers, practitioners, community activists, business leaders, parents, attorneys, and others will thoroughly read this book and ensure the necessary structures are in place that will (1) ensure all of the United States' facilities and facilities worldwide offer incarcerated youth an educational program and (2) assess, analyze and strengthen the relationships, expectations, resources and accountability structures within these facilities to ensure every confined youth is exposed to a high-quality education each and every day, without excuses or exceptions.

This book is divided into 8 chapters. **Chapter 1** begins with an introduction highlighting the lack of scholarly research in the area of juvenile justice education conducted to date.

Chapter 2 presents a contextual setting on America's incarcerated youth. Specifically, it includes the demographic data of our nation's incarcerated youth, a historical overview of our nation's juvenile justice system, data on America's juvenile justice facilities, the educational services provided for our nation's incarcerated youth, funding provided to rehabilitate America's incarcerated youth, our nation's accountability system for juvenile justice facilities, and finally, promising juvenile justice educational programs and practices in America.

For the purpose of this study, I chose to narrow my focus on a smaller subset of juvenile facilities and selected the state of Florida to research because of its quality assurance process and the ratings for each juvenile justice facility's education programs. For this reason, a contextual framework on Florida's incarcerated youth is also included in this section. This contextual framework includes demographic data of Florida's incarcerated youth, a description of Florida's juvenile justice reform (including a discussion of the landmark case *Bobby M. v. Chiles*, 907 F.Supp. 368 (N.D.Fla. 1995)), an explanation of the accountability structure for Florida's juvenile justice facilities, an overview of Florida's juvenile justice facilities and funding provided for Florida's juvenile justice facilities, and lastly, a description of the educational services provided for Florida's incarcerated youth.

In **Chapters 3 through 6**, I discuss the four Florida juvenile justice residential facilities where I conducted my research. The four sites are the Greta Olive Juvenile Justice Academy, the Hubert B. Juvenile Justice Residential Facility, the Gladys C. Juvenile Justice Academy, and the Philip I. Juvenile Justice Residential Center. Each site is presented as its own case. Pseudonyms are provided for the participants, the juvenile justice residential facilities, and their respective school districts. Each of these chapters includes an introduction to the facility, the school district, and the participants and an overview of the facility's educational program. Each participant is presented individually to take a deeper look at their perceptions and experiences, and each chapter concludes with a discussion section.

The Greta Olive Juvenile Justice Academy, a superior-rated, for-profit juvenile justice residential facility is presented in **Chapter 3**. Although the facility's CEO did not permit me to conduct observations at this site, the educators were very excited to participate in this study. Due to the dearth of information we have on juvenile justice educators, I also decided to include them in this book. Additionally, their facility consistently received a superior rating on their quality assurance visits for their educational program; there is much that can be learned from their experiences. Overall, these educators espoused positive relationships, high expectations, appropriate resources, and effective accountability.

Chapter 4 features the Hubert B. Juvenile Justice Residential Facility, a satisfactory-rated, for-profit juvenile justice residential facility. Overall, relationships were found lacking, expectations were low, some resources were in place but were often underutilized, and there were few efficient accountability structures in place. The educators employed direct instruction, round-robin reading, and one-on-one instruction. Students were brought to each class an average of 14 minutes late. The highest percentage of students on task was 50 percent (4 out of 8 students) in reading and 63 percent (5 out of 8 students) in math. An average of 1 disruption occurred every 52.8 seconds during the instructional time.

The Gladys C. Juvenile Justice Academy, a public juvenile justice residential facility rated marginal satisfactory, is presented in **Chapter 5.** This facility had positive relationships but incongruent expectations and resources, and it lacked sufficient accountability. The educators employed direct instruction, round-robin reading, and one-on-one instruction. Students were brought to each class an average of 3.5 minutes late. The highest percentage of students on task was 57 percent (4 out of 7 students) in reading and 100 percent (7 out of 7 students) in math. An average of 1 disruption occurred every 67 seconds during the instructional time.

Lastly, the Philip I. Juvenile Justice Residential Center, a for-profit, superior-rated juvenile justice residential facility is featured in **Chapter 6**. The educators demonstrated positive relationships, maintained high expectations, utilized the resources provided, and had an effective level of accountability. This allowed for significantly more students to be on task and significantly fewer disruptions occurring within the classroom as compared with the other two sites where observations occurred. These educators employed direct instruction, guided practice, assessments (checking for understanding), self-selection of texts, and two-on-one and one-on-one instruction. Students were brought to each class an average of 5.8 minutes late. The highest percentage of students on task was 100 percent (19 out of 19 students) in reading and 100 percent (14 out of 14 and 18 out of 18 students) in math. An average of 1 disruption occurred every 2 minutes and 50.52 seconds during the instructional time.

Chapter 7 provides a cross-case discussion focused on my findings from the four Florida juvenile justice residential facilities featured in Chapters 3 through 6. Finally, I conclude this book by providing implications for future practice, policies, and research and my concluding comments in **Chapter 8**.

Acknowledgments

Father God, thank you for putting this book on my heart and for the positive educational outcomes for all children that may transpire as a result.

A very special thank you to the Florida Department of Juvenile Justice, the participants, and the four residential juvenile facilities and school districts where I conducted my research, for without your participation, my study and this book would not exist.

Sincere thanks to my colleagues and friends at the Harvard Graduate School of Education, the Marion P. Thomas and North Jersey Arts and Science Charter Schools, the Center for Educational Excellence in Alternative Settings, and the various schools and programs I have been a part of for the past five years. Special thanks to Deborah Jewell-Sherman, Eileen McGowan, Maree Sneed, and Katherine Boles for your guidance and very helpful feedback. Thank you, Drew Echelson, Lizzy Carroll, Melissa Matarazzo, and Maqueda Randall-Weeks for your continual encouragement and support.

To my mentors, friends, and colleagues I've met during life's wonderful journey, I sincerely thank you for the role you've played in shaping and sharpening me. A heartfelt thanks to my immediate and extended families for your unconditional love, encouragement, and support. To my sister Patty and brother Neil, thank you for always loving me and for always taking great care of your "little sis."

Milt, thank you for being my awesome husband and best friend and for allowing me to be "free" to do everything God has placed on my heart. Shaquir and Nazarae, thank you for being such wonderful sons. May you seize every opportunity to be your very best!

1
Introduction

On February 6, 2012, during an Askwith Forum at the Harvard Graduate School of Education, I had the opportunity to ask U.S. Secretary of Education Arne Duncan:

> How much are we engaging our juvenile justice educators in . . . conversations to ensure that our children who are incarcerated . . . disproportionately children of color, disproportionately children of poverty and children with special needs, to ensure that while they are incarcerated the opportunity gap does not continue to persist?

Secretary Duncan responded,

> It's a great question. . . . I tell you some of the most inspiring educators are folks who have dedicated their lives to working with those young people, and there are huge challenges, technology challenges . . . transition challenges . . . so it's very difficult. But, you have some amazing educators who are in those tough situations every single day working very, very hard and making a real difference; but we have to continue to listen to them. We have to continue to learn, share what's working. But, I have to tell you a huge part of my focus is preventing more young people from getting locked up. I think it's so tough on the back end. . . . I think the voice of those educators is critical. . . .

This book provides the voices of 15 juvenile justice educators in four facilities in Florida. I hope this book will help assuage the current paucity of research conducted on juvenile justice education.

Many believe all children are entitled to a high-quality education, yet this sentiment becomes less pervasive when the children are our nation's incarcerated youth. The varied risk factors of incarcerated youth "make them arguably the most challenging population of school age students that are served in the public sector,"[1] with many being at least two academic years behind their peers.[2] Despite this, little research encompasses the demands that this unique context places on juvenile justice teachers and administrators.

Although juvenile justice courts were established in the United States more than 100 years ago,[3] there is very little research on education programs in juvenile justice facilities. For example, there are no studies examining the math instruction and only four studies examining the reading instruction provided for incarcerated youth,[4] despite our nation's mandates for proficiency in mathematics and language arts as required by the No Child Left Behind Act of 2001. Many states have adopted the Common Core State Standards as a way to introduce common rigorous academic standards throughout our nation, but to what extent are we ensuring all our nation's children are being exposed to these rigorous standards and challenged and supported to meet or exceed these standards? Among other assessments, nationally we have the NAEP (National Assessment of Educational Progress). Districts are selected, and students in grades 4, 8, and 12 take this rigorous assessment. Reading and mathematics are administered every two years. Upon analyzing the data, the overall results for our nation's students are bleak. We want rigor. We want to continually increase our competitiveness, but this won't happen until "all really means all"—until we challenge and support all children, especially our most disenfranchised youth, to achieve high academic standards.

My extensive literature review uncovered only two studies[5] and one memoir[6] aimed at better understanding the challenges faced and the educational practices utilized by juvenile justice educators. And, surprisingly, most of the national studies that have been done specifically focused on juvenile justice education are more than 10 years old.

Critics of the current system of education implore researchers to evaluate the educational programs provided for incarcerated youth. Foley contends that "the educational needs of these youth and the efficacy of correctional education programs must be examined by researchers, correctional administrators, and educators."[7] Despite what we know about youth who are incarcerated and the few studies conducted citing educational best practices, much less is known about the juvenile justice educators who are responsible for providing these youth with a quality education. Six years ago, Florida's Juvenile Justice Educational Enhancement Program urged researchers to "focus on this distinct population, their problems, and needs to inform policy."[8]

Despite the unique conditions of incarceration, the documented disadvantages of these youth, the importance of this rehabilitative opportunity for juveniles, and the costs to society that incarceration and recidivism incur, we currently have negligible scholarly research that takes advantage of the insights of juvenile justice educators whose careers are focused on their success.

Houchins et al.[9] conducted a study to better understand the facilitators and the barriers juvenile justice teachers in Louisiana face when working to provide incarcerated youth with a quality education. Seventy-eight teachers from three facilities completed a multiple-choice and open-ended response survey. The study revealed that personnel issues included poor staff morale, needs for professional development and increased classroom space, and racism. The study also found academic issues, including the need for more vocational programs (career and technical education), reductions in class sizes, and academic materials and Internet access in the classrooms.

Foley and Gao[10] surveyed 41 correctional educators in the Midwest who were responsible for providing educational services to incarcerated youth housed in juvenile justice facilities. These researchers sought to understand the teachers' educational practices for incarcerated students with and without special needs by using a four-part survey to collect data focusing on assessment practices, instructional programs, special education, and demographic data. They found that 90% of the facilities provided GED courses, 72.5% provided vocational education, and 70% had literacy programs. One-on-one instruction was provided almost 50% of the time, and the most frequent instructional materials used were textbooks, workbooks, and worksheets.

Wilder[11] provided her experiences as a teacher in a juvenile facility, located in a southeastern state, housing the largest concentration of male juvenile sex offenders in the state. She found that reading is not encouraged, supplies are limited, worksheets provide the main mode of instruction, and the televisions inside most of the classrooms are used to pacify the students. According to Wilder, "In this system, it does not seem to matter if the students are learning anything or even if they are attempting to learn."[12] She created hands-on experiences for her students and incentivized them with candy and food.

After reviewing the vital statistics of incarcerated youth on the national level and within Florida, I decided to focus more closely on four juvenile justice residential facilities within Florida. My study aimed at learning whether and how principals and teachers who are responsible for educating incarcerated youth housed in residential facilities perceive themselves as providers of high-quality education to incarcerated youth.

To gain a deeper understanding of these educators' perceptions of the educational services they provide, I interviewed the school district's principals, who oversee the educational programs at each facility, and a reading, math, and special education teacher[13] or vocational teacher within each of the four facilities. I collected documentation/artifacts that included the interviewed teachers' lesson plans, staff handbooks, professional development opportunities, student learning inventories, teachers' and students' schedules, and the staff meeting agendas from all four facilities and visited and observed classroom instruction and meetings at three of them.

Owing to the dearth of up-to-date research on juvenile justice educators, I conducted a qualitative study. According to Maxwell, "The strengths of qualitative research derive primarily from its inductive approach, its focus on specific situations or people, and its emphasis on words rather than numbers."[14] This qualitative study uses an inductive approach to effectively capture, analyze, and present my time spent interviewing and observing 15 juvenile justice educators in Florida.

To describe and organize the interviews, observations, and documentation/artifacts, I sought to use a conceptual framework, but my extensive search did not uncover an existing framework through which this research could best be analyzed. For this reason, my qualitative study required a grounded approach. I therefore used thematic analysis as a tool to interpret these phenomena[15] and organized this study using a multiple-case method.[16]

The Selection Process

I selected Florida because of the large number of youth housed in its residential facilities, its explicit expectations for providing a high-quality education for its incarcerated youth, and the accountability system provided through the JJEEP Quality Assurance process. In addition to using the FLDOE/JJEEP Quality Assurance process, which began in 1998, Florida sought to better meet the educational needs of their incarcerated youth by enacting Florida Statute 1003.52 (1a) in 2002:

> The Legislature finds that education is the single most important factor in the rehabilitation of adjudicated delinquent youth in the custody of Department of Juvenile Justice programs. It is the goal of the Legislature that youth in the juvenile justice system continue to be allowed the opportunity to obtain a high-quality education.

Florida's incarcerated youth, therefore, are required and expected to receive a comparable education to their non-incarcerated peers.[17]

Table 1 Demographic data for four Florida juvenile justice residential facilities

2008–2009 JJEEP Facility Rating		Facility Type/ Level	Facility Provider	Education Provider	# of males	Ethnicity W B H			ESE
1	Superior	Moderate-Risk Males/6	For-Profit	School District	Almost 100	30%	65%	2%	45%
2	Satisfactory	Moderate-Risk Males/6	For-Profit	School District	More than 100	25%	60%	15%	45%
3	Marginal Satisfactory	Moderate-Risk Males/6	Public-DJJ	School District	Less than 50	25%	70%	3%	40%
4	Superior	Moderate-Risk Males/6	For-Profit	School District	More than 100	45%	35%	20%	45%

After reviewing Florida's Juvenile Justice Educational Enhancement Program's (JJEEP) 2008–2009 Quality Assurance ratings for the educational programs housed in Florida's residential facilities, I found that 15% of the facilities were rated superior, 47% high satisfactory, 24% satisfactory, 12% marginal satisfactory, and 2% below satisfactory.[18]

Initially, I selected one facility in each of the three identified categories—superior, satisfactory, and marginal satisfactory—having the highest scores within their ranges and similar student demographic data. I sought to examine the factors that existed within facilities with similar student populations to further analyze the divergent ratings for the educational services provided. However, when I began seeking research approvals, the chief executive officer (CEO) of the superior-rated facility would not allow me to observe the classrooms within his facility. The school district approved my research proposal and the educators chose to participate in my study. Because I was unable to conduct observations at this facility, I added a fourth site, also rated superior, with similar demographics as the three initially selected sites. Using a data-driven approach, each facility serves as the unit of analysis (Sample A, B, C, and D), and each interview, observation, and review of documentation serves as the unit of coding.[19] Demographic data for each of the selected juvenile justice residential facilities are provided in Table 1[20] (approximate numbers are provided to increase anonymity).

I conducted all the interviews prior to my observations of classrooms and meetings. To learn more about the educational goals of each facility, academic supports for students and the support structures in place for the teachers and school leaders, I interviewed the principal at each of the four sites, two teachers at one site, and three teachers at three sites.

Students in juvenile facilities perform significantly below their peers in reading and mathematics.[21] For this reason, I interviewed both a reading teacher and math teacher at each facility to learn what strategies they employ to help students achieve grade level standards.

Because a disproportionate number of special needs students are incarcerated,[22] I also interviewed the special needs teacher, referred to as the Exceptional Student Education (ESE) Support Facilitator in Florida, at each facility to learn more about the special education programs that currently exist and how they work to ensure students are provided with the appropriate services as outlined in their Individualized Education Program (IEP). In Florida, students with disabilities or who are gifted and have an IEP (Individualized Education Program) are deemed as ESE, Exceptional Student Education. At the Greta Olive Juvenile Justice Academy (Chapter 3), all teachers are ESE certified, so I interviewed the vocational teacher. At the Hubert B. Juvenile Justice Residential Facility (Chapter 4) and the Philip I. Juvenile Justice Residential Center (Chapter 6), I interviewed the ESE support facilitators. However, at the Gladys C. Juvenile Justice Academy (Chapter 5), the ESE support facilitator position was vacant during my visit, so I conducted no ESE interview at this site.

The total time for all of the interviews conducted at each site lasted approximately 15.5 hours for an average interview time of approximately 1 hour each. However, it is important to note that I spent 1.5 hours longer interviewing the educators at the Greta Olive Juvenile Justice Academy than I did at the other three sites because I was not permitted to conduct observations within the facility.

During each interview, I asked questions from an interview protocol I developed, digitally recorded it and took field notes. The interview protocol was semi-structured in order to allow for flexibility to probe further.[23] I wrote down my field notes immediately after concluding of each interview to include my wonderings and collect additional questions to use as a basis for follow-up interviews, if necessary.[24] To capture the authenticity of the participants' experiences, I did not edit direct quotes for clarity or grammatical correctness.

Observations

To gather additional data, I spent two days at three of the facilities to observe (1) the facility, (2) reading and mathematics classroom environments and other classrooms where the ESE support facilitator was providing academic support to students, and (3) the educational staff meetings and treatment team meetings. Treatment team meetings are facilitated by the juvenile justice staff and allow youth the opportunity to discuss their progress with the various supports they receive during their time at the facility, including medical, educational, and counseling. I used three different observation protocols.

During my observations of the classroom lessons, I wrote scripted notes on what I observed and also wrote notes using an observation protocol I developed for the facility and the individual classrooms, including what signs were posted, what physical supports were in place for students, and what the overall environment looked like, smelled like, felt like, in addition to my own reflections.

Another observation protocol was used during my observations of the reading and mathematics lessons and observations of the ESE support facilitators. I wrote scripted notes on what I observed and also noted how many students were in the classroom, the race/ethnicity of the students, the teacher's words and actions, the students' words and actions, the classroom conditions, the materials provided, and any disruptions or interruptions.

Finally, I devised an observation protocol for use during my observations of the educational staff and treatment team meetings. In addition to my scripted notes of what I heard and observed, I also noted what routines existed, any protocols or norms, the purpose of the meeting, attendance at the meeting, the topic of discussion, and the focus of the meeting.

At the end of each of my visits, I wrote a reflection journal entry about what I observed and noted questions to be included in any needed followup interviews to probe more deeply so I could better understand the context and to study participants' experiences.[25]

Documentation/Artifacts

I gathered pertinent documents/artifacts, such as copies of the teachers' lesson plans of the teachers I interviewed, staff handbooks, professional development opportunities, student learning inventories, teachers' and students' schedules, and the staff meeting agendas. I thoroughly reviewed each document/artifact and took anecdotal notes on my findings to further determine what support structures are in place for the incarcerated students and teachers at each facility.

Analysis

After completing the fifteen interviews, I transcribed each interview and read twice through each transcript. During the second reading, I studied and analyzed the text and marked what was of interest in the text.[26] I also analyzed the observation and documentation data to identify themes and code the data. I then reduced the raw information, identified themes within subsamples, compared themes across subsamples, created codes, and determined the codes' reliability by applying the codes to another subsample.[27] I wrote analytic memos including my thoughts and wonderings, and I created concept maps in order to better understand the concepts and relationships among the data.[28] I also had another doctoral student adept in thematic analysis and coding code a sample of my transcripts. When the coded transcripts were returned to me, I compared them with my codes to confirm the validity of the four major themes that emerged: relationships, expectations, resources, and

accountability. Although these were the major themes that the participants espoused and that the observations and documentation reviews
most frequently revealed, other themes, such as empathy, role complex-
ity, assertiveness versus nonassertiveness, lack of funding, pride, cel-
ebration, challenges and limitations, and educators' use of data, also
emerged. Most of these themes, however, were aptly framed within the
four major themes.

After identifying the four major themes, I reviewed each of the fifteen
transcripts again, validating them and using the identified codes,[29] further coding the observational data and the documents. Based on my
observations, I also added two codes for disruptions and instructional
practices to further analyze whether or how these were affected by the
four major themes.

Validity

My study focuses on the perceptions of eleven teachers and four principals as to their experiences in providing educational services to incarcerated youth. Because this is a qualitative study, it is important to avoid
making generalizations. There are more than 100 juvenile justice facilities
in Florida,[30] and there are nearly 2,700 juvenile justice facilities nationwide.[31] I conducted my research at only four sites. However, my study
allowed me to gain a greater understanding of some of the issues faced
by educators responsible for providing an education to students within a
juvenile justice system that has a state-mandated requirement of quality
and assessment that may also be applicable to other facilities and states.

Because I selected four sites and only interviewed three to four educators at each facility, someone might attempt to decipher the identity of
the study participants. To minimize this possibility, I present my data as a
collective whole when possible and use pseudonyms for the juvenile justice facilities, the counties/school districts, and the fifteen participants.

Additionally, the information provided by the participants was self-
reported. It is possible that participants chose to reveal what they thought
I wanted to hear. One way that I addressed this issue was by assuring the
participants that my study is not an evaluation or test of their teaching
or leadership ability. Rather, my study is an independently constructed
research study whose purpose is to gain a better understanding of the
realities of their teaching and leadership experiences—the challenges
they face and the supports they receive. Furthermore, in three of the
facilities, I was able to substantiate aspects of what was shared during the
days I spent observing the educators and students within the facilities.

While this study provides insight into how the teachers and principals perceive their experiences in providing education to incarcerated youth, it is important to note that it does not assess the students' educational outcomes.

Because I am a former teacher, a school administrator, and a prison volunteer, it was important to ensure that my own biases regarding high-quality education and support structures for teachers and students did not taint my data collection. Although I did expect to see a higher quality of education provided at the superior and satisfactory-rated facilities than at the marginal satisfactory rated facility, it was crucial that I keep an open mind when conducting each interview, observing each setting, reading through each transcript, and reviewing documentation and artifacts. This was fairly easy for me, because this was my first time observing classrooms in a juvenile justice setting. I found myself more eager to focus on listening and observing than on making judgments or premature analyses.

2
Contextual Setting

This chapter provides two contexts for incarcerated youth and the juvenile justice system—the United States and the state of Florida. Demographic data, historical context, educational services, funding, accountability structures, and promising practices are provided from a national perspective. The state of Florida provides a smaller subset for this study, with corresponding data to orient the reader to this state's incarcerated youth, historical context, accountability structures, facilities, funding, and educational services.

Demographic Data of U.S. Incarcerated Youth

In 2009, our nation's juvenile justice courts handled more than 1.5 million juvenile delinquent cases; and more than 130,000 youth were incarcerated.[1] These numbers account for the more than 70,000 youth confined within our nation's juvenile facilities on any given day.[2] Although the number of female juvenile arrests is steadily rising,[3] the majority of our nation's incarcerated youth are males;[4] boys represent almost 87% of incarcerated youth.[5]

Incarcerated youth are overwhelmingly economically disadvantaged[6] and disproportionately youth of color.[7] Even though nationwide only one-third of the American youth population in 1997 were of color, these youth "accounted for nearly two-thirds of the detained and committed population in secure juvenile facilities."[8] Even when Whites and youths of color are adjudicated for the same types of crime, with identical prior records, youths of color are still confined at a much higher rate than their white peers.[9]

The majority of our nation's incarcerated youth are children of color. Almost 20% are Hispanic, and 40% are African American,[10] the largest overrepresented group of color. Based on a study conducted from 1980 to 1993, Arum and Beattie contend that even with 12 years of education, African Americans "are 4.8 times more likely to be incarcerated than

Whites with similar educations."[11] Baltodano, Harris, and Rutherford also assert that "African American males are 5 times more likely to be incarcerated than White males."[12]

In addition to youth of color being overrepresented in the juvenile justice system, students with special needs are also more likely to be incarcerated.[13] Although the percentage of public school students classified with an Individualized Education Program (IEP) in 2005 was 12.7%, the average juvenile justice facility had special education students at a rate of 34%, almost triple the proportion of non-incarcerated juveniles.[14] This rate, however, varies from facility to facility and state to state. Wolford analyzed 20 state agencies responsible for providing juvenile justice education and found that 41% of the students in these states' juvenile facilities were eligible for special education services, ranging from Georgia having only 12% identified special needs students to Colorado having 70%.[15] Quinn et al. conducted a national study to determine the number of special needs students held in juvenile facilities. Although 33.4% of the students were identified as having special needs, the range within the facilities was 9.1% to 77.5%, with emotional disturbance (47.7%) and specific learning disabilities (38.6%) most prevalent.[16]

Despite the disparities that exist among incarcerated youth, there are clear indicators, regardless of race or special needs classifications, which put children on a downward trajectory toward delinquency. There continues to be a strong link between school failure, lack of education, and crime.[17] Incarcerated youth typically have poor school experiences,[18] lack academic achievement,[19] have behavioral challenges,[20] and experience little school success.[21] Even for those who complete school, the reality is grim for poor academic performers. According to Arum and Beattie,[22] a male high school graduate with a 1.0 grade point average (GPA) is 14.1 times more likely to be incarcerated than a male high school graduate with a 4.0 GPA.

Most incarcerated youth are at least two academic years behind their peers[23] and tend to have significantly low reading levels.[24] Project READ was the first national study linking juvenile delinquency with low reading skills.[25] Based on an analysis of more than 4,000 incarcerated students nationwide, the average age for incarcerated youth was 16, and the average ability for these youth to decode words and comprehend text was at the fourth-grade level.[26]

Typically, youth who are incarcerated have been retained at least once or twice,[27] yet they continue to function lower than their non-incarcerated peers academically[28] and experience social problems in school.[29] Incarcerated youth also typically drop out of school earlier in their schooling years.[30] An estimated 75% of incarcerated juveniles nationwide are high school dropouts.[31] Furthermore, youth with foster care experience are four times more likely to be incarcerated, and youth with a family member convicted of a felony are twice as likely to be incarcerated.[32] Unfortunately, incarcerated youth lack the much-needed political influence[33] to ensure that they are not denied the comprehensive educational services required for successful transitions back to their home communities.

Historical Overview of the U.S. Juvenile Justice System

The first juvenile court opened its doors in Chicago, Illinois, in 1899.[34] Society and lawmakers sought this change to remove youth from adult prisons.[35] By 1920, most states and several foreign countries established juvenile courts similar to the one set up in Illinois.[36] In addition to separating adults from juveniles, these courts were established to help civilize and provide social controls for delinquents[37] and provide needed rehabilitation for these youth.[38] During this period, it is noteworthy that juvenile delinquents were viewed as victims of society's social ills[39] and in need of treatment.[40]

The early juvenile court hearings were rather informal,[41] and it was up to the juvenile judges, who were often untrained, whether to speak to the delinquent in a formal or informal manner, seated next to the youth or from behind the bench.[42] The informal, inconsistent, and unstructured format of the juvenile courts, however, made itself vulnerable to lawsuits.

As a result of the informality and lack of due process for juveniles, the Supreme Court decided two key cases in the 1960s—*Kent v. United States*, 383 U.S. 541 (1966) and *In re Gault*, 387 U.S. 1 (1967). These decisions resulted in juveniles' being afforded more legal rights, including entitlement to a hearing before being sent to adult court.[43]

According to Small, "Previous changes to the juvenile justice system were driven by judicial efforts to protect juveniles. More recent changes are being driven by legislative efforts to protect society from juveniles."[44] Jenson and Howard argued that violent crimes escalated only after punishment-based tactics were employed.[45] As more time passed and juveniles began to become involved in more serious crimes,[46] they became viewed as criminals rather than juvenile delinquents, in need of punishment rather than rehabilitation.[47] As a result, the juvenile courts began to take a much more punitive stance,[48] emphasizing responsibility and accountability.[49] There continues to be tremendous vacillation between these divergent philosophies of rehabilitation and punishment.[50]

According to Cannon, "Many youth who are incarcerated have been unduly exploited and assaulted by others."[51] Numerous class action lawsuits have ensued at the state and local level over the last three decades.[52] Cases citing mistreatment of incarcerated youth, overcrowded facilities, lack of or poor educational services, and deplorable living conditions continue to be heard in courts across our nation. One example is the 1998 lawsuit filed by the U.S. Department of Justice against the state of Louisiana alleging the lack of provision for educational services for incarcerated youth.[53] Louisiana's spending for juvenile justice before the legal settlement was $50 million; after the settlement, Louisiana spent $85 million,[54] a 70% increase.

U.S. Juvenile Justice Facilities

In 2006, there were approximately 2,700 juvenile facilities in the United States.[55] Incarcerated youth are placed in one of several juvenile justice centers. The three predominant types of facilities serving incarcerated youth are residential treatment centers (35%), group homes (28%), and detention centers (27%).[56] More than half of these three types of facilities are privately operated[57] and are either not-for-profit/non-profit or for-profit.

Educational Services for America's Incarcerated Youth

According to Black, "Youthful offenders who lose their freedom shouldn't lose their chance for a good education."[58] Despite our nation's compulsory school attendance laws, however, only 65% of the juvenile residential facilities in the United States offer educational services to all of its incarcerated youth.[59] The numbers are even more staggering for children with special needs, who are not receiving the free and appropriate education (FAPE) mandated by the Individuals with Disabilities Education Act (IDEA).[60] Read and O' Cummings found that only 46% of students with special needs that were identified before their adjudication reported receiving their FAPE while incarcerated.

There is tremendous variance between states in which organization is responsible for overseeing the education programs[61] and what levels of support juvenile justice educational programs receive.[62] As of 2000, in most states, school districts were primarily responsible for providing education to youth housed in juvenile justice facilities within its jurisdictions.[63] Some states, such as Alabama, Georgia, and Illinois, established separate school districts solely for incarcerated youth; other states, such as Arizona, Delaware, and Michigan, require juvenile justice agencies to provide educational services.[64]

Much like our traditional public schools nationwide, there is tremendous variety in the types of educational services provided for incarcerated youth. For example, a 2000 study found that some states maintain a mandatory curriculum, maximum class size ratios, and statewide assessments for their incarcerated youth, whereas other states did not maintain such requirements.[65]

Some states and facilities choose to focus solely on the academic basics; others emphasize hands-on vocational training. According to Zabel and Nigro, "correctional education programs must provide a variety of transitional educational services, including instruction in basic academic skills, GED preparation, vocational awareness, pre-employment, and occupational experiences."[66] In a national survey conducted by Read and O'Cummings,[67] they found that 69% of juvenile facilities nationwide offered special education services, 63% offered GED preparation, and 32% offered vocational or technical education.

To properly rehabilitate incarcerated youth, practitioners and researchers make several recommendations. For example, a study by Blomberg and Waldo[68] recommends that incarcerated youth be housed in smaller facilities, because the youth tend to make greater academic progress in smaller facilities than they do in larger ones. Additionally, Leone et al. recommend placing incarcerated youth with high needs in classes with smaller numbers of students.[69]

Furthermore, research shows that incarcerated youths' strengths and areas of need must also be properly evaluated. An assessment should be provided to effectively evaluate their academic needs,[70] learning styles,[71] occupational aspirations,[72] functional needs,[73] and life skills needs.[74]

Researchers also emphasize the importance of the following skills being taught to youth while they are incarcerated to increase their opportunities for success once they are released. Juvenile justice facilities should teach high-level employment skills[75]; provide job training[76]; provide direct and intimate relationships and social skills learning[77]; teach effective instruction in basic reading[78] and mathematics[79]; provide a holistic curriculum focused on adjustment, employability, vocational, resiliency, and literacy needs[80]; focus on literacy development[81]; provide essential skills and career development projects[82]; teach at least the basic skills[83]; offer vocational training[84]; focus on building resiliency, including locus of control, autonomy, and self esteem[85]; and provide visual arts education.[86]

Delivery of instruction is equally important for incarcerated youth. Researchers recommend students receive instruction that is hands-on[87];

project-based and within small cooperative groups[88]; based upon students' IEPs for students identified with special needs[89]; direct, including decoding and comprehension and whole language reading instruction, peer tutoring, and teacher read-aloud[90]; culturally relevant, year-round school with a daily schedule comparable to that of the community school[91]; based on relevant material and positive reinforcement[92] focused on acceleration instead of remediation and curriculum alignment between the facility and the local public school[93]; taught to students' strengths[94]; and motivating and engaging.[95]

Additionally, several support structures should be in place to ensure that students receive a high-quality education, including use of principles and standards of exemplary programs,[96] retention of high-quality teachers,[97] provision of ongoing professional development,[98] and provision of transition planning and supports.[99]

Funding for America's Incarcerated Youth

In 2008, a total of $241 was spent every day for each youth who was incarcerated.[100] At this rate, the cost for incarcerating one juvenile for one year in 2008 was $87,965, an amount five times greater than the annual $17,131 total tuition, fees, room and board costs for a student attending a public four-year in-state college.[101]

In addition to the varied structures and diverse services provided for each state's juvenile justice programs, the per pupil allocation for education also differs. In a 20-state comparison of educational services conducted in 1999, per pupil funding for education ranged from $2,259 to $9,000.[102] Some states, including Alabama, Colorado, Kentucky, Pennsylvania, and Washington, allocated much more per pupil funding for incarcerated youth than for traditional school children, whereas others, including Illinois, Missouri, and Ohio, provided less funding for this high-need population.[103]

America's Accountability System for Juvenile Justice Facilities

Although there are still great discrepancies between facilities, educational providers, services, and funds allocated to help rehabilitate incarcerated youth, NCLB provided some standards and levels of accountability for juvenile justice facilities nationwide. According to Blomberg, Pesta, and Valentine, "Overall, NCLB has served as a catalyst for state juvenile justice education administrators to improve services and develop needed accountability systems."[104] Additionally, a 2004 study reported that some states required accreditation for their juvenile facilities.[105] Other studies found that some states provided quality assurance standards and conducted site visits.[106]

Promising Juvenile Justice Educational Programs/Practices within the United States

Despite the numerous challenges juvenile justice facilities face, researchers have identified promising educational programs and practices throughout the United States. Examples of these programs and practices are discussed below.

One promising program was Project READ (Reading Efficiency and Delinquency), the first national study to assess and improve the reading levels of incarcerated youth. Project READ's main components included teacher training that provided sustained silent reading, functional reading packets, and a Language Experience Approach taught to students' strengths. This initiative also used paperback books in the classroom. Ninety percent of the schools in this study had libraries for the students. In a four-month period, an average reading gain of one year was observed.[107]

Another promising program occurred in 1998. An intense six-week summer reading program was designed for 45 incarcerated youth who were low academic achievers. Training was provided for the teachers and instruction provided for students. Students received 2 hours and 50 minutes of direct instruction daily for decoding and comprehension, whole language reading instruction, peer tutoring, and teacher read-aloud. Students improved their reading rate, accuracy and comprehension.[108]

In 2003, a program for incarcerated youth and college students was facilitated on a college campus. A restorative justice college course was taught to a classroom of 18 students; 10 were college students, and eight were incarcerated youth, mostly aged 15 and 16. Selection criteria included a requirement that the student read at at least a ninth-grade level and desire to take the class. The incarcerated youth attended class on the college campus every Tuesday for 16 weeks. They were able to tour the college campus, and the college students were able to tour the juvenile facility. This was a positive experience for both groups.[109]

An additional promising program is located at a facility in Texas. An independent charter school in Texas runs a training center for its incarcerated youth. In addition to counseling and aftercare services, juveniles receive academic and vocational courses and real work experiences. Students receive two hours of classroom instruction daily and complete a 915-hour vocational curriculum. Students are able to enroll in automotive technology, building trades, bricklaying/stone masonry, construction carpentry, culinary arts, horticulture-related occupations, office support systems, or painting and decorating. Youth from this center are half as likely to be reincarcerated as other incarcerated youth housed in similar moderate-security residential facilities in Texas.[110]

Another promising program is located in Oregon. A juvenile facility in Oregon provides a career development curriculum for its incarcerated youth. In addition to learning how to develop resumés and complete job applications, students are required to complete a career development project in a field in which they are interested. For approximately 6 to 17 months, students research career interests, plan their projects, work with mentors, complete their culminating projects, and prepare and deliver their oral presentations. Students shared positive feedback for this real world, hands-on approach to learning.[111]

Demographic Data of Florida's Incarcerated Youth

Although my research for incarcerated youth initially focused on a national level, I decided to narrow my research on a smaller subset—incarcerated youth in one state. I decided to focus on a smaller subset so that I could study the educational opportunities provided for incarcerated youth in more depth and study the perceptions and practices of the educators responsible for providing them with a quality education.

My qualitative study was conducted in Florida, the fourth largest state in the country based on population, where approximately 10,000 youth are confined in juvenile facilities.[112] I chose Florida for three primary reasons. First, as of 2009, Florida exceeded national norms in the number of students placed in residential juvenile facilities.[113] Second, Florida has a state law that includes requirements for educating incarcerated youth (Florida Statute 1003.52 (1)). Third, Florida's law includes a unique quality assurance accountability process for its juvenile justice educational programs.[114]

Similar to the demographics representing youth throughout the United States, in 2005, Florida's incarcerated youth were disproportionately male (76%) and African American (47%), and 38% were identified as students with special needs.[115] Moreover, 75% of Florida's incarcerated youth are one or more academic years behind their peers.[116]

Florida's Juvenile Justice Reform

A lawsuit against the state of Florida served as the catalyst for the state's juvenile justice reform. *Bobby M. v. Chiles*, 907 F.Supp. 368 (N.D.Fla. 1995), the key juvenile justice civil rights class action lawsuit in Florida,[117] involved four plaintiffs, one of whom was female, three of whom were male, and two of whom were special needs students, with one English Language Learner (ELL). The lawsuit, filed in 1983 against the state of Florida, focused on three of Florida's highest-security facilities. Some of the allegations included significant overcrowding, mistreatment of juveniles, and lack of educational materials and services for the youth within each of the facilities.

While the *Bobby M.* case was still being decided in the courtroom, the Dropout Prevention and Academic Intervention Act was enacted by the Florida Legislature in 1986, requiring all juvenile justice facilities to provide its incarcerated youth with a basic academic, vocational and special education.[118] And in 1987, the parties of the *Bobby M.* case entered into a consent decree that required immediate closure of one facility, disallowed housing of females in training schools, and mandated a maximum number of youth enrolled in these facilities. The consent decree also required the state to improve educational programs in the two remaining facilities and that staff be provided proper training. Finally, pursuant to the consent decree, the Florida Department of Education (FLDOE) was charged with the task of improving and overseeing the educational services in juvenile facilities statewide.

By 1993, Florida's Department of Juvenile Justice was established,[119] and after some legislators visited juvenile facilities and attended juvenile court proceedings, the Juvenile Justice Act of 1994 was created[120] with an attempt to balance both punishment and prevention and place a stronger emphasis on academic programming.[121] The defendants implemented the requirements of the *Bobby M.* consent decree, and in 1996, the *Bobby M.* case was officially closed.[122]

Florida's Accountability System for Juvenile Justice Facilities

Simultaneous with the oversight provided to close the *Bobby M.* case, in 1996 the Florida Legislature also required the Florida Department of Education (FLDOE) to conduct annual quality assurance reviews for each of its juvenile facilities.[123] Standards were generated and the process for holding juvenile facilities accountable ensued. In 1998, the FLDOE provided a grant, renewable every three years, to the Florida State University's College of Criminology and Criminal Justice Studies to carry out the charge given a few years earlier. The Florida State University's School of Criminology and Criminal Justice launched the Juvenile Justice Educational Enhancement Program (JJEEP) in 1998.[124] The main function of JJEEP was to incorporate research-based best practices into an accountability mechanism for the state to gauge the degree to which it makes progress toward the expected outcomes articulated in Statute 1003.52(1) which states that "the goal of the Legislature (is) that youth in the juvenile justice system continue to be allowed the opportunity to obtain a high-quality education."

Despite the large proportion of juveniles the state of Florida incarcerates each year, Florida serves as a model for program accountability for its juvenile justice education programs and its use of common assessments.[125] The Florida Department of Education (FLDOE) is responsible for oversight of all educational programs within the juvenile justice facilities[126] and the Juvenile Justice Educational Enhancement Program (JJEEP) was responsible for evaluating research-based practices for effective educational strategies, evaluating the educational programs for each of Florida's juvenile facilities, and providing technical support as needed.[127] Each year, JJEEP conducted a site visit to each of Florida's juvenile facilities that had an educational program. JJEEP's Educational Quality Assurance process emphasized three main quality assurance components—quality teachers, quality instruction, and quality entrance and exit transition services.[128]

During the 2008–2009 school year, 15% of the juvenile facilities were rated superior, with a score range of 7.00–9.00; 47% of the facilities were rated high satisfactory, with a score range of 6.00–6.99; 24% were rated satisfactory, with a score range of 5.00–5.99; 12% were rated marginal satisfactory, with a score range of 4.00–4.99; and 2% were ranked below satisfactory, with a score range of 0.00–3.99.[129]

In order to increase its level of accountability, the state of Florida, beginning in 2006, also adopted one common assessment for use in all its juvenile facilities.[130] Before this, 32 different assessments were being used throughout the state, preventing comparisons or consistency when youth transferred from one facility to the next.[131]

Although the state of Florida appeared to be moving in the right direction for its accountability structures, the Florida Department of Education is now working to develop a new, viable accountability system for its juvenile justice education programs. The 2009–2010 school year marked the end of the JJEEP's quality assurance reviews when the state opted not to renew its discretionary grant. According to the Juvenile Justice Educational Enhancement Program's 2009–2010 Annual Report, as the twelfth year came to an end, it brought, "perhaps, the end of comprehensive, systematic on-site quality assurance for Florida's juvenile justice education programs for the immediate future."[132]

Florida's Juvenile Justice Facilities

Florida has approximately 145 juvenile facilities,[133] a decrease from the approximate 200 facilities eight years earlier,[134] which are residential commitment programs, day treatment programs, and detention centers. Florida has more residential treatment facilities than any other type of juvenile facility. A security level is assigned to each facility, beginning with minimal risk for non-residential facilities and progressing to low-risk, moderate-risk, high-risk, or maximum-risk for its residential facilities. There are more level 6 programs (moderate-risk) in Florida than any other security program,[135] and the majority of incarcerated youth are detained in level 6 facilities.[136]

Eighty percent of all Florida's juvenile justice facilities[137] and 95% of its residential facilities[138] are privately operated. The first (Chapter 3), second (Chapter 4), and fourth (Chapter 6) facilities found in this study are owned and operated by for-profit organizations; the third (Chapter 5) facility is owned and operated by the Department of Juvenile Justice.

Funding for Florida's Incarcerated Youth

The state of Florida provides the funding for each of its juvenile facilities. The amount of funds each facility receives is based on the type of program—i.e. low-, moderate-, or maximum-risk—and the number of incarcerated youth housed within the facility. The average cost for program completion for a moderate-risk facility in Florida was $34,784.[139] The average cost for a low-risk program completion was approximately $18,000, compared to $119,000 for maximum-risk program completion.[140] These figures provide a total cost including funds for education based on the youths' average length of stay—an approximate $165–$200 per day per incarcerated youth. Based on the state of Florida's per pupil expenditure of $8,741[141] and the minimum of 180 days of school mandated by Florida's state law, Florida spent less than $50 per day to educate its youth. This amount indicates that Florida spends three to four times more money to incarcerate its youth than to educate them within local school districts.

Educational Services for Florida's Incarcerated Youth

Florida has 67 counties, and each county has its own school district. Each school district is responsible for providing educational services to all incarcerated youth housed in the juvenile facilities and the adult prisons located within its district. School districts, however, have the option to contract out these educational services. In 2002, the percentage of variation in providers was almost equal, with 53% of the educational services for juvenile populations provided by local school districts and 47% provided by private education providers.[142] In Florida's residential facilities, the percentage of local district providers was 60%; not-for-profit providers encompassed 28% of these programs, and 12% were for-profit providers.[143]

School is in session for 240 days each year at the four facilities featured in this book. This enables students to be exposed to an instructional program regardless of when they enter the facility.

3
Greta Olive Juvenile Justice Academy[1]

Introduction

The Greta Olive Juvenile Justice Academy is owned and operated by a for-profit health organization that has been in existence for more than 30 years and that owns and operates more than 200 facilities nationwide. Approximately 100 incarcerated youth are housed in this level 6, moderate-risk facility. Approximately 70% of the population are youth of color, with 65% African American and 2% Hispanic; 30% are white. Forty-five percent of the youth are classified as Exceptional Student Education (ESE). During the 2008–2009 school year, the Greta Olive Juvenile Justice Academy was rated superior, the highest rating given by the Juvenile Justice Educational Enhancement Program (JJEEP), for its educational services.

The Milton County Public Schools is responsible for providing a high-quality education to its more than 25,000 students, including the incarcerated youth housed at the Greta Olive Juvenile Justice Academy. The Milton County Public Schools' demographics are quite different from the demographics of the youth housed at the Greta Olive Juvenile Justice Academy. The majority of students served by the Milton County Public Schools are white—almost 75%. African Americans and Hispanics make up less than 20% of the school district's population. The district's ESE population is approximately 20%, and 33% of the district's students qualify for Free or Reduced Price Meals (FRPM). During the 2008–2009 school year, the Milton County Public Schools was rated an A-level school district by the Florida Department of Education for its high level of student achievement.

While on my way to interview the educators at the Greta Olive Juvenile Justice Academy, there were no fences or bars visible to indicate that this space housed incarcerated youth. Its entrance resembled that

23

of a small shopping center or a medical facility. After I parked my rental car and began to make my way to the entrance, I noticed beautiful stonework next to the flagpole. I later learned that some of the youth housed at this facility created the display as a project for their vocational class.

I entered the door of the facility much as I would any office space. Approximately four feet from the door, immediately facing me, was the main reception desk with someone to greet me and inquire why I was there. Had I not known what location this was, the only indication I might have had that this was a facility warranting security was the large walk-through metal detector off to the right and the signs posted reminding guests to lock their car doors or risk having their cars towed away. Something else that caught my attention was the "Excellence in Service" signs posted throughout the office.

Unfortunately, I cannot provide a description of the classrooms, because the CEO of this for-profit facility would not allow me to conduct my research at this site. The educators, however, were interested in participating in this study, so I conducted my interview with the principal at his district office and my interviews with the teachers and documentation review in the conference room at the facility, but not within the confines of its educational space.

My findings are based on what I observed within the environment of the front of this facility, the data collected from the four interviews I conducted, and my review of the following documents/artifacts: master schedule, including teachers' and students' schedules; math inventory sheet; professional development opportunities; educational staff meeting agendas; and copies of math, reading, and vocational lesson plans.

Participants

Table 2   Greta Olive Juvenile Justice Academy participants

Juvenile Justice Educator	Position	Tenure at the Facility
Alexander	Principal	5 years
Kyle	Vocational Teacher	10 years
Mae	Math Teacher	9 months
David	Reading Teacher	10 years

Educational Program

Each day, school begins at 7:25 a.m. and ends at 2:30 p.m. The following courses are taught each week: reading, employability skills, math, intensive math, language arts, science, social studies, and vocational studies. Students are on a rotating block schedule. Students take three classes daily that last 1 hour and 40 minutes (100 minutes) each, for a total of 300 minutes of daily in-class instruction. Scheduled classes alternate days.

The teachers begin their day at 7:10 a.m. and end at 2:40 p.m. They have 1 hour and 50 minutes each day for lunch and a common planning period. Their class size ranges from 8 to 13 students. All the teachers at this facility chose to be there and are ESE (Exceptional Student Education) and CAR–PD (Content Area Reading–Professional Development) certified beyond the certifications they have for the content area(s) they are responsible for teaching.

Findings

The CEO of this facility did not permit me to observe the classrooms, staff meetings, or treatment team meetings, which limited my ability to thoroughly investigate and analyze the educational opportunities provided for the youth incarcerated at the Greta Olive Juvenile Justice Academy. All the information reported is based on self-reported data and review of the documentation/artifacts provided. Although the educators substantiated several statements, the information was provided by the participants without any additional corroboration that could have been accomplished through observations. However, despite this limitation, my interviews with the educators provide insight into their understanding of their roles and perceptions of the educational program—a program consistently rated superior by the Juvenile Justice Educational Enhancement Program's Quality Assurance process. For each of the four themes that emerged from this study, it was evident that there were positive relationships, high expectations, appropriate resources, and accountability.

Principal Alexander

Alexander has been working in the Milton County Public Schools for more than 20 years as a teacher and administrator. He has been the principal of the Department of Juvenile Justice (DJJ) schools for this school district for five years. He is responsible for overseeing the educators at this facility and at six additional DJJ sites. Principal Alexander has one assistant principal who also provides support to this and the other six facilities. He appears to be a jovial gentleman who passionately shared with me his belief that incarcerated youth should be afforded the necessary supports and programs while confined to be successful when they transition back to their communities. He espouses positive relationships, high expectations, and adequate resources and believes that the necessary accountability components are in place at the Greta Olive Juvenile Justice Academy for his students to be exposed to a high-quality education.

Relationships

There are a multitude of positive relationships that exist at this facility. Principal Alexander spoke with pride when he described the relationships he has forged and encouraged his teachers to do the same. He attributed the positive working relationship he has with the juvenile justice staff to their rich history. Principal Alexander has been in the district for many years, and several of the guards are his former high school students. The positive relationship he established with them continues to strengthen the partnership between juvenile justice and education. Principal Alexander shared, "Some of the guards are kids I had at [a local] high school. They tell those kids all the time, 'If you do what you're supposed to [Principal Alexander] will help you. If you don't do it, you can forget it.'"

Principal Alexander also spoke proudly of the autonomy and the reciprocal relationship he and his staff have with the juvenile justice leader and staff. The educators are allowed to make the decisions they feel are best suited for the youth, when the issues are educationally related. The juvenile justice staff has their role to play, and the educators recognize that they also have their roles. He believes educators are more inclined to provide efficient record keeping, and both he and the CEO of the facility want to ensure they continue to receive high scores during the quality assurance reviews. According to Principal Alexander, "They just leave us alone. We do education and we bail 'em out when it comes to Q&A, quality assurance control. We bail them out, 'cause we keep records."

At the administrative level, Principal Alexander includes his assistant principal on interviews when he is looking for teaching candidates for any of the seven facilities he oversees. He believes this demonstrates to her that he values her opinion.

He also described the close relationship of the educators at this facility: "They love kids. And they're very close. They have a meeting every week on Thursday. Somebody'll bring a dessert. . . . They share ideas and they share strengths of those kids." During this time, the teachers are able to focus on students who are also in need of additional support. Principal Alexander elaborated, "They may have one every now and then; they might say, 'Something's going on somewhere, 'cause he's having a rough week and he typically doesn't do it. Can anybody figure it out?'"

Principal Alexander shared that he was "taught to respect people, and that's what it should be." Much like the way the teachers talk to, respect and collaborate with one another, Principal Alexander also stresses the importance of these same principles when working with students. He believes that students will "talk to you if you show them back that you trust them and that you respect them." He explained how he prepares and expects his teachers to establish positive relationships built on trust and respect. Principal Alexander stated, "I train my teachers to establish that trust with these kids, more so than any public school, you know. . . . 'Is there something I need to know about you? Why are you here? What made you make that decision?'" He elaborated,

> When I first got here . . . there were no goals, so I developed 10 goals. And I tell the teachers, if you can get seven of these goals, you're gonna be a highly effective teacher. . . . Sit down with the kids and go over, "Okay, here's what I've gotta do, so somehow I've got to get you to do these too. We gotta be a team."

Principal Alexander ensures that he gets to know his students and takes pride in speaking with them and building the same type of trust and respect he expects of his teachers. He shared several stories of conversations he's had with students. He introduces himself to the incarcerated youth and tells them a little about himself and asks them to share a little bit about their hopes and experiences. He also takes advantage of these times to share his expectations while he is establishing a positive relationship with the youth. Principal Alexander divulged,

> Like yesterday, that runner. I asked him why he wasn't out there. He said, "'Cause I'm a runner, they won't let me go." So I asked him, "What's your goal?" "What do you mean goal; what's that?" I said, "What do you want to accomplish with your life?" He said, "I'd like to be out there learning how to work with that concrete and lay block and all that." I said, "Well, you gotta get out of that white suit [worn to designate youth who will attempt to escape]. . . . He said, "Well

how do you do it?" "Number one you gonna start respecting people. Number two, you're gonna get rid of that reputation as a runner. You're gonna be where you're supposed to be, do what you're supposed to do."

Principal Alexander talked about the great dividends because of the time he takes to have these conversations with the youth. The results of these positive relationships with students were exemplified as he shared a recent incident:

> About two months ago, we had some riots and it was on a Friday night. And I don't like getting called out on a Friday night, but they couldn't get 'em calmed down and . . . when the Sheriff's Deputies come in, they're not used to dealing with kids. . . . So, I walked in there and I walked down the middle of that facility. I said, "Okay, stop. Everybody sit down." And they did and so, the cops said, "How'd you get that done? How'd you do that?" I said, "Well number one, they respect me," and I said, "That's half the battle, is respect. They know that if you do right, you do what you're supposed to do, I'm goin' help you."

Relationships with colleagues within the school district, with community members and organizations within Florida are also something in which Principal Alexander takes great pride. He boasted, "We can call [a city in] Florida and get a kid a job. We've got that kind of connection all over the state of Florida and vice versa." This is very important, because many of the youth who transition are looking for ways to earn money to make a living.

A multitude of partnerships have been established between the educators at this facility, the local school district and outside entities. Community members reach out to them to offer their time as mentors. Principal Alexander described an honor student who was matched with an ideal mentor at this facility:

> [We had] an honor student. . . . Well, one day this guy walks in. He says, "I'm from [a city in] Florida." He said, "I'm just looking. I don't care who it is." He said, "I don't know who you got here, don't care who it is, but I want to give a young man, a deserving young man who's got a chance to be successful in college, a full scholarship to Florida State University." "Sir, is this a joke?" "Is this, you know—." "Nope."

So, I went down there (laughs), I walked down there and got that kid, you know what I mean. So, through his probation officer, he had to check in with probation, we had all that, 'cause we had to go through DJJ and blah, blah, blah. Well, the kid graduated from FSU (Florida State University) with a master's degree and this guy paid for the entire thing. He had his degree in electrical engineering and a master's degree in architecture. That's how smart the kid was. I got a letter from him, this kid. Man, I tell you I cried for an hour.

In addition to partnering with local community members who serve as mentors, the educators in this facility also maintain that they benefit greatly from the collegial relationships they have with their colleagues located within their school district. Principal Alexander spoke about a time when his budget was significantly cut. Because of the relationship that existed, he was able to arrange for some additional monies to be set aside for his educational programs. Principal Alexander disclosed, "I did some creative financing and got some money back, plus the bookkeeper, the finance director, is a good friend and she said, 'I'm gonna give you some extra money 'cause that's not right what they're doing.'"

Expectations

The educators stated that they deeply value education, and because of this, they have placed high expectations on themselves as they deliver their instruction daily to their students. Principal Alexander recognizes that his thinking must be different if his students are to receive the high-quality education they deserve. He shared, "I've been accused of thinking out of the box, and, they're right, I do. But also, I think being out of the box sometimes helps kids learn." He further divulged, "I believe very heavily in multiple intelligence." And, with that belief he ensures he provides professional development for his teachers to meet the needs of all the learners in their classrooms. All of his teachers are certified in ESE (Exceptional Student Education) and reading.

According to Principal Alexander, "As far as the teacher is concerned, it takes a special, special breed of person. You've got to want to be here." He expects the teachers who are at this facility to be there by choice. He stated, "Most of our teachers are veterans. They want to be here. And . . . that's the unique thing about it." Principal Alexander was adamant:

You can't be assigned, "You go to DJJ," you know, and expect to be real successful. You got to have a passion and a love for working with these kids, which I'm the luckiest guy in the world, because I would say I don't have any teachers that don't want to be with me here at the DJJ.

Training is provided which reinforces the expectations of the educational staff. Principal Alexander spoke about the sensitivity training that is provided by the school district's director of human resources before the teachers begin and during the school year, as needed. According to Principal Alexander, "He goes over a lot of things; professionalism, how you dress, how you act, sensitive to each different kind of kid that you got in your class . . . I had a teacher I sent back to him one time." He described an incident of a relatively new teacher who used profanity after a student threw a chair, emphasizing again, the very unique context of working with incarcerated youth and the need for such training.

Principal Alexander also recognizes that students must be able to read. He stated, "You just got to be able to read and when the kids can't read, they can't read." And because of this he reiterated, "It's awful important that these teachers understand how to teach reading across the curriculum." Because of the population they are working with and the expectations outlined in the Common Core State Standards, Principal Alexander expects all his teachers to be certified in reading. He explained, "I send my teachers to, and they never got this 'til I got here but I'm a big proponent of it. I got 'em all certified in reading—CARPD."

He ensures that teachers receive proper professional development and says that this was a flaw of his predecessor. Principal Alexander shared, "I want to bring those teachers up to where everybody else is, I mean those poor babies, that other guy before me, I mean, he did nothing."

Principal Alexander expounded, "I believe in a comprehensive education. Now what do I mean by that? Everybody's not doctors and lawyers. There are mechanics and bricklayers. So comprehensive meaning that we're gonna educate everybody to what they are capable of doing." Although the capabilities of his students remain unknown, Principal Alexander wants to ensure his teachers are properly trained and equipped to provide them with the necessary educational program to help them be successful.

In addition to their preparedness and the resources provided, Principal Alexander expects his teachers to build relationships with their students. He informs them of this as they return to teach each school year:

I tell the teachers—. We started school August 18 and I, then I tell them do it at Christmas, right before Christmas, and then in the middle of spring. Take a week. Forget math, English, science, and all that stuff. Take a week and sit down and talk to the kids and that will help you get their confidence. Explain to them, that you're there to help 'em and not to hurt 'em . . . and have a plan.

Principal Alexander also believes heavily in the power of respect and feels that teachers must do everything they can to ensure there is always a mutual level of respect; otherwise, the learning won't take place. He shared, "I just think you can't teach without first that child respecting what you're trying to teach." Certifications also matter in this facility, and the educators believe multi-certified teachers serve as resources for their students and also allow them to not get transferred out if more budget cuts occur. Principal Alexander shared, "Our teachers are all multi-certified. They've gone back on their own, 'cause they didn't want to get moved out, and got multi-certified."

Believing that his expectations are clear, Principal Alexander recognizes that teachers need a healthy balance of autonomy and accountability to be successful. He expects teachers will use the state standards and teach in a way that motivates their students:

I'm not a micromanager and I believe in teaching incarcerated kids you gotta give those teachers some flexibility to where they can teach; but at the same time, you gotta watch, make sure they're teaching Florida Sunshine State Standards 'cause we follow those too. . . . You can't be a preacher–teacher, in our situation. You can't be that in public schools either. You gotta move around. You got to be a little bit of a movie star, little bit of a ham. You gotta move around the classroom. You gotta circulate. You got to let the kids know that you are looking at what they're doing. And then they're more conscious about it, you know.

Principal Alexander expects that the juvenile justice staff will continually ensure that students are not disrupting the learning environment. He shared his expectation if a student's language is too inappropriate or if his behavior becomes disorderly. According to Principal Alexander, "Now, if it gets real bad, that guard's job is to get him out of there, get him out of that classroom."

Principal Alexander also expects that the juvenile justice staff and the educators will work collaboratively to reward positive student behavior. As a way to incentivize students to complete their school work, Principal Alexander makes special requests to the juvenile justice director which positively effects the classroom environment:

I worked out a deal with the director out there. I said, "Look, if these kids have a good day in class, educationally, can we let them watch TV tonight? There's a ball game on." I said, "Our teachers will give you a list."

Well it started out one or two kids, but then all of a sudden they found out, "Ya'll getting to watch the ballgame? How ya'll get to do that?" And so, (laughs) the teachers said, "All of a sudden our discipline problems got cut in half."

Not only do the educators maintain high expectations for themselves and their peers, they also maintain high expectations for their students. Principal Alexander believes Milton County has higher standards and expectations than any other school district in the state. He shared, "[Milton] County's been rated [a] number one school system in the state of Florida for years." He believes the youth have greater difficulty here because they are not accustomed to Milton County's standards. Most of the residential facilities within the state of Florida do not house youth in the same county where they lived before being adjudicated. Principal Alexander explained, "We're asking kids that come from different parts of the state of Florida who probably don't have the school improvement plan or the pupil progression plan that we have to perform under our plan, which is tougher."

Principal Alexander also takes a more authoritative stance with his students; yet his comments demonstrate his commitment to providing a quality educational environment for every youth. He asserted,

Are some of 'em tough? Yeah. And I just tell them straight up; I always meet all the new ones. I tell them straight up, "I run the school." "It's my building." "Now, either you do what you are supposed to do, or you gonna be somewhere else, but you're not going to deprive another kid of an education.

Principal Alexander expects two things of his students when they leave—that they will have a vocational certification and have a diploma or be on their way to successfully obtaining a diploma. He shared, "I believe every kid ought to at least have that certification, that little card says I'm certified concrete man, I'm certified this, certified that. I want them to either have that vocational certification or diploma or both."

The educators also recognize the importance of celebrating students as they meet or exceed expectations. They hold a graduation ceremony for their graduates each year. According to Principal Alexander, "You would be surprised and shocked how many kids come back." He described how the graduates are celebrated: "We give them robes, caps; we do the whole thing. We play pomp and circumstance, march them down. Their families come. Mommas and daddies are crying you know because they never thought their kids would ever graduate." Principal Alexander stated, "Maybe we instilled enough pride in him that he says, 'You know I can go on and do this.' . . . Because, I will not accept and I tell them straight up, 'I won't accept your second best.'" Throughout our time together, Principal Alexander reiterated the importance of instilling pride in students and his expectations for students to always put forth their best effort.

The educators believe students have a capability level and seek to provide instruction "according to their level." Principal Alexander explained, "I go back to what level can a child achieve? What are they capable of achieving? Now . . . if I teach them to their multiple intelligence learning level they got a chance to receive a high school diploma." This uncertainty of what someone is capable of is the case for every child in every one of our nation's classrooms. We have no idea what one is capable of and the danger of not creating learning environments that foster self discovery with appropriate challenges and support, cause educators, like Principal Alexander, to just want the best yet still not have a matrix that demonstrates how close they've helped make that happen for each of their students.

Moreover, the educators are proud to provide their youth with a quality instructional and vocational program. Even amongst the Department of Juvenile Justice (DJJ) staff within the facility and other DJJ employees throughout the state who visit them, there is great shock that the incarcerated youth at this facility are allowed to work with the vocational materials. Principal Alexander, however, is adamant that expectations matter:

> We got table saws; we've got circular saws; and we got the kids using 'em. And they say, "I can't believe you're doing that." "And they got a hammer?" I say, "Well, you need to understand the whole program and the whole program is, is first it starts with safety. Second part of the program is, you mess up, you're out. Now you mess up, you could hurt yourself bad, but if you mess up or you do something, or you break a safety violation, you're no longer in vocational education." And, what they don't understand is, the first chapter of the book that we start them in is all about safety. If you can't pass that, I mean 100% or for some reason, we don't think you can be trusted,

you don't get in there. You don't get in the program. So you can have a kid not in a vocational program, but it's because of them, not us.

There were visitors from the Florida DJJ and several school districts who came to visit the facility and see some of the work the incarcerated youth completed at various schools. According to Principal Alexander, the visitors couldn't wrap their minds around what was accomplished by the youth and the fact that there weren't any incidences of youth attempting to escape. Principal Alexander once again emphasized the importance of expectations:

> They said, "Well, ya'll are outside the facility with one guard and a teacher?" "Yeah. What's the problem?" They said, "Well, they don't run?" I said, "We don't take the—, we not gonna bring any runners out here (laughs)." I said, "No, because of Mr. [Kyle]. . . . They respect that man and they know that he's going to teach them and they know when they leave that facility . . . they're gonna have that certificate. They know that Mr. [Kyle's] gonna call and say, "Hey you need to hire—. He's certified in this, that and the other."

Resources

Principal Alexander believes he has the support/resources needed to be successful in his role. The strong working relationship he has with district personnel, including the director of human resources and the business manager is evident with the training provided for his teachers and the additional monies he received for his educational programs. Principal Alexander is also able to attend professional development sessions, as needed. He shared,

> I can't tell you how many professional developments [I've been to]. As a matter of fact, I got one on that computer I got to go to in October and . . . it's about . . . transitioning prisoners; and, it's not necessarily our kids, but I'll go to it 'cause they may give us some ideas on transitioning. 'Cause we transition differently with our kids than what they do at a adult prison.

The teachers at this facility receive ongoing support. The administrators make themselves available and visit classrooms regularly; and, according to the educators, there are also ample professional development opportunities. A positive working relationship also ensures district personnel provide support whenever needed.

According to Principal Alexander, "I go to those facilities every day, either me or my assistant, because I believe if they see me, the teachers appreciate it." In addition to observing the learning environments, Principal Alexander also visits this facility when teachers reach out to him to help discipline students. He described a recent incident:

> We've got kids, for example, that their language is just really not very good. I got a call the other day from one of my teachers and she got called something. And of course, "He's not coming back to my class until you talk to him, you know." And so, I had to make a special trip up and talked to him.
>
> But I tell them, I said, "Just let, let the language fly because if you ever, ever show that it bothers you—." I said, "They lay in those dorms, they lay in those rooms at night and think of ways to bother you and if you ever let a kid know that they can get to you some way, they got you. And then you need to go ahead, we need to move you somewhere. 'Cause they got ya." So I said, "Just keep right on talking. Keep right on teaching."

Principal Alexander ensures his staff is kept informed and they receive the necessary professional development to be highly effective. He shared, "They would tell you very quickly that number one, I keep 'em informed." He elaborated, "When I go to a principal's meeting, I come back, I have a faculty meeting . . . I tell them exactly what was said and done, give 'em all the paperwork they need." Furthermore, Principal Alexander explained, "All of our teachers are certified reading teachers . . . because this Common Core that we're going through right now is all about reading across the curriculum." He provided an example of the training that was provided:

> A math teacher may not want to teach reading across the curriculum, because, how do you do it? Well, we took our math teachers, our science teachers, our history teachers and history being probably one of the easiest one, to read across the curriculum and we trained CAR–PD, reading, whatever it takes to get these teachers ready.

Professional development topics also include handling disruptive students and keeping students on task "from bell to bell." Principal

Alexander shared, "So we'd have professional development. I say, 'Today we are going to talk about bell to bell.' I said, 'Bell-to-bell means this. You start when the bell rings and you end when the bell rings.'" This transferred to the reading and math teacher as both teachers discussed what they normally do as their "bell ringer" or starter for each class.

Principal Alexander emphasized professional development is provided not only for the teachers, but also for the substitute teachers. He stated, "We train 'em. We don't just throw 'em. You can't throw a DJJ teacher into the pit. Because, number one, we teach 'em how to get in and out of the facility."

Principal Alexander also continually seeks out other resources that will help to further develop his teachers. He recently ordered the book *I'd Like to Apologize to Every Teacher I Ever Had: My Year as a Rookie Teacher at Northeast High* by Tony Danza and plans to do a book study with his teachers. He explained, "I think it will help them because their frustration sets in when they don't think that they're making a difference . . . and that's the reason why I got it for my teachers to keep some of these kids out of incarceration."

The educators themselves are a resource to one another. Principal Alexander proudly shared, "They share ideas. They work tremendously together. And the kids know that and they see that." Principal Alexander also provides his teachers with advice, suggestions, and strategies for being more effective:

> I talk to 'em about things like, you know, letting foul language go over your head. But then stand by the door and when that child walks out, say, "You know, I've done a poor job teaching you. I'm going to work on your vocabulary tomorrow." And they'll come back and say, "What do you mean?" "Well apparently, your vocabulary, you don't have any vocabulary, 'cause if that's the only word you know then I've done a poor job teaching." Well, that kid goes back to the dorm says, "Yeah, that teacher done a poor job teaching; my vocabulary—."

Technology has been another resource and source of support for teachers. Principal Alexander explained the benefits of some of the tools they purchased:

> When I took over they didn't have very much as far as materials and things to work with and one of my goals in my evaluation is to bring more technology in and that's what we've done. We've bought

Mimios, Mimio pad, and why Mimio pad? Because a teacher can stand in the back of the room and he can look at the back of their heads instead of him being at the front of the room on the board with the kids throwing things at him looking at the back of the head. So, the Mimio pads have been successful.

The educators at this facility ensure an abundance of resources and support is provided for their students. Principal Alexander has made a concerted effort to ensure students have the necessary resources to be successful. Because many learning manipulatives are considered contraband and cannot be brought into the facility, Principal Alexander ordered Mimios/Gizmos for the teachers to use with the students. He explained, "Without those things, you can teach science. We teach science, but you couldn't [dissect] . . . I mean, we can do that now. And, with a little joystick, you know, they can dissect a frog or whatever animal you want to."

Many students are also able to participate in the vocational training and take a test in order to receive a NCCER (National Center for Construction and Education Research) certificate, a national certificate that allows them to work on construction or industrial sites. The fees associated with this certificate are paid through the school district's educational budget. Academic resources such as Read 180, a computer program designed to increase struggling readers' literacy levels, are also provided at the facility for the youth. Principal Alexander shared, "We do have Read 180 in every facility." Furthermore, mentors, Treatment Team meetings, quotes used to spark class discussion, hands-on activities, books, newspapers, and magazines are regularly provided for students.

Having teachers who really want to be there is also a tremendous resource/support for students. Principal Alexander said, "We never have any transfers. Nobody, we have that, 'I'm not going to DJJ' mentality.'" He proudly indicated, "They know the kids by name."

One resource that Principal Alexander recognizes the need for more of is money. He shared, "So many people don't understand how we're funded." The facility receives funds based on the full-time equivalent, or FTE, per student. Four times each year—February, June, July and October, a count is taken to determine the number of youth housed at the facility. This determines the amount of funds the facility will receive for the upcoming months. Principal Alexander added, "It's tough, but with the funding like it is, we're probably doing the best we can do." He elaborated,

It's one of them dang if you do dang if you don't things, you know what I mean? You want more prisons, but you don't want more prisons. And that don't make no sense, but that's exactly what it's like. So if I don't have more [youth], I don't [get] any money to educate them and do what I'm supposed to do.

Despite the lack of funds, Principal Alexander does all he can to ensure students are exposed to as many different resources as possible. In addition to the core courses provided at this facility, he explained, "We got the Ready to Work program, we got the votech (vocational-technical) computer program down there and basically that program we hold it. . . . We have someone that does computer with them, teaches them how to do the computer."

The teachers also serve as tutors for students. Principal Alexander shared, "A lot of my teachers stay after school and work with—, to tutor the kids, come up on the weekend and tutor them." Additionally, he assigns ancillary staff to work with students. According to Principal Alexander,

I've got an aide, couple of aides that go and I keep them in the math class and they'll go to math classes and they'll work with the kids, the lower kids, the business math, the Math-I and then the math teacher will actually work with the trig[onometry] and the geometry kids. So, there's two teachers there, you know, and the biggest thing is keeping 'em busy to where they don't create a disturbance and those kids that are higher achievers, you don't slow them down. They don't get bogged with what's going on maybe with some of the others.

Resources are also provided to students who transition back into Milton County. Principal Alexander explained his role as the transition coordinator:

When . . . one of our kids comes back into our county, transitions back in, one of the first things I ask him, I say, "Where you gonna live?" "I'm gonna live on the street." Or, if we have a kid leaving here going back with transition, I'll say, "All right, when you get back to [another town in Florida], where you gonna live?" "On the street." I said, "Well, where's your mom and dad at?" "I ain't seen 'em in *x* amount of years." Well, when they come back here and they give us that line we have some facilities, the . . . Methodist Church up here has a homeless facility, we have homeless facilities in [Milton] County.

As an additional resource for his students, Principal Alexander actively seeks out mentors for the incarcerated youth housed in the facilities he oversees. He described the tremendous benefits of having mentors serve as resources and support for these youth:

> I go out and get mentors, so by luck I get this guy. He works out at the [military] base. So I had this kid . . . and every time I walked by his desk . . . he was drawing airplanes. I said, "What, you want to be a designer of airplanes?" He said, "No, I wanna be a pilot." That's when I said, "Look . . . I got this mentor so I think he'll really help you."
>
> So I brought him in here, introduced him and the next thing I know he comes in my office. . . . He says . . . "I'd like to take [the student] flying." I say, "Agh" (laughs). I said, "Are you gonna fly, fly, or, he is gonna fly?" He said, "I'm gonna teach him how to fly." . . . I said, "Well, I can't let him go with you now. He'll have to take a guard with him." He said, "I believe I can handle him." I said, "No." So, I went to [the facility's CEO] and he said, "No we can't do that. That's against DJJ rules."
>
> . . .
>
> So, finally, they found a guard that wanted to go. And he took 'em out to [the military base]. It was a four-seater and he rode him around one day for about an hour and then he'd take him the next week. Finally, he's got the kid, he's got the kid flying and he's coming to school and he's teaching the kid all this stuff, you know what I mean. . . . But, that kid ended up getting his pilot license. . . . But see, it meant something to him and he . . . and we got lucky. We found a guy that was sincere about helping a kid, you know; and God, how beautiful is that?

Accountability

Principal Alexander believes the necessary accountability measures are in place to ensure teachers and students are on task. He visits the facilities and walks through the classrooms regularly. Describing a recent visit, he shared, "I was in a class the other day and it was too quiet. I said, 'There's something going on' . . . I got to watching and walking around and those kids were working their back ends off. . . . That just made me so happy."

The facility also holds the educational staff accountable, particularly when it comes to safety and security matters. Principal Alexander stated, "You only get one piece of paper at a time, one little . . . golf course pencil. . . . And, you can't leave the room until everything's accounted for 'cause they can take that paper and make stuff out of it to hurt you."

There are district and state expectations for which the educators are held accountable. According to Principal Alexander, "We follow the pupil progression plan of [Milton] County, which means that everything that a kid in public school or student in public school is responsible for, our kids are responsible for." Part of the DJJ requirement is that every student is assessed upon entry and exit of the facility. "To start with, we give them an entrance test and an exit test required by the Department of Juvenile Justice and the DOE [Department of Education]," said Principal Alexander.

Students at this facility are also responsible for taking the FCAT (Florida Comprehensive Achievement Test), an assessment administered to fulfill a requirement outlined in the NCLB (No Child Left Behind) Act. Principal Alexander embraces this challenge: "My goal is to score on the FCAT—as high as the other schools in the county. That's my goal. People think I'm crazy, but I probably am."

Kyle

Kyle is the vocational teacher at the Greta Olive Juvenile Justice Academy. He teaches vocational classes and an employability class and is shared between two sites. He has been working at this facility for more than 10 years. He believes in establishing positive relationships, and he espouses high expectations for himself, his peers, and his students. He also works hard to ensure that appropriate resources are provided and is adamant that accountability mechanisms be in place to hold all stakeholders accountable.

Relationships

Kyle believes that the school's success is largely because of the positive working relationships between the educators and the juvenile justice staff. According to Kyle, "We have the best working relationship with program [the facility] here of any place in the state." Almost immediately into our conversation, Kyle offered,

> The cooperation between education and program (the facility) here is one of the reasons for our success. And, I don't know if you picked us for a reason or not, but we have a reputation of being one of the best programs in the state, okay. I would say a full 50% of that reputation is because we have such a good relationship between program (the facility) and education.

He further disclosed, "I've spoken to a lot of my peers across the state. We have a better relationship between program and education. . . . There's a lot of cooperation given to us by the program that allows us to do things."

That cooperation comes in the form of a reciprocity that exists between the educational staff and the juvenile justice facility. With the vocational program Kyle teaches, he actively seeks out opportunities for the youth to receive as much hands-on training as possible. As the youth work to beautify the facility, Kyle recognizes the mutual respect and collaboration that coincides with these efforts. He explained,

> We do have a lot of, give and take here . . . like the floor. I don't have to do that stuff, but they still have to learn how to square out the room. They still have to learn how to figure materials. They still have to know to use a trowel and how to use a cutter and you know, how to use all this other stuff. Which, is basically in support of everything that we're doing here.
>
> So why not do it here and let them have some hands-on practical experience and at the same time make them happy and at the same time, earn blue chips? So that when we say, "On the 4th of July, can we have a big picnic? And you're gonna pay for all the food, boss [CEO of the facility]. But, we're gonna have a big picnic, we're gonna have a barbeque; and we're gonna bring the boys out and we're gonna play some basketball, and some bean bag toss, and some, you know tug-of-war and this, that and the other stuff." And he's like, "Sure, no problem."

The educators and the juvenile justice staff also work cohesively to ensure they are meeting the needs of the youth and are continually rated a superior facility. Although educational staff meetings are just for the educators, Kyle explained that the juvenile justice staff also join them whenever there is a need. He shared, "They want to try and tie in with education 'cause we all try to work hand in hand to make this whole process work."

The partnership amongst teachers was also evident as the participants spoke. Kyle explained how he sought assistance to assess the reading level of the core book he is using for his vocational class as he has had several students who have attempted to read it, yet encountered tremendous difficulty. He shared, "I had the reading teacher do the classification on the book. . . . She said, 'You know, [grade] 11 to 14, that's tough.' And I'm like, 'Well, it's a post secondary book really.'" Because of what

Kyle learned from the reading teacher, he recognizes he has to "work with students on . . . vocabulary and stuff like that; stuff to help them get through." He provides additional resources to further enhance students' understanding, rather than deny them access to this vocational program because of possible learning deficiencies.

Kyle takes pride in the relationships he establishes with his students and is also committed to continuing the relationships he has with the community, including the parents of the youth housed in this facility. His examples demonstrate how personable he is and how his approach has the potential for great dividends. He shared a conversation he had with a parent who came in to pick up her son who was allowed a home visit on the same morning I was scheduled to interview Kyle:

> One of the number one things that I found that the boys who like drawing is tattoos. They want to be tattoo artists (chuckles). It just so happened that one of them that likes to draw that's in my employability class was going on a home visit this morning. . . . I was able to talk to his mother and I explained to her; I said, "I hope you're not upset with me but I am trying to get him to run with it. 'Cause I've seen him draw, I mean he is really good and he loves to do it. If you don't watch him, he won't be doing his work, he'll be drawing. Okay?"
>
> So, I told her, I said, "I'm trying to get him to go to school," I said, "Because if he goes and he gets advanced education beyond high school in drawing, it's going to provide him with not only skill and talent but also some credentials." And I said, "Then he has a leg up over the person that just has skill." Okay, not only that, but I said, "This is his sprout, you know, and a sprout, when it comes up you can't tell what it is, but when it becomes this tree, you know, it might be a tattoo sprout now but after he gets his education, he could be in graphic design, he could be you know, it's a means for him to learn the other things that's out there and you know, and how to get into it."
>
> And she was like, "Ah, you know, I never really thought about that." 'Cause she's kind of—. She doesn't mind him being a tattoo artist. I don't know. I think she looks at it as kind of an area that she's not wild about him being involved with the people in that industry (laughs). So, uh, so that, you know, that made her, you know, take a breath of relief, you know, she was like, "Yeah, that's true; I never thought about that. He might decide that there's something else he

wants to do." And I said, "Well you know, the only way to expose him to that stuff is to put him in school. You know, with grants and scholarships and he just turned 15 today, you know." I said, "He's young enough that he can still do well enough in school to start getting some grants and scholarships."

There is a reciprocity that also exists between the educators at this facility and their local school district. Because of their relationships within the school district and the vocational component of their educational program, these educators are able to reciprocate many favors to their colleagues. Kyle shared,

I'm a [Milton] County schoolteacher. As such, I know a whole lot of [Milton] County schoolteachers (laughs), and they know what I do, and so they will ask me, "Can you do this or can you help me with that or can you help me with this?"

Describing some work his vocational students recently completed at a local school, Kyle further explained,

We did all the landscape stuff but a friend of mine who is the horticulture landscape management teacher over at the [vocational–technical high school], he donated and had his guys install the plants. Okay? So basically, all the school had to pay for was the paving stones and the concrete, you know, so it was pretty good.

Expectations

In addition to the positive working relationships the educators have with the juvenile justice staff, Kyle believes the other reason for their success is because they have "teachers that really care." The teachers in this facility have been recognized as school, district and state teachers of the year. They hold one another with high regard and esteem. With these titles come great expectations. Kyle listed all the teachers, including himself who have been recognized for their excellence in teaching and explained,

So I mean we've got good people here and . . . 90% of us have between 10 and 12 years. . . . Most of us have been here for a while and we're here because . . . this is what I want to do. And, not only that, but I'm the kind of person, if you're here, I'm hoping it's what you want to do too, because they'll know. They know. You cannot, you cannot go in there and pull the wool over their eyes for more than a couple, three classes. And then they've got you pegged, "Oh, you here for the check, big boy, okay."

Educators at this facility are committed to ensuring that they provide students with as many opportunities as possible. Instead of going through the motions, they maintain high expectations as they seek out ways to increase their effectiveness. They take the initiative to bring about changes that will further enhance the students' learning experiences and benefit students. Kyle shared, "The Florida Sunshine State Standards for masonry didn't necessarily fill the bill for what the contractors were looking for when youth would step out and want to go get a job. So I began looking for an alternative." Kyle was influential in establishing the vocational program that is now offered at the facility that provides the youth with a national certification upon exiting.

Kyle believes in the importance of maintaining high expectations for his students and providing them with ample hands-on opportunities to practice the skills he teaches them in class. He was very proud as he shared,

You know all the stuff that you saw coming in around the flagpole . . . the stonework . . . all the boys did that. You know the floors out here. Did you see 'em? That's done throughout the building. The boys did all of that. . . . If you have the opportunity to use the administrator bathroom . . . all the tile work, all the painting, all the installation of fixtures . . . were all done by the boys. . . . My room, that I teach in has porcelain tile floors, ceramic tile on one wall, parquet flooring, has a wainscot around that the boys did, and on the back, we took brick and cut them into 3/8-inch slabs and we put 'em up on the wall and it looks like we have a brick wall in the back, but, it's veneer . . . I try to expose them to as many things as I can.

The educators wholeheartedly believe in the necessity to differentiate instruction and meet the needs of their students. Kyle explained, "As a teacher, you have to differentiate your instruction . . . and every one of my students are on different chapters, okay, so, you know I have to help the students that really need the help." He is determined to put his best effort forward to help students achieve no matter their educational strengths or weaknesses. He elaborated, "I need to do the best I can for 'each one of them in the level that they're going to be able to obtain and try to push them to go on to increase their education level."

Additionally, the educators also celebrate up to six students every other week—four or five students of the week and possibly one most improved, which reinforces the expectations they have for students. With their own money, the educators take turns to purchase lunches and snacks to share with the students they've selected. According to Kyle, "We eat lunch with them while they eat all of their junk that we just bought for them for student of the week." Believing this to be a unique experience for incarcerated youth, Kyle divulged, "Some of the facilities don't do that."

Because of the positive relationships Kyle has established with his students, he expects his students will make better choices when they leave. He shared, "They know that I love them. They know that I want them to do well. But they also know that my expectation is, that they're going to put their effort into it." He expounded,

> If they don't put their effort into it, they know that I'm not going to be happy with 'em. Because, you know, they've got to get out of the habit that things are just going to fall into place. . . . Because you had the ability to not be there. I say it's choices. You know, you gotta make the right choices and you got to follow through and that's really, you know. Yeah, I teach masonry and I teach employability but in both of my classes, I'm not ashamed to tell you that I try to teach them also how to be a man, you know. That's important to me and you know, and sometimes, it might go beyond the norms.

Kyle believes it's all in what you expect of students. He recognizes, "There's some of 'em that they receive their full accommodations, differentiated instruction and stuff like that because they truly need it." However, he also strongly believes many youth are misclassified and he refuses to allow them to use their ESE label as an excuse. He divulged,

> Oh, me, I've passed the ESE certification exam but I'm not qualified to say what's wrong with a kid or what's right with a kid, or whatever. But I have seen a lot of kids that have come in here that their records for years have been that they're EBD (emotionally–behaviorally disturbed). And, basically all it takes is, take him aside saying look, "Do you know why you have this? Do you understand that your, your desire to just speak out, out of turn; your desire to you know, want to

be first; your desire, you know, all these things makes it appear that you do not have control? I know you do. Okay, so, if you want to use your title in other classes, that's fine, but it's not going to work here, okay?"

Resources

Kyle wanted to ensure students were able to leave the facility with a certification that would allow them to be hired to work at construction or industrial sites. He taught a vocational course for several years that only provided certificates for students demonstrating their hours within the course. To provide a much-needed resource for his students, Kyle was instrumental in establishing a new vocational class which provides national certification, to ensure students have a greater opportunity for success upon leaving the facility. He shared,

> I began looking for an alternative and I came across NCCER. . . . It's a nationwide program that basically these people got together and they sent surveys out to contractors, supervisors, stuff like that; and wanted to know, what is it that you want to know when a person comes to work for you in a construction/industrial site? The result of that is this book. . . . The core book is the first step that you have to accomplish in your NCCER quest to obtain your card. Now when you finish this book, you do receive a card. This is a national certification.
>
> It's, it's better for the guys. They get to focus in the small amount of time that they have . . . to obtain these positions across the nation and construction and industrial work settings. . . . It's working well. I have my last year's results that I have 32 people that were able to pass this and obtain their certifications.

The education side also pays the fee for the students to obtain their cards, another resource for students. Kyle disclosed, "Now, we have to pay $25 dollars per person to do that. Now, that's a small price to pay for what they get and my boss has absolutely no problem doing that."

The educators at this facility are also committed to putting forth their best effort despite the realization that they may not be able to reach each student. Their desire to see students succeed leads them to differentiate lessons and allow as many students to be exposed to the vocational course to receive national certification—a tremendous resource. Kyle expounded,

I've come to the conclusion that out of all the people that I teach— and this is just from doing it a year so far—out of all the people that I try to teach this information, I'm going to have just a little under half be able to get their certification. But my, my objective is to make sure that those people are at least highly qualified and able to get jobs as laborers, tenders, and other people that work on construction and industrial sites that aren't necessarily responsible for the higher-level requirements of the job.

Kyle thinks it is important to provide an adequate education for the youth based upon what students hope to achieve and are capable of achieving. He explained, "I will take the kids that absolutely just are not cutting it in this book, and I will, I will teach them to be the best laborer that they can be, you know, give them as much as I can." He continued,

I'm'a tell you right now, I've got a couple, they'll never get through that book. . . . We've got 70 IQ here and, and he's in my class and . . . there's no way that he's . . . going to get through that book. But he does learn very well hands-on. He learns very well. He can go out there and he can precisely mix mud to the exact specification that you want it, you know, because he learns very well with hands-on. He can do that kind of thing.

And, it takes us to be able to recognize that and say, "Okay, well you know what, we're not going to put him out of this program [vocational class], because he can't do this program. If this is what he's going to do, then what we're going to do is modify the program to teach him to be the best at what he can be within this program." You know, and that's what we need to start doing. I mean, we need to start basing our education and what we do and what we teach, based upon what the kid can do and needs to do, you know, not what we want the kid to do.

Kyle shared how he received permission from the district for the vocational program and how Principal Alexander, "gives us the leeway to do the things that we need to do that's best for the child." This includes making what they believe are the appropriate modifications for students.

Treatment team is another resource for students. Although this falls under the DJJ (Department of Juvenile Justice) umbrella, teachers are expected to provide the team with updates on a regular basis. According to Kyle,

The reason they call it treatment team is because once a month we meet with the youth, with the parents on the phone, a therapist is there, a program representative is there, education representative— . . . they consider all three legs of the triad [education, therapy, program rehabilitation] being, you know critical in making this functional; make it work. And it has. The students have a better opportunity not being a statistic of recidivism.

Accountability

Kyle is a firm believer in the importance of accountability and believes everyone should be held accountable. He admonished, "It's my opinion that every school in the district, whether it's private or whatever, should answer to somebody."

The educators at this facility ensure they are being held accountable. This comes in various forms. The questions that were posed to Kyle over the years regarding the vocational classes students were taking was a form of accountability which led him to look into the NCCER certification and provide what is currently being offered. He stated he kept "hearing the question" and decided it was time to act. Kyle shared the dialogue he had years ago. According to Kyle, people asked, "'What kind of certification do they get?' And I'm like, 'Well they get a certificate that they can transfer?' 'Well, what kind of programs could be taught where they can get a certification during the time that they're here?'" The juvenile facility also determines which students can participate in the vocational program, another level of accountability. Kyle stated,

Once their names are on a list, unfortunately at this point, they have to have at least 60 days in the facility for a security observation period, to make sure that they're not going to abscond or do anything else. And then once they've passed that point, then the director approves by name each one of those that can come into the [vocational] class.

Kyle is adamant that the teachers at this facility really care—if they don't, he and other teachers will not stand for it. He divulged, "We have teachers that really care, and if they don't, I'm gonna snitch them out." He further explained this was a shared level of accountability by the other teachers in this facility as well: "[MA] will snitch 'em out. [GV] will snitch 'em out. We got somebody that wants to show movies all the time, oh, okay, 'Well maybe you need to go work for [another facility], okay, not here.'"

Mae

Mae teaches math at the Greta Olive Juvenile Justice Academy. She received this teaching position just nine months before I met with her. For more than 10 years, Mae was involved as a volunteer and teacher's aide at traditional schools and various DJJ sites within the district, including this facility. Mae espoused positive relationships, high expectations, the importance of appropriate resources—particularly for teachers and students—and multiple forms of accountability.

Relationships

The educators espouse a strong cohesiveness existing between the juvenile justice administrators/juvenile justice staff and the educational staff at this facility. This is important because of the need to be in sync as it relates to scheduling for the students and establishing support structures. Mae explained the significance of this type of relationship: "So program [the facility] works with education . . . scheduling the students in classes, who can be with who, who can't be around who, you know—that type of a thing when it does come up."

Mae also expressed the importance of working collaboratively with her colleagues. She shared, "It is nice to be able—, if a child isn't cooperating with me to be able to talk to their reading teacher. . . . I will talk with her and see, you know, what she says about it, you know. . . . We work together."

This collegiality is also seen among the teachers, particularly because of the bond that has been established over the years. Mae shared, "So . . . when I came back this February . . . a lot of the same people in here [knew] me already and my other experience in other facilities."

Mae shared how she uses math inventory sheets to get to know her new students when they enter the facility. She explained, "I'll talk individually with the student and sometimes they're forthcoming with what they know, sometimes not, which is another reason it's kind of nice to have a little something that they've already done."

There's also a long history of relationships between the other educators at this facility and the school district. Most of the teachers at this facility have been teaching or in the field of education within this location or the school district for at least 10 to 12 years. Mae explained how she ended up working at this facility:

> The principal at [another school] at the time . . . went from being principal at [a school] to being principal of DJJ. . . . This was between 10 and 15 years ago. . . . He knew a lot of us from [his previous

school] and he invited a lot of us to come visit and there's still . . . some of us around at the different facilities here in [Milton] County; they're still DJJ. And we've had several principals since then, but that's how I got into it.

Expectations

All the educators at this facility are certified in reading. They expect that they will provide the appropriate strategies needed for students to succeed. Mae explained, "We could be their reading teacher. I could be their reading teacher and their math teacher as long as they're level 2 [on the Florida Comprehensive Achievement Test] or higher." This also demonstrates her expectation to be prepared to work with her students.

Mae wants to ensure that students are exposed to an equal or better educational environment in this facility. The teachers here expect to work at the same pace as the regular schools so students won't be completely lost upon returning to school after exiting the facility. Mae stated, "I try to keep the same pacing as the regular schools, for example [at the local] high school and I give the students a pacing chart." Mae also believes her role in providing her students with a high-quality education involves more than "just teaching math." She elaborated,

> Even though I teach math, a lot of people think out in the real world that it's just your computational part and it's rote. No, the student has to be able to read and comprehend and you have to use the reading strategies. They have to be able to write in math . . . so . . . I do talk to the reading teachers. I have gotten SRI (Scholastic Reading Inventory) scores. I do want to know what a child's reading ability is.

The educators at this facility also bring a wealth of knowledge with them that has developed over the years. The educators expect themselves and the other educators within the facility to have a wealth of experience. Referring to the other teachers I was scheduled to interview, Mae shared, "I mean, they've been here for a while, too (laughs), and so no none of us are new or evenly vaguely new. So we're long-timers."

Mae believes her experience assisting for many years in the district allows her to now experience tremendous successes as an educator in this juvenile justice setting. The expectation Mae had before accepting this position was that she wouldn't teach until she believed she was well equipped. She explained,

When I started, my first day was at [the] detention center and I was a volunteer . . . so I was able to gain a lot of experience with these type of students before I ever took a dime of anybody's money. And then, I was also a sub for instructional and non-instructional in DJJ. . . . I kind of worked my way into this. I was a teacher's aide for three and a half years and between that and being a teacher, I was a long-term sub, which gave me the additional time to get my act together to teach.

Mae believes she can meet students' needs better in this environment than in a traditional setting:

I feel like we can actually do more here . . . because I don't have a whole class of Algebra 1, and everybody—. It's not that structured that everybody has to be in this certain place. And, even with my middle schoolers where I try to keep them as a group generally on a certain track to be able to fulfill all the standards and for them to be ready for FCAT, I still have the ability to be able to individualize it and meet them where they are and I feel like I have that ability more here in DJJ than I would if I was in the regular school system out there.

The educators expect that the juvenile justice staff will be in the classroom with them to help maintain order in a positive way and will work collaboratively with the educators to provide the incarcerated youth with an optimal learning environment. Mae expects the juvenile justice staff to be in the classroom during class time. She explained, "We're supposed to have and most of the time we have . . . youth care workers here and there's usually one at your, in your room, at the door or you know within calling distance."

Throughout my interviews, the educators at this facility continually emphasized the importance of instilling pride in students. They celebrate students by displaying their work on the walls. Mae said, after students worked on a "Graphiti" (graphing coordinates) activity, she displayed their work "because there's a little bit of boy in some of these, even young men, and they'll say they want to see their artwork on the wall."

Mae believes students should be aware of what is expected of them if they were in a traditional school and ensure their transition is smooth. At this facility, although students are encouraged to work at their own pace, they are expected to be on target when they return. Mae explained,

[This] shows what the regular schools are doing conceptwise, Sunshine State Standard wise, the first nine weeks, first quarter, second, third and fourth. And a student is very aware of what's going on out there in the real world so that they can transition to that when they leave here. So there, there are no surprises; however, they still are working at their own pace here and they can still work at a faster pace if they want to catch up and earn, for example, a half a credit in Algebra 1A.

Resources

Having the necessary resources and support are vital to ensuring students have the opportunity to receive a high-quality education. The educators at the Greta Olive Juvenile Justice Academy believe they have what they and their students need to be successful. Mae takes professional development seriously and believes the district has served and continues to serve as a tremendous resource. Mae explained, "It's all been professional development, meaning whatever I could do to further my education for free." In her role as volunteer, substitute, and teaching assistant, she has also been able to learn many strategies that she uses today. She shared, "I . . . basically got to practice teaching before I was an official teacher with the school district and here in [Milton] County." Mae elaborated,

So I've had the privilege of observing in a lot of classrooms, and spending time in there without being the teacher on record. . . . Like I said, as an aide, I walked around with a letter of eligibility which said I could be hired as a teacher, but I wasn't official and so I got to do a lot of practice that way . . . I've gone to different gang trainings . . . In my math trainings, we developed what are called pacing charts and . . . we're considered a regular school just like any other in the district, and so I go to the same workshops as everybody else in the district, and of course there are other DJJ teachers from the other facilities there.

I'm blessed in the fact that I do work for, even though I am program [juvenile justice], I'm also [Milton] County school system, and I have access to any and all of it that I want. I consider that a blessing.

Mae has also established additional strategies for her students. Describing a daily activity she does with her students, she shared, "One thing I do together with all of my students in the class is we have math vocabulary and . . . that's what I do for a bell ringer." She stated that, "Over the years I've developed my own vocabulary list, 10 terms per list, and they have two terms per day and I put 'em up on the board and we discuss." She elaborated, "We talk about the morphemes, we break 'em down, prefixes, suffixes, roots, or base words, and we talk about how those terms are used."

There is also a mobile library from which students choose reading materials. Mae said, "I call it a moving library. We have these huge metal book carts, and, during the main school day, we shove them all out in the big hallway and they're up against the wall. Students have access."

The educators continually seek out additional resources for their students. Mae shared a recent experience about a student who just left. According to Mae, "Math was his worst subject. I emailed . . . our teacher on special assignment . . . I need an end-of-course math re-exam for [my student]. . . . He ended up passing it and . . . that was the last thing he needed to get promoted to high school." She also described other ways she has helped students attain their goals:

> I've had a student and he had all his math requirements already met . . . but he was wanting to go into the military when he got out and he did get his high school diploma by the way, and graduated this past school year, and so I worked with him out of an ASVAB [Armed Services Vocational Aptitude Battery] book. We worked on, you know passing the math part of some of that.

To serve as a greater resource to her students, in addition to the required assessments administered to students when they enter the facility, Mae provides an assessment to see where students are so she can begin providing the appropriate instruction and resources to help them strengthen their math proficiency. She explained, "I give them their little handy dandy test which gives me, before I can get any other test results, it gives me an idea of what they know and even before I have their schedule and we have their records."

In addition to the hands-on training the youth receive while in the vocational class, Mae explained how she provides hands-on learning opportunities for her students, including by teaching

> [p]robability and odds with Skittles. Which, you know, I can go to Sam's [Club] and buy the big box and everybody has their big individual packets, so I like to do things like that. I have like, around holidays I can take certain shapes, Valentine's for example, with construction paper and hopefully plastic scissors we can do the perimeter

and area of a heart and the heart is made up of, the two side circles that make the whole circle, your two right triangles, so we can get into the Pythagorean theorem . . .

Accountability

Mae expounded on the matters of safety and security for which the educators are held accountable. According to Mae, "We . . . provide the paper and program [the facility] provides the little golf pencils. . . . They're on a little block and they have to be counted in and out. We can't use staples. We can't bring in anything metal into the facility."

Although Mae understands the importance of these safety matters, she also acknowledges the limitations they place on her ability to provide students with myriad hands-on experiences. Mae explained,

It limits you as far as if I wanted to do hands-on math projects and all, you know, scissors, or if I wanted to do constructions in geometry. I can't hand them a traditional compass. I have these special little what they call safety flap compasses but it does limit doing some of the constructions and all. . . . I can't hand them a regular compass with a nice metal point on the end. . . . Because it is a program [facility] and again because I'm a math teacher, everything gets counted out, everything gets counted in.

You know, you have to go through the proper channels to get approval. For example, if I do a probability and odds project with Skittles, it literally goes through all the chain to the top. It's a big deal, but I like to do it with Skittles, 'cause then the kids can eat the skittles when they're done and I don't have to count 'em back in (laughs). You know, you gotta count calculators. The staff has to deal with the pencils. If the pencils aren't all there then, you know, it's like, "Nobody's leaving the classroom."

There is also an accountability mechanism in place to identify students who are not allowed to be on the computers. The teachers and juvenile justice staff are regularly kept up to date on the students who are banned from using the computer. Within the master schedule, the teachers, and the teachers' students for each class, are listed. Any student who is not able to be on the computers is identified in red.

While Mae was a substitute teacher, before coming on board as an official math teacher, she was also held accountable. She shared that even as a substitute, she "had somebody that looked if I did lesson plans or I did any of that."

Mae also shared the monthly data updates for which the educators are responsible. Mae explained, "I use that [data] to help develop their PMP [Progress Monitoring Plan]. All students have a portfolio and PMP . . . and we update those once a month and we try to update those with the students."

The participants also often referred to the Florida Sunshine State Standards. Mae highlighted the importance of "fulfilling the Sunshine State Standards which are required by law . . . the minimum guidelines that the student needs to know . . . so you have the differentiation in order to be able to help that student where they are." Additionally, she further described what she is being held accountable for within the NCLB (No Child Left Behind) requirements. According to Mae, "Part of what I have to do as a math teacher is . . . backtrack to be able to—, sometimes to get to where you are now, and fulfill what you need to fulfill, in order for that child to progress."

Students at Greta Olive are also held accountable for passing the state end-of-course exams. Mae explained,

> Now, technically if it's algebra 1B or geometry since we have the state end-of-course exams on the computer, they can't technically get that credit until they have completed that coursework for the year. They complete the coursework and they have to pass the state online test. We offer all the regular tests here that you would in a regular school in [Milton] County.

The educators in this facility also use the FCAT (Florida Comprehensive Achievement Test) as a bar to measure their effectiveness. Although there is great debate about No Child Left Behind and high-stakes tests, accepting this as some standard measurement that all students are expected to attain, the educators at this facility use FCAT as their benchmark. Mae shared, "I want them to do, learn certain concepts so at the end of the year they'll be ready for FCAT."

David

David teaches reading and social studies at the Greta Olive Juvenile Justice Academy and another facility operated by the same for-profit organization. He has served as a reading teacher at this facility for 10 years and has more than 12 years' teaching experience. David stresses the importance of establishing positive relationships with students. He maintains high expectations and believes even the most basic materials are all that's needed to teach students effectively. He appreciates the accountability mechanisms that are in place.

Relationships

The principal and the teachers at this facility recognize the importance of establishing relationships with their students. Time is taken at the beginning of each school year and as new students arrive, to get to know students and allow students to share their strengths and weaknesses and how they feel they learn best. This is important because of the mobility of the incarcerated youth. Although the average length of stay is six months for the youth housed at this facility, there is tremendous variability when youth begin serving their time. On any given day in one classroom, there could be five students who are in their sixth month at the facility and three students in their fourth month; four students may only be completing their first week. David stresses the importance of getting to know the students. He divulged, "I think that's the key for new teachers coming in—to really try to understand where these kids are coming from and understand how to talk to them."

Expectations

The educators at this facility espouse high expectations for themselves, their peers, and their students. David stated, "It's all in what you expect." These educators expect a lot and celebrate their accomplishments. While they also have expectations for the juvenile justice staff, they take the ownership for what is happening in the classrooms each day. David described the daily challenges he faces:

> Ninety percent of the time, I'm thinking less about the standards and I'm thinking more about how I'm going to teach them or what I'm going to say to these kids to make them do this work that I put in front of them you know, 'cause that's what it's all about.

David is committed to his role as a classroom teacher at this facility and believes he doesn't need much to be an effective teacher:

> I mean, I'm old school, you know? It's nothing wrong with sitting down and getting a book, reading what's in the book and then answering questions about it. That's the way we learned and we turned out okay. You know, got a pencil, piece of paper, that's all I need to teach. . . . I would like to think that I could go teach in a hut in Africa somewhere as long as they had a blackboard and some

chalk, you know, and that's the way I think teaching should be. You know, get them involved in that.

He recognizes the importance of getting to know his students and understanding what might be happening with the youth. He expects that he will get to know his students to ensure the time spent with them is maximized. David explained, "they could care less about what you're trying to teach 'em, when they're thinking about, 'When am I going to see my mom again?' . . . You gotta wrap your mind around that and understand that's what's going on with these kids." Because of this, he stresses the need for having a tremendous amount of patience that's required when teaching incarcerated youth:

> You have to have a lot of patience. You know, I guess I use more of that psychology thing, you know, and you just have to. I don't know, I guess my thing is I just stay on focus. You know, I just focus on what we're doing in class and try to get them focused, 'cause they're all over the place. They got all these other stuff in their head. They'll try to get you off course and off track.

Educators at this facility believe in measuring students' growth to determine their effectiveness. David expects students will improve three to four grade levels within the time he has with the youth. This demonstrates the high expectations he has for students, particularly because they are only with him for six to nine months. He also realizes the importance of him instilling confidence to ensure that students continue their progress long after they leave the facility. David indicated,

> You know, if I have a kid coming in here and comes in reading at the third grade level and in six months he leaves here reading at a sixth- or seventh-grade level I feel like I did a pretty good job. That's how I—. That's how I measure myself, and their growth. . . . And, like I said at the beginning, my goal is to get that kid confidence so that he can feel like he can go back to the regular classroom and not have to skip school all day and he can actually do that, and sit in class and get his grades and move on.

David further acknowledged it's his responsibility and he expects himself to keep his students on task. Similar to Principal Alexander, David takes an assertive stance so students can take full advantage of the learning environment provided. He divulged, "I am the instructional program (laughs). You know, when I step in that room, it's my class, and it goes the way I say it goes, and these kids understand that." David expects that he will ensure the students are focused and on task each day:

> If they can get over on you, they will. But if you, if you're like, "This is what we're here to learn, and we're focusing on this." They're gonna come up; they're gonna ask you a bunch of questions. "I'm not author-ized to answer that right now, so I'm trying to get my mind focused and ready for class, please have a seat (chuckles)." It's just like that. You have to stay on point with them all the time and then after they're done with their lesson and everything, yeah, "You can ask me about . . . whatever (laughs)." But until that happens—; I always tell them, "You don't get what you want until I get what I want, and I want you to do your schoolwork and until I get that done, don't talk to me about anything else. Do you have a question about your schoolwork, sir?" (Laughs.)

The educators also emphasize the importance of meeting students where they are. David shared, "You gotta meet the kids where they are. You can't throw some curriculum in front of them, that there's no way they're gonna do. . . . You gotta find something they do well and you got to go from there." He described the importance of infusing positive reinforcement in his classroom while simultaneously helping to build the youths' confidence:

> My goal is to keep 'em in school, you know. Most of these guys haven't been to school in weeks, months, some of them, years, you know. But, if I can build some confidence in them and show them, you can sit in a classroom even if there's 30 other kids in the class and not feel lost and not feel like you gotta cut up in class 'cause you feel stupid or you don't know, you know? That's what's going on with them. You know, when kids act up in class, it's because they don't understand, you know and that's what—. You gotta recognize that. When they start getting mad and everything and they're like, "Oh, I'm not doing that. This is stupid." It's 'cause they don't understand what's going on. If you go over and show them how to do it and say, "Hey, I knew you could do it, man. That's a great job." He's like, "All right man, I got this." You know, and they'll just get right into it, so it's all about positive reinforcement.

David believes in the importance of educators' being positive, regard-less of what students say or do:

You know, it's not about negative reinforcement with these guys. They get a lot of that. They know how to deal with that. It's about positive reinforcement. You know, I've always said, "If you ever find yourself raising your voice with these kids, you lost." So (laughs), you know, 'cause they know. That's what they want. They want that conversation. If they can sit up there and argue with you all day long in class, they're good. They're not doing your schoolwork, right (laughs)? So, they won.

David expects the students to complete their work regardless of the excuses they provide and he reemphasizes their need for continual positive reinforcement. He shared, "You just have to meet 'em where they are and then give 'em a lot of positive reinforcement . . . even if it's just their handwriting. You say, 'Man, you have excellent handwriting. That's great man, keep going.' . . . Just find something." He cited a recent example that demonstrates his expectations for his students:

I got this kid. I think he's 16 or 17 and he's reading at a seventh-grade level. He's enrolled in the eighth grade, and he's just never done any thing in school, you know. He's always told his teachers that he couldn't do stuff. He's been thrown out of a bunch of schools for fighting teachers and stuff like that. . . . He's been here for two weeks. So I finally got him to do one assignment yesterday, and he just keeps hitting me with all these excuses, and I'm like, "I don't have time for excuses."

"I have ADHD." "Yeah, me too," whatever (laughs). I don't have ADHD, but I told him that, you know. "I don't have time for your excuses. You sit down and do your work. If you need some help with it, let me know, but I don't have time for your excuses." And I don't take excuses from any of them. You know, all these labels they put on these kids. "I expect you to do your work and I know you can do it, so do it."

The educators ensure that there are incentives for students, recognizing the leverage they have with their expectations and what needs to be in place to further encourage students to make good choices and complete what they're supposed to complete. "They like to fight over the magazines and stuff, but they know, 'You're not going to see that until you get done with your regular assignment.' So you know, it's instilling that kind of thing, work before play," stated David. He elaborated,

[The students ask], "How come we never have fun in here?" And I'm like and I go Joe Pesci on 'em. I'm like, "What, am I here to entertain you? Am I some kind of clown? This isn't fun. This is work. Do I look like I'm having fun? We're working here. This is about work. You come to school to work." And I think that's what kids don't get you know. You have to work to be successful in life, period. And my students know when you come in the class, you're going to either be reading something or writing something. We're going to be working. "Don't talk to me about play. You work first, and then you can play."

While the educators at this facility recognize the importance of being positive with students and focusing on the positive it is this same expectation David maintains for the juvenile justice staff. He asserted, "I think there's too much negative reinforcement going around here. You know, they take away their points for everything you know. And all this stuff is going on in these kids' heads." He elaborated,

You know, personally in class, I don't care if they're sitting on a wall as long as they're doing their schoolwork. You know but these, you know, just sitting wrong in their seat, if they're slouching, or something like this, you got people yelling, "Sit up in your seat. Do this. Do that." I'm like, "Leave the kid alone man. He's reading (laughs). Let him do his work."

So now the kid is thinking . . . "Aw man, she's gonna take my points," instead of reading the work. And he's gone, you know, it's gonna take me a half hour to get him back and doing his reading again and that's, that's happening in, you know, in 10 other spots all around the room (chuckles).

I would give 'em points for doing positive things. You know, even if they're faking it just to make it you know. If you fake it for six months, some of that might rub off (laughs), you know.

Resources

David believes he and his colleagues teach in a very supportive environment, one with appropriate resources to help him successfully fulfill his responsibilities as a juvenile justice educator:

We have all sorts of support, you know, from our peers to our principal. I think our principal is very supportive. He understands, you know, what's going on with the system. He understands the kids, which is very important. And I think the district supports us as well, you know. If I ever need anything for the classroom . . . it's there. It's all there. They're very supportive.

David recognized that his administrators are "here all the time." He further emphasized this resource when he shared the frequency of the classroom visits and the feedback he receives. David told me that the administrators are "here at least once a week, sticking their heads in the door. If they don't think I'm doing something well, they'll pull me out of class and say something, but, most of the time, they just give thumbs up."

The educators see themselves as resources for the students. David believes his psychology degree comes in "very handy here." He also believes his status as a writer allows more students to respect the skills he tries to teach. He brings his writings into his classroom for the students to critique and discuss. He shared, "I think I have a bit of an advantage 'cause I'm a novelist. I write books and I write books about kids that have been through a lot of adversity."

The monthly team that comes together to discuss the youths' progress, called the treatment team, also serves as a tremendous resource for students. David stated, "They get input from the teachers every month." He explained, "We do treatment team notes and attend treatment team meetings, so we're involved in their progress and updating their progress so their case managers and their therapists and everybody knows how they're progressing."

The educators also recognize how much students benefit from interactive discussions focused on the standards or subject the teacher is trying to teach. Each day, David places a quote and has the students respond to questions in writing and verbally:

I put a starter on the board, and it's just a daily quote, and I ask them three questions about it. Like today's quote was [recites from memory] "Nobody gets through life without hardships, not even saints or sages." And it's a good opportunity to go over vocabulary with them, 'cause a bunch of 'em will say, "Hey, what's a sage?" You know, so we'll talk about that. Then I ask them three questions. I ask them: What does it mean? Do you agree with it and then try to relate it to a real life situation. And, you know it doesn't have to be something about themselves. It could be something they saw on the news, read in a book or saw in a movie or something like that. And that just gets them thinking, gets them going.

In addition to the "moving library" that serves as a resource for students, teachers bring in reading materials for students and use this as an incentive for students to complete their work. David brings in books from the library and other reading materials like newspapers, for his students. He shared, "I bring library books in that they want to see, want to read. They're all reading the *Hunger Games: Catching Fire* right now. I bring in magazines, national geographic, sports magazines, all that kind of stuff."

Accountability

David believes there is an appropriate level of accountability within this facility. His administrators visit his classroom often and provide him with feedback. The Florida Comprehensive Achievement Test (FCAT) also provides a level of accountability as students who are in the facility during the testing times are responsible for taking the assessment. David shared his expectation of wanting the students to do well on FCAT and how he prepares his students:

> What I'm doing is I'm basically teaching them how to do a paragraph and I do a lot of this. We do a lot of quick write paragraphs. You know, so that . . . when it gets time for FCAT and essay times, and it asks them to put together a five-paragraph essay, they don't look at me like "What?" "We've been writing paragraphs, don't play with me, you know how to do this."

Discussion

Relationships

There are myriad relationships amongst the educators at the Greta Olive Juvenile Justice Academy that are varied and appear healthy, as evidenced by their open communication and the apparent affection they have for their colleagues as they spoke about them working as a team and being recognized as outstanding local and state educators. The ongoing communication with the reading teacher is key because incarcerated youth tend to have significantly low reading levels. There is an evident reciprocity of respect and favors done for one another and at the various sites within the school district. The educators demonstrate respect and admiration for their peers. This was evident as they shared their stories.

As evidenced by the descriptions provided by the educators, the relationships between them and the juvenile justice administrators and juvenile justice staff also seem to be strong. There is open communication and an apparent reciprocal partnership, which allows the youth to benefit tremendously.

Longevity is highly valued and seems to contribute to the strong relationships. Each of the participants has spent more than 10 years working for the Milton County Public Schools. This has allowed them to build relationships over time that now overlap in their roles as educators at the Greta Olive Juvenile Justice Academy.

Because of the school district's and the facility's reputations, community members become involved and provide resources to the youth in the capacity as mentors and potential employers. Principal Alexander cited two examples of the roles mentors played for the incarcerated youth at this facility because of their relationships, which further provide the youth with additional resources and support.

While maintaining positive relationships with youth in any setting are important, Principal Alexander stresses its importance in this environment because of the number of incarcerated youth who are dealing with issues of trust. Principal Alexander makes it a point to introduce himself to the youth when they arrive and maintains ongoing conversations. The effectiveness of this approach is evident in the example he provided when the youth were rioting and the sheriff's department was called to the facility. When the sheriffs couldn't get the youth calmed down, Principal Alexander was successful because of the relationships and trust he previously established with the youth.

Although it's questionable that the district's bookkeeper was able to find and give Principal Alexander additional funds for his DJJ schools, it is obvious what can happen when positive working relationships exist between the school leader and the district personnel. The educators appear to be invested in each other and the school district.

Expectations

The educators maintain high expectations for themselves and one another. They believe their school district maintains higher standards for their teachers and students than any other school district in Florida. This is evidenced as Mae only accepted her role as a teacher in this facility after multiple years of serving as a volunteer and teaching assistant to gain what she felt was much-needed experience to make a difference with this population.

The educators have a desire to work with incarcerated youth and they maintain high expectations for themselves, each other, the juvenile justice staff, and students. They believe their commitment, expertise, provision of hands-on, relevant instruction and ability to motivate the youth at the facility are the essential ingredients for ensuring the incarcerated youth housed at the Greta Olive Juvenile Justice Academy are provided with a high-quality education.

The educators are convinced, however, that there are different ways of measuring and providing a high-quality education based on where the student is academically. They often used the phrase, "teaching or working a student to his level" or "working with students based on what they're capable of." Despite this ambiguity, the educators maintain high expectations for their students, supporting them to pass the FCAT, the state's end-of-course exams, and expecting them to improve at least three grade levels during the time they have with the youth. The educators recognize the need for, and expect that they will continue to instill, a sense of pride and confidence with their students by being explicit about what they expect, while also being positive, and incentivizing and rewarding the youth.

Resources

Because of their positive working relationship with the facility, their district and one another, and the high expectations they maintain, these educators are able to provide myriad resources and support for themselves and their students. The district serves as a tremendous resource for the educators, and Principal Alexander ensures his teachers take full advantage of the courses and professional development offered. Knowing the disproportionate number of incarcerated youth who qualify for an Exceptional Student Education (ESE) and that most incarcerated youths' literacy levels are low, Principal Alexander ensures his teachers are certified ESE and CAR–PD reading to further support the learning for their students. The vocational program also serves as a tremendous resource for the youth as some of them have the opportunity to work on a construction or industrial site after they successfully complete the coursework and pass the exams to receive their NCCER card. David provides daily quotes for discussion, and Mae provides hands-on learning for her students as often as she can, providing the materials are approved to be brought into the facility. The youth are also provided with a moving library cart and other magazines and books brought in by the educators. Furthermore, Principal Alexander extends the provision of academic supports for the students with the utilization of teacher aides in the math class and Mimios and Gizmos for learning.

The most significant resource Principal Alexander believes they are lacking at this time is funding. Although he doesn't want to see the numbers of youth in the facility increase, Principal Alexander recognizes this is the only way to receive more funding to purchase additional resources or services his students or teachers may need.

Accountability

There is strong evidence that the educators at this facility hold one another accountable to provide their incarcerated youth with a high-quality education. Principal Alexander and his assistant regularly visit this facility and Kyle shared how he and his colleagues ensure the teachers who are there truly want to be there and are being effective. After being asked several times about the vocational classes Kyle once taught, he took the leadership and was supported by Principal Alexander to investigate a vocational program that led to the implementation of the NCCER national certification vocational class.

Outside the facility, there are several accountability mechanisms in place, which allow the educators to measure their effectiveness. Although they seem to be in agreement with and open to the expectations that students pass the FCAT and the state's end-of-course exams, they disagree with part of the state's requirement. The state requires the youth who score low on the reading portion of the FCAT to take an extra reading class, which prevents the students from participating in the vocational program. The educators believe this decision is detrimental to the youth who probably have the greatest need for hands-on, vocational experiences.

The extent of the quality of the instruction provided to the incarcerated youth is not assessed in this study. Because I was not allowed access to the facility for observations, I am unable to substantiate whether or not the espoused values, as articulated by the participants, are actually aligned with their theories in use.[2] While this is a significant limitation when analyzing the data, the consistency of the themes identified across interviews within this study such as strong relationships and high expectations, coupled with the high state grades on school district rankings and consistently high-quality assurance ratings, provides compelling reason to believe that the educational program at the Greta Olive Juvenile Justice Academy offers a number of highly effective and potentially best practices for ensuring the incarcerated youth receive a high-quality education. More research, including observations, is needed to confirm my initial findings.

4
Hubert B. Juvenile Justice Residential Facility[1]

Introduction

The Hubert B. Juvenile Justice Residential Facility is owned and operated by a for-profit treatment organization that has been in operation for more than 20 years. It owns and operates approximately 15 facilities throughout several states. More than 100 youth are housed in this level 6, moderate-risk facility. Sixty percent of the youth are African American, 15% Hispanic, and 25% White; 45% are classified as Exceptional Student Education (ESE). During the 2008–2009 school year, the Hubert B. Juvenile Justice Residential Facility was rated satisfactory by the Juvenile Justice Educational Enhancement Program (JJEEP) for its educational services.

The Carmen County Public Schools District is responsible for providing a high-quality education to its more than 75,000 students, including the incarcerated youth housed at the Hubert B. Juvenile Justice Residential Facility. Most students in the Carmen County Public Schools District are children of color, with approximately 40% being African American, 30% Hispanic, and 25% White. Fifty-four percent of the district's students qualify for Free or Reduced Price Meals (FRPM). During the 2008–2009 school year, the Carmen County Public Schools District was rated an A-grade school district by the Florida Department of Education for its high levels of student achievement.

The Hubert B. Juvenile Justice Residential Facility is located in a multi-complex containing housing, businesses, and other buildings. The facility is located in a one-floor building that appears dated. As I approached this facility, I did not see anything indicating the incarceration of juveniles. While driving into its parking lot, I did notice a large banner highlighting the facility's satisfactory status rating by the Department of Juvenile Justice/JJEEP.

The only way to enter this facility was to be buzzed in through the main door. Inside, the strong smell of ammonia certainly gave me the impression that this facility takes cleanliness seriously. I noticed a tinted window, the security booth, as well as a small waiting area with the feel of a modest waiting room in a rather comfortable atmosphere and setting. On the wall, I saw a plaque marked Fa-mi-ly, three certificates, and a few pieces of framed artwork. After being buzzed in past the waiting area, I noticed the security hand wand on the counter, the only indication that any form of security screening takes place. Just down the hallway from the waiting area was the bathroom, which appeared to be newly remodeled with beautiful 16-inch tiled floors and granite countertops—the feel of a four star hotel. Unfortunately, it stood in stark contrast to what the students face each day as they enter their classrooms.

As I walked from the main entrance to the classrooms, I immediately noticed the open courtyard and saw large numbers on the doors, indicating classrooms. There was also one area with large glass windows, the cafeteria for the youth.

By the time I entered the classrooms, the scent of ammonia was long gone. The 12-inch linoleum-tiled floors were scuffed, and rust stained many of the tiles; small pieces of debris lay on the floor and around trash cans. In the first period of the day, the trash remained from at least the day before.

In the reading classroom, there was very little indication that it was a learning environment for youth. Although the classroom featured a few store-bought teaching charts, a few stacks of textbooks, some trade books, and a posted bell schedule, four locked boxes once housed computers but were now empty, and the teacher's desk was completely empty.

In the math classroom, there were a few store bought charts as well, but the teacher also listed her rules: (1) Raise your hand for permission to speak or to leave your seat. (2) Follow directions the FIRST TIME given. (3) Keep your hands, feet, and objects to yourself. (4) No profanity. Two reminders to students were also posted: "Show Your Work!" and "Do Your Corrections! Return for a Grade!" There were shelves of math textbooks and one shelf of trade books. The teacher's desk had various items on them, including her laptop. She had a filing cabinet with a padlock on each draw, where she was able to store her items. The computers had also been removed from her classroom.

In both classrooms, large poster paper listed the facility's classroom rules: (1) Be in your assigned seat and ready to work when the bell rings. (2) Obtain permission before speaking or leaving your seat. (3) Listen and stay seated when someone is speaking. (4) Follow directions the first time they are given. (5) Turn assignments in on time. (6) Respect everyone and all property (school property, personal property, and others' property). Treat computers with care.

Participants

Table 3   Hubert B. Juvenile Residential Facility participants

Juvenile Justice Educator	Position	Tenure at the Facility
Patrick	Principal	3 years
Mary	Math teacher	1 year 2 months
Karen	Reading teacher	1 year 2 months
Susan	ESE	2 months

Educational Program

Each day, school begins at 7:45 a.m. and ends at 2:20 p.m. for the students. The following courses are taught each week: reading, research, careers, math, English, social studies, and unified arts. Students are on a rotating block schedule. They take four classes daily that last 1 hour and 15 minutes (75 minutes) each, for 300 minutes each day; their scheduled classes alternate every other day.

The teachers begin their day at 7:30 a.m. and end at 2:30 p.m. In addition to their duty-free periods before and after school, totaling 25 minutes, the teachers at this facility have 1 hour and 15 minutes each day for lunch and a common planning period. Their class sizes range from 5 to 14 students. All the teachers at this site were assigned to teach at this facility.

Findings

Based on the four themes that emerged from this study, I found few positive relationships, overall low expectations, disparate resources, and lack of accountability. The instructional methods used to work with the students at this facility were direct instruction, round-robin reading, and one-on-one instruction. Based on the 5 hours and 16 minutes spent observing the reading and math classes at this facility, students were brought to class by the juvenile justice staff an average of 14 minutes late, equating to a loss of 20% of students' instructional time each class period. The range of students on task at any given time during a reading lesson was as low as 21%, or 3 out of 14 students, and as high as 50%, or 4 out of 8 students. The range of students on task at any given time during a math lesson was as low as 40%, or 2 out of 5 students, to as high as 63%, or 5 out of 8 students. Disruptions occurred frequently during the lessons. Disruptions included student outbursts, singing, rapping, use of profanity, talking, requests for water or to use the bathroom, requests for toilet paper, laughter, throwing paper, entering and exiting the room after the lesson began, juvenile justice staff speaking with one another or with a student, and walkie-talkies transmitting. During the instructional time, an average of 1 disruption occurred every 52.8 seconds.

Principal Patrick

Patrick serves as the principal of the Hubert B. Juvenile Justice Residential Facility. Although he is responsible for the educators placed here, his primary role is serving as principal of an alternative middle/high school, which currently serves more than 1,100 students. He is also responsible for overseeing four additional DJJ facilities and a district adult education school. Patrick is in his third year as principal and has worked as an administrator in a similar capacity for longer than five years. He has three assistant principals who are also designated to provide support to the facilities he oversees. Principal Patrick believes that positive relationships are important but struggles to establish these relationships under the demands of his many responsibilities. He wants these students to receive a high-quality education but doesn't think that is possible with the teachers he assigns to this facility. Much like the mixed bag of resources his district provides, he also has divergent resources for the educators and students that are either unknown, not sought after, or completely underused. Little is done to hold stakeholders accountable.

Relationships

Although Principal Patrick recognizes the importance of a positive working relationship with the leader at the juvenile facility, he acknowledges that their relationship remains wanting. At this facility, there are divergent views that exist between the juvenile justice side and the education side. According to Principal Patrick, "The flow of the day—it's not designed for education. It's not. The structure is not set up for education. . . . They're required by law to provide it. They do it reluctantly. . . . That's what you see when you walk in there." He further divulged,

> It's not something that is a unified front between the school district side and the program (facility) side. There's tension and that's

partially because they have to sit on their hands between, you know, 8:00 and 2:30, 3:00, waiting for school to end, so they can get to their job.

Principal Patrick understands very clearly that the facility's primary responsibility is to provide safety and security, and there are several required juvenile justice components, including counseling and group therapy for the youth, that the facility leader must also ensure is appropriately scheduled. Principal Patrick feels that these obligations take priority over education. He sees the need to have a variety of educational programs for the youth there, including a vocational component, but because of the lack of relationship needed to have such conversations, these support structures do not exist. Principal Patrick shared, "The principal and the facility director [should be] on the same page. Now, I'm not saying that I have the answers, you know. I may have fallen short in really forcing the hand and really having that conversation." He continued,

> We have just been responsible for overseeing an educational process through a cooperative agreement. . . . The success or failure always starts with the leadership, and so, however that program goes educationally, is really based on . . . the leadership of both the principal of the school as well as the leader of the facility itself. Both of us, would, you know, we have to be on the same page. We have to work together to make the success for those students educationally happen.

Although Principal Patrick recognizes its importance, there has not yet been a positive working relationship established between him and the facility director.

Principal Patrick believes the relationships between students and teachers are also pertinent. Although he disclosed his belief that those relationships are also lacking, he believes that the students see their teachers and school as a great option to their day-to-day monotony of incarceration. He stated,

> I noticed that whenever we have any type of disaster, storm, or have a break in school they're always excited that the teachers are finally coming back. They hate when there's a long series of substitutes. They always like to have their teachers there. So, it contradicts maybe me saying that the [lack of] relationship is there, but, you know, it's like an abusive—. It's still like a parent-to-child relationship.

Principal Patrick recognizes the importance of having relationships within the district, and according to him, that's typically how people in his district obtain leadership positions. Unfortunately, he's an outsider; he believes this is why a relationship between him and the district is lacking. He explained,

> You know, there's a relationship built, and yeah, you may have to perform, but there's some connection. I mean, when you pull the cover off of people, there's people who grew up in certain communities. They got the backing. . . . They're related. There's something there. Me, coming from [another city in], Florida, here, nobody knows. What I had over everyone—nobody understood this program and nobody wanted to put their hand on putting somebody here that would get this.

Moreover, Principal Patrick believes this lack of relationship causes him to work in isolation. Although the district provides him with adequate funding for the facilities he oversees, there is an apparent lack of a much-needed relationship. Principal Patrick divulged,

> This is a school the superintendent does not want to have to think about. "I got enough schools with enough problems that I . . . shouldn't be worrying about schools that aren't graded, that don't have community involvement, that kids already at risk of dropping out. You know, we give you enough money to do what you need to do for them. You have more money, more resources than you need. . . . Don't call me."
> That's sort of how the relationship is. "Don't call me with the problem that you can't fix." 'Cause nobody can fix my problems. So now I got bad teachers and they know. I mean, they used to send us lots of bad teachers, so you know, if I have a teacher—"[Principal Patrick], really, when was the last time I asked you about your learning gains?" This is the answers that I get. "When was the last time I asked you about learning gains? When was the last time we talked about the achievement of your students?" . . . So, you know, that's—. I sort of work in isolation.

Disappointingly, this disconnect also exists amongst the teachers. Principal Patrick's attempt to deter burnout leads him to rotate teachers between his alternative school and the other facilities he is responsible for overseeing every two years. This rotation provides little time or expectation for teachers to develop collegial relationships among themselves, nor is this a priority between some of the teachers and their students.

Expectations

Principal Patrick expects that he is making the best decision for who he places in this facility, particularly with the competing interests of the various schools and programs he oversees. He explained, "There's more than one teacher in that situation down there. 'This is not what I signed up for. Why am I here? [Principal Patrick] must not like me.'" He elaborated,

> People outside looking in will say, "[Principal Patrick], you put all the bad teachers in [the Hubert B. Juvenile Justice Residential Facility], didn't you? Didn't you? Just be honest with me." But if you ask the teachers themselves, "Well, I heard [Principal Patrick] puts all the bad teachers at [the Hubert B. Juvenile Justice Residential Facility]." They'll say, "Which of you are the bad teacher?" None of them are going to say, "Well, no, I'm the bad teacher. I'm the good teacher. I'm the good one that's left (laughs)."

His comment foreshadowed the sentiments shared by one of the teachers, who believes that she and the other "good teachers" at this facility should be commended for the work they are doing with the youth each day. One teacher implored,

> I really feel that what we do needs to be exposed to people. I don't think people know what we do and I really think that people in these settings . . . I'm talking about the ones who are really working and trying—they need to be commended. I think they are special teachers. I really do. And what we do needs to be brought to the forefront. The general public doesn't know what we do. And like I said, if you have a good teacher, people who do this type of work, they need to be commended.

Principal Patrick explained why he faces such a dilemma with the teachers he places at this facility and his belief that he has been given many more responsibilities than was initially agreed upon. He shared,

> Truth be told, I have to make a conscious decision about where I place teachers and . . . I believe that there should be; that DJJ should

have its own principal . . . one principal, the AP (assistant principal), you know, the staff is all DJJ and I'm the principal. I mean, I didn't sign up for this, either. I get high school pay.

Unfortunately with the numerous responsibilities Principal Patrick has with his 1,100-student alternative school and other juvenile justice facilities and responsibilities, and the fact that he assigns teachers to this facility every two years, none of the educators who participated in this study felt like they were well prepared or highly qualified for their roles.

Also, because the teachers are assigned to this facility Principal Patrick expects that the teachers are not intrinsically motivated. According to Principal Patrick, "There's no intrinsic— . . . Those teachers didn't sign up to be there. I assigned those teachers there. . . . They don't ask to go there. They go." He elaborated, "I'm the principal of [the main campus-alternative school] and I say, 'You're in room 138. You're in room 200. You're in [Hubert B. JJ Residential Facility] room 1. That's your assignment for this year.' So, that's a huge problem." Although he sees this as a problem, he finds it very difficult to find other appropriate ways to address this dilemma he faces year after year.

What's remarkably interesting, however, and perhaps a bit of cognitive dissonance within his own mind, is that Principal Patrick acknowledges that his teachers are not there by choice, yet he still recognizes the importance of having a highly qualified teacher in each classroom who is able to establish positive relationships with the students. He shared, "It's all about the teacher. It's about being able to put in front of those kids a quality educator." And, he expressed the need for "highly qualified teachers in each room, teaching in-field, that have some expertise in what they're teaching that, that I would consider them an expert in their field as an educator." Principal Patrick, however also believes a teacher must be willing and able to establish relationships and make learning relevant for students. He divulged, "In this environment, a teacher [must have] the type of with-it-ness to understand that relationships come before any type of instruction can take place." According to Principal Patrick, the ideal teachers for this environment

recognize the diversity of the population . . . use strategies and use curriculum, use materials that will engage them in the learning so that the learning is authentic . . . understands the importance of relationships, understands that you infuse the curriculum that's relevant to the lives of kids . . .

> The teachers make the difference. . . . I guarantee you, I can take strong teachers. . . . Here's the textbook, here's paper and pencil. . . . I guarantee you, I can remain on par or achieve at higher rates than teachers who don't have a passion, don't have relationships, don't understand the kids that they're serving and give them everything.

Despite what he knows and expects of the teachers at this facility, he places the educators he considers to be his best teachers in the classrooms on the main campus where his alternative school is located. He stated, "All of my resources, all of my energy, all of my best people are here [at the alternative school]." This is done because he believes that the students at his alternative campus recognize that their alternative school is the last option for them to earn a diploma or GED. Principal Patrick also recognizes that there is a strong possibility that only 10% of the youth housed at the Hubert B. Juvenile Justice Residential Facility are actually Carmen County students, so why invest the best resources in a place for such a small percentage of students who actually "belong" to the school district? This quandary, affecting so many students' lives, is one that no educator should ever have to face in isolation.

Unfortunately, Principal Patrick doesn't have very high expectations for the juvenile justice staff, particularly with the history they've had together and his perception of what's lacking when working with a for-profit provider. He reasoned,

> You get what you pay for so, the quality of the employee is the difference maker I think and in the success of the follow through. I mean you're asking people to work for $10, $12, $15 an hour, but you're expecting $30- to $50-an-hour type of work, and that's just a hard thing to do. . . . It's a for-profit corporation that makes its money on therapy and medication. So, when you don't pay high wages, people look at that as a job, and not a career.

Students are also continually brought to class late. For this reason, the educators in this facility expect the juvenile justice staff will always bring the students to class late, particularly for their first period—immediately after the students have breakfast, and their fourth period, which follows lunch. One teacher explained, "They usually come to class, but it might be late." During my time at the facility, students were an average 14 minutes late to each class, equating to a loss of 20% of their allotted class times each day. The significant lateness occurred before their first period, as more than 30 students were seen lined up to eat at 7:40 a.m., even though their first class began at 7:45 a.m., and before their last class of the day, which followed lunch.

In addition to the lateness, after students finally arrived to class, there was still significant movement within the classroom. Unfortunately, the teachers have come to expect that students will be removed from class frequently. Many students at the Hubert B. Juvenile Justice Residential Facility were brought or sent in and out of class during my time there, but Principal Patrick stated that students are not supposed to leave class for non-educational purposes. He expects juvenile justice staff to refrain from pulling the youth out of class. According to Principal Patrick, "They're not supposed to pull kids that have therapy. They're not supposed to pull kids for things unrelated to education." He elaborated, "They need to clean up, you know. They need to do this. They need to do that. But, they're not supposed to do it during the school day." Despite Principal Patrick's expectation, however, as the teacher in one classroom called attendance, students responded with, "He's on clean up. . . . He's on the unit."

In addition to the youth not being pulled out of class for non-educational purposes, Principal Patrick expects the juvenile justice staff will administer medication to students who require medicine after school, rather than before the students begin their classes. There were students in each observed classroom who appeared drowsy. Most of these students chose to put their heads down on their desk or against a wall to go to sleep. Principal Patrick asserted, "We have a disproportionate number of kids there who are taking psych meds, among other things while they're there, so it makes them sleepy." Again, he expressed the importance of having open communication with the juvenile justice staff to ensure that the decisions made are in the students' best interests. Principal Patrick divulged, "Once again that's a leader, an administrator having that conversation about giving meds in the morning time that have side effects that include drowsiness."

During the 5 hours and 16 minutes (316 minutes) I spent observing classrooms, there were 359 disruptions, including outbursts, singing, rapping, use of profanity, talking, requests for water or to use the bathroom, requests for toilet paper, laughter, throwing paper, entering and exiting the room after the lesson began, juvenile justice staff speaking with one another or with a student, and walkie-talkies transmitting. 316 minutes/359 disruptions = .88 × 60 seconds = 1 disruption every 52.8 seconds. The educators believe the juvenile justice staff must do a better job to eliminate these disruptions and further help with student discipline.

Furthermore, the educators keep everything locked. Because they are "the guests" in this facility and, as Principal Patrick mentioned, the juvenile justice staff at this for-profit facility are not compensated at the same level other juvenile justice workers would be in a not-for-profit or public facility, the educators have come to expect their items to be stolen. Items such as student textbooks and computer monitor screens have gone missing. According to Principal Patrick, "We've had a lot of situations where things are walking out and now you're looking on camera. . . . So how does stuff end up missing?" He continued,

> It's usually [the juvenile justice] staff, not only taking textbooks for their own families, but taking the monitor screens. And you know, because some of the staff is so young, they're using it, they're taking it to hook up their computer game systems to it. It's like, what in the world is going on?

Although there are expectations posted for student behavior in the classrooms, the educators at this facility believe the students will complete their work only when the students choose to work. They recognize there are times when the students don't want to work and believe there is nothing that can be done to change the students' mindsets. This was evident in one class with as few as five students: two students had their heads down, one student was singing, and only two students were on task. The educators believe that if they demand that students do their work, the youths' negative behaviors will intensify. Principal Patrick believes one of the reasons students may put their heads down in class is because they are sleepy or they want to avoid conflict and if so, they should not be bothered. He explained, "Kids who don't want to create a problem . . . who feel as though they're not going to engage in education; to avoid conflict, they go to sleep." Principal Patrick elaborated,

> They put their head down so they don't have conflict with either the teacher or another student. . . . When the kids are forced to stay up and pay attention, whether it's the [juvenile justice] staff or the teacher making them do it, they're going to let you know how to leave them. "Leave me alone. So I'm gonna act a fool in the classroom and next time you'll know. I'll just put my head down and we won't have any problems."

Despite the expectation that students may disrupt the class or choose not to participate, Principal Patrick recognizes that the students actually enjoy being in school. He shared, "The irony is the kids love their teachers. They love school, 'cause it's 6, 7 hours of their day that goes by pretty quickly and for many of them it's the first time they really paid attention in school." He believes the primary reason for this is the distractions have been removed, opening the door for a much-needed opportunity to reach the youth while they are incarcerated. Principal Patrick divulged,

> There are no girls. There's something to be said about single-gender schools. There are no other distractions, you know. . . . There's no rush to go home to watch TV. There's no rush to go to the corner. There's no rush to go to football practice. None of that. So, and for many of our kids at [this facility] they were drug abusers, you know, drug users at the very least, or casual so, a lot of them are sober which is some type of—. It's an epiphany, like "Wow, it's actually not that bad."

Principal Patrick believes that the youth should be job ready but most importantly earn their diploma, and acknowledges the conflict that arises when students are significantly over aged for their grade level. According to Principal Patrick, "Job training [is needed] if we want them to . . . walk away from that lifestyle many of them . . . glorify, or engage in. They have to have something that they can do that will give them an opportunity to earn legitimate money."

In addition to the job training, Principal Patrick insisted the youth must also receive a quality education. While he believes a diploma is ideal, he recognizes that the GED (General Educational Development) test may be the most suitable option for the youth housed at this facility. He explained,

> The most important thing they can get is their diploma. I mean, you can't do anything without it. However, the realities are when you're asking a 17-, 16-, 18-year-old with no credits prior to going to a program (facility) to get 2 or 3 credits and then to go back and finish your other 20-something credits, pass both, pass all your state tests, get your 40 service hours, *x*, *y*, and *z*, it's not going to happen.

Resources

Unfortunately, there are not many resources or support mechanisms in place for this school leader. Principal Patrick disclosed, "There really isn't anything in place formally designed to address the needs. As a matter of fact, there aren't a lot of support systems for leaders who work with this population. . . . It's the sink or swim here." Moreover, he doesn't get the support even when his requests are about ensuring students have a high-quality teacher. He blames the local teachers' union for part of this shortcoming:

> In the large urban school district with a strong union, it makes it very difficult to have control over who walks through that door. You know, as quickly as I put [the teachers] in [the facility], I can move [them] around within the [alternative school's main campus], but it's not like I can do anything and you're not going to get the type of support it would take to move a bad teacher.

If the teachers were at this facility for longer than two years, they could potentially have stronger relationships and serve as greater resources for one another. While this is not the case, Principal Patrick believes placing teachers two years at a time at this facility serves as a resource. According to Principal Patrick, "I don't allow any teachers to stay there more than two years at a time. So if they work two consecutive years, I'm going to move them, put them in a different environment and replace them with a teacher." He explained his rationale for this decision:

> I was here as an assistant principal, and one of my responsibilities was to oversee the DJJ program and I did it for three years. I left and went on to work in other schools and I returned as principal with some of the same teachers in place, and it was shocking and it was saddening to see what had happened to the teachers over time. They work year-round with no break. They're not required to work beyond a 196-day calendar, but because of the economic times, they were choosing to work all summer, the winter break, the spring break, without any rest.
>   During that time, we lost several teachers. They passed away. Several other teachers got sick, and I could also see the—the quality of their instruction was deteriorating. And what I found was that, you know, it's a tough job in a traditional environment. It's a tough job, even tougher in this environment. And, having teachers work year-round . . . it's detrimental to, you know, what you can provide for kids because, you know, you have to have with any job in any profession, you have to have, you know, a mental, physical break from it or it will wear you out.

In addition to this "break," Principal Patrick also recognizes that teachers do need varying degrees of support. He believes he addresses this with the ancillary staff members placed at this facility to provide teachers with additional support, particularly because he has his hands full running his 1,100-plus-student alternative middle/high school and overseeing several other facilities and programs. Principal Patrick cited,

> We have . . . several teachers that are in a support role and their role is to support the teachers. . . . I have three teachers and an assistant principal who are scheduled to be there, to go to each classroom to make sure that the teachers have what they need. Work—, you know, pull out students if need be, push in with them as necessary . . . help them get materials and supplies; you know, do things for the teachers so that it can help them.

He added, "In addition to the eight classroom teachers, we have a guidance counselor assigned to that location, we have an ESE support facilitator assigned to that position, we also have a transition specialist that's assigned to that position." Interestingly, though, during my observation period, when I asked about the roles of two of these individuals, teachers said they didn't know. Although these individuals are expected to provide support, this resource is not fully used, because teachers are unaware of the ancillary staff's roles and responsibilities.

Principal Patrick also realized the instructional focus calendar served as a resource for his teachers, but it was removed to incorporate the Common Core State Standards. This demonstrated yet another example of how he and his educators in many ways, work in isolation. He looks forward to having a similar resource for his teachers and students in the near future. He remarked,

> With the Common Core, they've gone away from the . . . instructional focus calendar, so that used to be during the New Generation Sunshine Standards. You know, for reading you had the instructional focus calendar and it addressed the benchmark each day or each week and you know, along with your word wall and focus of the day. . . . And we incorporate all those things as well, at least that's what we should be doing; but now, everyone's sort of, you know, revising what we're doing. So right now, as a district, we're in transition, and then our most fragile programs are sort of out there on their own.

Despite what is lacking, there is an abundance of funding that can be used to purchase the needed materials for the teachers and students. However, owing to the constraints within the facility, the educators and students cannot fully use the resources to which they are entitled. According to Principal Patrick, "Truth be told, one of the things the district has done an exemplary job of doing is funding the programs. I mean they're funded. We get more than we can actually fit into [the facility]." He expounded,

> [The Hubert B. Juvenile Justice Residential Facility] probably doesn't have as much as they are entitled to, because we physically can't put it all there. We don't have a place to store things there. We don't have a secure space there. So it makes it difficult to put all the resources. And, there's not enough space for all the staff that I can potentially put there to serve them. The rooms are small—the office, I mean, all the teachers can't be in there at the same time.

Often times when schools are faced with dilemmas and educators are not feeling supported, we think if we just provide them with more funds, they'll be happier, better prepared and we will see the desired results and outcomes. Principal Patrick's dilemma is a perfect example of how an overabundance of funds does not ensure appropriate resources, expectations, relationships or accountability will be in place. All of this can be fostered, more than likely without changing any line item. Even with access to funds, Principal Patrick still can't provide the number one resource that he believes is pertinent for the students at Hubert B. to receive a high-quality education—having a highly effective teacher in every classroom. He divulged,

> How do we help our most vulnerable students get the best education if I don't have the best teachers there? If they're not getting the best services and I'm acknowledging that, you know, in many cases, you know, they're not getting . . . the best that they could get from the district.

Because of the various schools and programs Principal Patrick is responsible for, he feels very conflicted when he has to decide what teachers he should have teaching in his alternative middle/high school and what teachers he should place at the DJJ facilities. Although Principal Patrick recognizes the greatest support that he can have for his students is a high-quality teacher, he believes the teachers at this facility are substandard. Principal Patrick disclosed, "Unfortunately with the DJJ programs, they're getting, you know, in my opinion, inferior teachers and I know it's a huge emotional sacrifice that I had to make, but I had to make a conscious decision." He described his dilemma:

If I take my best math teacher and put 'em at the detention center where kids are only there for up to 21 days, they're in and out every day, most are only there two or three days. How am I maximizing this? If I send them to [the Hubert B. Facility] and work with kids four to six months that may or may not even graduate, that may be going to other counties that are going to learn Mr. Such and Such's way, but when they leave—. Do I take that best teacher or if when they come to this [alternative school], he's their math teacher 'til—. 'Cause, this is it. You leave [this alternative middle/high school] without a diploma, no one's even taking you anywhere else, unless it's a GED program. Like, this is it, and that's how these kids operate—in desperation. Like, if I don't make it at [this alternative school], I'm not making it.

When asked about a specific teacher at Hubert B., Principal Patrick responded, "I don't have my best teacher teaching that class. It's not a teacher that I would . . . say, 'This is the classroom that I would want everybody to see.' It's a teacher who is marginal and I know is marginal." Because only about 10% of this facility's youth actually belong to Carmen County, Principal Patrick confirmed what site takes priority:

All of my best teachers, among the group that I have, all of them, in my opinion, are on this campus [at the alternative school] serving [Carmen] County kids, 'cause this is where they will start and finish. If any kid has a real chance of making it, they're on this campus.

Despite this reality, Principal Patrick recognizes that the continuity of an educational program is a resource for the youth, even if it might not be one of high-quality. He explained,

It's therapeutic for the kids to have education go on. It normalizes their experience there. Though as a professional, I don't think I'm getting the best out of my staff, and that's partly my fault, I do think for the kids' sake, they enjoy having the teachers there.

Principal Patrick believes the quality of the teacher affects the resources provided to the youth, but he also believes that six months with the youth is not enough time to truly give them the support that's needed. He concluded, "My heart hurts every time I walk into one of the facilities because, you know . . . our young people are suffering. . . . I can't get the teachers to be vested in kids they only see for a small window of time."

He also recognizes the need for a variety of educational programs for the youth specifically focused on a vocation or career, but this also is a resource that is void for the youth at this facility. He explained that he understands "the standards for DJJ education infused vocational, career exploration or opportunity" and disclosed, "I mean, truth be told . . . we have eight teachers. Probably three of 'em at the minimum should be vocational teachers or some type of career." Despite this acknowledgement, no vocational or career course is provided at this facility for its incarcerated youth.

Furthermore, Principal Patrick described the types of learners he has and the fact that they are not being provided with the right tools or resources. According to Principal Patrick, "[They] need hands-on. And then once again, we get back to the types of learners we have; disproportionately kinesthetic learners, right-brained kids. Kids who need to manipulate things—our black and Latino boys." He elaborated, "Boys need to be able to move around, run around, talk, you know, get involved. . . . You want to teach a boy about math? Give him some blocks and let's build something." It's clear that he recognizes the things that need to change, yet he operates as if he lacks agency.

At one time, there was a vocational program offered to the youth through the juvenile justice program. It was, however, disbanded due to funding. Principal Patrick mentioned the facility had "a Home Builders program. . . . for a long time, however, it only served about 12 to 15 students, but it didn't serve the 100-and-something kids that it could have." This is also further evidence that the lack of relationship is hampering the necessary resources for students. Although the facility did not continue this program because of funds, the district's excess of funds for the youth at this facility could have potentially been used to continue this service or a similar program to support many of the youth with the necessary job training skills and support.

To help prepare students to enter the workforce, he shared what they have recently implemented through the educational side. Principal Patrick stated, "What we've added though is the career readiness piece which was not something that has historically been in place through the school system." Career readiness is a course designed to help students write cover letters and prepare for job interviews.

Principal Patrick recognizes the need for growth in providing the youth with the quality educational programs they deserve. He described the ideal programs that he believes would serve as tremendous resources for the incarcerated youth at this facility:

If I was able to give them you know, the four core subject teachers with maybe the reading teacher and two electives, you know, whether it was physical education, art, music, drama, a career technical program. You know, if I could have on site, you know, a traditional schedule, that I could deliver and they can get all of the caveats of a secondary program, that would be I think a huge starting point for them. Right now, they're not scheduled that way.

Tutoring was available at one time for the incarcerated youth at this facility. Principal Patrick shared, "Through our Title 1 Part D funds, we have the opportunity to hire both tutors and other resource staff that can work with the students outside of the school day." The teachers shared that this was disbanded due to a lack of funding for this service. Again the dissonance: How could there be this overwhelming abundance of funds, yet no use of funds when it's time to provide additional services to students?

The computer lab serves as a potential resource for the youth housed at the Hubert B. Juvenile Justice Residential Facility, although Principal Patrick believes taking classes via a computer is "impersonal." Despite the seemingly impersonal nature of computer courses, many online courses are provided for the students to recover credits and earn credits. Some of the computers have been removed, however, and without computers accessible to the students, they cannot take advantage of such resources. According to Principal Patrick, "We do have computers and we have a couple labs, you know, we do have, you know, LCD projectors and things like that that you can utilize and wire, but it's a challenge using technology in an incarcerated environment." Because of the type of youth they are working with, he believes many resources that could be provided to them are not provided. He asserted, "Many of them have a criminal mentality, not by any fault of their own; it may be the environment they grew up in. So they're always looking at how to get over, how to take advantage of situations." Principal Patrick described some of the youths' destructive and criminal behaviors: "You can use the Promethean board . . . pose questions and have them . . . use the little mouse thing to click, well, then you have to worry about that being contraband and walking away or kids having an altercation and tossing the equipment."

Principal Patrick discussed the credit recovery option but also explained the challenges his district faces with this potential resource: "The district has had some challenges. . . . it's been referred to as a diploma mill because there aren't the type of protections on there . . . that will ensure that the students don't have an easy way to get answers." The good news for students is that they are able to get credits and be promoted while at this facility. Principal Patrick offered, "We try to help them to get their credits to go to the next grade level . . . have them get promoted, get their credits . . . towards high school promotion to the next grade level." Students meet with the guidance counselor upon entry to determine what courses they need to be enrolled in while they are housed in this facility. Principal Patrick explained its importance:

> We do support students attempting to get their GED, because you know, the statistics show . . . if they don't have a high school diploma when they leave a DJJ program and they have to go back to the community in which they came, the chances of them returning back to school are very low.

Though limited with technology, fortunately for the students, within the structure of the juvenile justice program there are myriad supports in place, including treatment team meetings. Each youth is reviewed once each month to determine his "level" and assess his progress toward achieving his program goals, a requirement for transitioning out of the program. Principal Patrick described the many stakeholders involved during the Treatment Team meetings: "teacher, therapist, case management, and in some cases, the facility supervisor." He explained how effective these meetings are: "They constantly go over what their achievement, their goals need to be both academically, behaviorally, you know, whatever it is that their goals are and they communicate that with the parent." Unfortunately however, during my observations of the treatment team meetings, I learned that the classroom teachers had not submitted the progress reports for their students for at least two weeks, and no classroom teacher was sitting in on the meetings to provide the team with an update of the youths' academic or behavioral progress.

Accountability

Much like the lack of accountability evidenced as I sat through several treatment team meetings, teachers also expressed a desire for more accountability. During my time at the facility, several teachers wanted to speak to me. Because my study only focused on the math, reading, and exceptional student education support facilitator, I only had informal chats with others and yet took notes while in my researching mode. One teacher was so proud to share the library he helped to create and the data he compiled on the types of books the students were most likely to check out and how he made a correlation with the progress students made on the TABE (Tests of Adult Basic Education) with the number of books they checked out. This teacher was split between Hubert B. and the adult prison, which held approximately 12 youth during the time of my study. This was his own version of accountability that he created.

While walking through a History teacher's classroom, one teacher averred, "Off-campus schools are like how black schools used to be during segregation. There's a need for accountability. Some facilities are up just as cash cows. Facilities like this, that need the resources, don't receive them." Unabashedly, Principal Patrick also shares the view by the teacher noted in the above poignant quote. He recognizes the accountability structure is lacking tremendously at this facility and candidly shared, "The monitoring piece is weak and that starts with me. I mean, I own that. I mean, because, being an off-campus location and having one administrator over multiple sites . . . make sure that what's happening is happening [is difficult]." Principal Patrick further divulged, "The accountability is not placed on the school the same way it would be on a school in the community." He elaborated,

> There's no outside pressure or internal accountability to make sure that these teachers are, you know, delivering on what should be happening. . . . If I place a teacher in documentation for performance that I go to once a week or once a month, to talk about and try to explain to a district that's not even clear about what this is supposed to be and then teachers saying, "We're in a different environment and . . . the rules don't apply." It's a tough sell. So . . . it's a battle that you have to decide how much is it worth. . . . How bad are kids getting hurt? And it's an ugly answer to you know, a very important question.

Fortunately, there are some forms of accountability that Principal Patrick believes are helpful. He described the state components the educators are held accountable, for the students to achieve:

> We are still following the Common Core, which, from the Sunshine State to the New Generation [Standards] we've tried to align what we would call our learning plans, which is also commonly known in the facilities as contracts. Contracts is an ugly word now because it basically says, it's a packet that you throw at the kids that they sit there and do. The learning plans are really, are designed, I'm

not saying that it's the practice, but they're designed to be a guide for benchmarks that students should be working towards that are aligned with the Common Core, or the Sunshine, the New Generation [Standards] . . .

Although the JJEEP (Juvenile Justice Educational Enhancement Program) is no longer conducting quality assurance reviews, Principal Patrick explained how helpful this process was, because it served as an accountability tool to ensure he received the necessary funds and materials for his teachers and students. According to Principal Patrick, "The district has provided more than, you know, our fair share of technology, you know. They've signed off on whatever we've needed and that came through the process of the quality assurance." While signing off on whatever they've needed appears to be some support, there is much more that must happen at Hubert B. for the students to be exposed to a high-quality education.

Mary

Mary is the math teacher at Hubert B. She is in her second year teaching at this facility, and she has more than five years' teaching experience as a teacher in a traditional setting, in an alternative setting, and at another DJJ site. Mary believes in establishing positive relationships, yet finds this quest difficult as she tends to move from facility to facility every year or two. She believes she maintains high expectations for herself and is also adamant that the youth be treated appropriately. Mary wishes there were more resources available for the educators and students and questions the accountability structures in this setting, particularly because of its unique context. She recognizes that teaching incarcerated youth is a daunting task.

Relationships

Unfortunately, the relationships at this facility aren't as positive or effective as they potentially could be. Principal Patrick assigns the teachers to this facility and usually rotates them every two years. Although the teachers do converse with one another, there is an apparent lack of relationship and knowledge about what each teacher does. When asked about other teachers or staff members within the facility, the response most often given was, "I'm not sure what he or she does. . . . I don't know what that class looks like." There are only eight classroom teachers and an additional three teachers in support roles. Additionally, the teachers share the same lunchtime and have common planning time every afternoon. Mary shared, "I'm not sure what Ms. [Z] is teaching right now, because we had some changes. . . . They have some other type of language thing with Ms. [X]. . . . I think right now we're not doing computers." Mary described how she taught her personal careers class at another facility, but when asked what was done here, she responded,

> One of the things I did was, I gave them a lot of job descriptions you know, like this is what a plumber does, you read up on it and then they answer the questions. . . . Gave them a lot of information about jobs . . . how to write a cover letter, how to write a resume, things like that. So that's what I did at that time, but what's being done now, I don't know. I'm not sure.

There was one teacher in particular with whom Mary appeared to have a positive working relationship. As it turns out, they were both at another facility together before it was closed. As I entered her classroom, the two of them were sharing some of their frustrations they were facing as well as a few recollections about the "good old days" at their previous site.

Positive student–teacher relationships were evident as Mary greeted the students when they were in the classroom; she knew most of them by name. She began each class with, "Good morning/afternoon, gentlemen."

Fortunately, the juvenile justice requirement for treatment team meetings requires students to receive monthly updates from their teachers about their grades and participation in class. Mary explained how she manages this and makes time to share her feedback one-on-one with her students. She shared, "Once a month . . . I have a talk with them. . . . 'From the time you started, these are all your grades. This is where you are. This is what you need to try to work on.'" She believes these check-ins further strengthen positive relationships with her students and also demonstrate for them that she cares about their progress.

Expectations

Although Mary expects to be an effective teacher, she realizes how difficult it will be to accomplish this feat with so much transition every two years. She divulged,

> Your first year is like, "What's gonna work here?" And then the second year you have something to go on: "That didn't work," or "I gotta fix that." And then after that, your third year, you know, it starts to get easier; but I don't tend to remain in place for more than

two years, so that makes it what I find to be difficult to be a highly effective teacher.

Within the juvenile justice setting, it is highly probable that several students within one math classroom will be on different levels. Mary recognizes how astute she must be as the math teacher in this setting teaching multiple math content areas at the same time. She believes her experience helps bring about some degree of expertise:

> So I get a question from a student, say, in formal geometry, and I answer that and the very next person is in pre-algebra, so my thinking has to switch. And then the person after that is in basic math. . . . So you really need to know your math . . . because you're, you know; you're in different books one question after the other.
>
> Sometimes, I have to tell them, sometimes, "You know what, I need a few minutes to look at this question." But for the most part I'm able to sit with them and help them. What happens a lot of times and from experience now, I know what questions they will have trouble with. So when he comes up to me, I've seen that question before, maybe several times.

Although Mary doesn't feel she is highly qualified, she has higher expectations for herself and for what she does than she believes other people expect. She explained, "I know people are going to think that I'm probably insane, but I have my standards and I don't just, like, look over the paper and give them a grade." She continued,

> I grade every single question, because I really need to see what you're doing . . . I have signs. You've got to show me your work. Just give me answers, I give it right back to you. I've got to see what you're doing and I take the time to grade each question for me to see what it is you're doing wrong; and, is there a common thread here? You know, "Why did you get all these 10 questions wrong?" "Oh, you didn't reduce to the lowest terms. That's one concept that you don't know." So it's important for me to know.

Despite what some may believe when working with youth in an alternative learning environment, Mary believes her students who are confined should be provided with the same opportunities as their peers who are free. She is adamant,

Because they're in a facility and they're academically deficient, you don't treat them like less people, you know, like they're subhuman or something. You have to, you know, give them the same thing that you would to the students out there.

She believes with her support, the students will improve at least one grade level from the time they enter her classroom until the time they leave. All youth are required to take an academic assessment when they arrive at the facility and again before they transition out of the facility. Although her goal is to get the students to at least the next grade level, Mary expects this task to be quite demanding for her and expects that she will at least impart some knowledge while trying to meet each student's needs. She shared, "I like the fact that we try to meet their individual needs and the situation is unique. . . . They're all in different books but . . . you try to help them with their work. I try to do a lesson that will hopefully help everyone."

Mary went on to explain how difficult this task is: "Sometimes, it's insurmountable because it's you know, it's so many months, yes, but remember, they're academically deficient. So, he's not even at his grade level and then you have to try to pull him up." If a student doesn't make it to the next grade level, Mary believes her expectation will change and takes solace that she's "hopefully ma[d]e him a better student, you know, [and] he has more knowledge."

Mary expects to continually provide positive experiences for students with the hope that those experiences will continue to lead to more positive experiences when they return home. According to Mary, "My hope is that they would learn something and start to have a more positive attitude towards math, because if you're helping them and they don't get it, and then, 'Wow, I get it, and I'm not getting Fs.'" Because of this belief, Mary is focused on doing the best she can to provide the information to her students. The rest is up to the youth. Mary disclosed, "I'm going to provide the information. You don't want to learn it, that's on you, not on me. But I want what I do, my conscience to be clear. I've tried doing the best that I could."

Mary believes "it takes a special teacher" to work in this environment and expects the educators will serve as a resource to her and the other educators within the facility. She explained, "If somebody does that, you know what I'm saying, 'I will help you' or 'I could go to—'. . . . It makes such a big difference even though I'm not, like, officially your mentor." She further shared the need for supporting one another: "I've been doing this for a while, so I'm a little more experienced, I think. But that's why I think you have to help the new people, 'cause it's overwhelming. . . . You have to support."

The educators also expect the juvenile justice staff to have a better handle on discipline. During my observations, Mary made the following requests to the juvenile justice staff: "Mr. J, these students need to be in their seats;" and, "If you can't control him, maybe you need to get a manager." Mary explained, "If the staff were a little bit better, you know, can control things a little better, it would help, you know, with the discipline."

Mary also expects students will have bad days, and she is accepting if they don't participate in class as long as they do not disturb the other students. She commented,

> Sometimes they'll still have charges pending. So you have to be aware of some of this, and they're people too. . . . But if you're having a bad day or something, just say, "Miss, today, you know—" and just be quiet. But don't be disruptive and nasty. I can understand that. If you need to be quiet today or whatever, fine, because of whatever is going on; okay, not a problem. But that doesn't give you the right to lash out and curse us. . . . A lot of times you have to deal with their, their frustration and sometimes you have to set them straight.

Mary also believes the youth should receive a quality education to better prepare them for when they transition back home. She expects her students to demonstrate their knowledge by showing their work. According to Mary, "You haven't shown the work, a big component of it is you got to show the work, 'cause the other thing is who knows who's doing the work? See, that's the other thing, who's doing the work?" She believes students will be motivated the more A's they see in her class, which may translate to the youth returning to school once they are released. "If you can start getting them to see passing grades, maybe they will be motivated. Maybe they'll get hooked and want to continue even when they leave here," Mary surmised. For this reason, she provides multiple opportunities for her students to receive passing grades. She believes this provides students with an opportunity to experience success—something many of them desperately need. Mary asserted,

> You've got to have them do each assignment and if they get under a 60, it's given back to you for remediation. "Just correct the ones you get wrong and I give you the higher grade. I don't average it. I just

give you the higher grade." Because my hope is that they will learn something. And if they start seeing, "Hey . . . I can't get an F, I'm getting C's and B's and A's." And one time I had a student tell me way back when, "I've never had A's and B's" . . .

That is the whole focus of doing this the way I do it. . . . If they haven't passed it, give them an opportunity over and over if they need to, until they get a passing grade . . . And, even some cases, which is extra work for me, they already have a passing grade and I say, "Look, you just had 4 × 2 and you put 7. That's a very simple thing to correct. Correct that and I'll change the 80 to an 85. I give you the option, you want to fix it or do you want to stay with that?"

The educators also believe students will take advantage of the learning environment here which is set up to allow students to work at their own pace. Mary informs the youth, "You work at your own pace if you're slow, but also if you really can do the work, you can get it done quickly and move on to another contract and have an opportunity to get another math credit." While students are working at their own pace, Mary expects them to understand when she has a new student, the youth won't receive assistance. Mary explained,

First of all, I already told them, "When you see I have a new student, don't expect to get any help." Because that new student comes in, I've got to see what contract he's in. I have to put his folder together. I have to talk to him, explain to him, this is his book, contract, what I want, show your work, do this, do that—not that he remembers half of it. I have to do that. . . . "Once so and so comes in, don't expect any help." I'm not even being mean. I'm being honest, 'cause I have to spend time with this student.

Resources

Without hesitation, Mary offered, "We need a lot of support." Although the educators at this facility didn't know much about what the other educators were responsible for or what they did on a daily basis, they stated that they serve as a resource for each other. According to Mary, "We just help one another. We rely on each other for support."

While teachers serve as a resource for each other, this is an area that could also use some improvement according to Mary. She shared, "I think we just help one another (chuckles), to tell you the truth. I really feel that, you know, in a place like this, you need to support one another." Mary also disclosed,

Teachers need to be more supportive and they should not be against you—we all in this. And, if you've not been in the classroom, you need to be aware of what's going on in a classroom, in a setting like this 'cause we get cursed out and everything like that too. . . . Having somebody there that we can be able to talk to and supporting one another, if you are having a bad day, "Well come to me, that's okay." So that I can see and say, "Yeah I know what you're going through just give me your problem."

Unfortunately for the educators and the students, not only are the teachers placed at this facility without having a say in the matter, they also do not receive training before they begin. Mary described her reaction when she found out she was being placed at this facility: "I was just told I was going to be put in a residential facility (laughs). I'm like, 'Oh, my God. What is this?' You know, 'And they have guards?'" She elaborated, "No, no training, as I said, it's just when I got there, I looked at what was there and I was like, I don't like how this is operating."

Although the educators didn't receive training before they began working at this facility, they do have access to professional development throughout the school year. While they haven't attended any training sessions specific to working with incarcerated youth, they are able to attend workshops, conferences and have monthly professional development sessions on the main campus (at the alternative school). Mary shared, "Well, we do [have professional development] with the main campus, and so it's sort of general topics. We talk about Common Core, 'cause everybody's going to be doing Common Core. . . . We can go to workshops."

Another recognized form of support for the educators is the process of being observed and provided with authentic feedback for improvement. Mary said she had three classroom observations last year. And, according to her, "All three were on the computer. I think they met with me once, 'cause they're still trying to do this merit pay thing." While this has the potential to serve as a resource for Mary's growth as an educator, it didn't appear that this is being actualized to the extent possible.

There is an apparent disconnect with how principal and teachers view confinements. Mary believes many of the necessary resources for students are lacking. Despite the abundance of funding Principal Patrick spoke about, Mary expressed the need for more support to further assist students and help her with grading the students' work. She pleaded, "I wish I had more help, because I cannot always get to everybody, and it's tough because they're not all on the same page, you know. They're in all these different books . . . and the grading is . . . a lot of work." Mary also spoke about the basic materials that would serve as helpful resources for the students. Other teachers further conveyed this during their weekly staff meeting. "We need to make sure we have supplies like paper, pencils, basic stuff," said Mary.

The instructional focus calendar served as a resource for the teachers, but that was since removed. Mary is left to design lessons and plan how she sees fit. Mary explained, "I pretty much was told what I could teach for my whole group and then they would break out into their individual, do their own, what we call contracts or learning plans." She shared how much the instructional focus calendar is needed and how she used this experience to develop her own resources:

> Now we go to end-of-course exams. . . . There's no more instructional focus, but yet your class is not a pure class, so you can't say, "Okay, let's all do page 5 in the pre-algebra book." You have them all in different books, so it took me a while . . . and I started to think, from helping them, I started to realize that there were topics that were universal, and that's what I do now is I've taken those topics and I've turned them into my whole class lesson, so I've made, so to speak, my own instructional focus based on topics that are in all their books.

The teachers at Hubert B. also believe a vocational program would be an added resource for the youth. Mary mentioned, "I think [vocational training] is an excellent idea. . . . Hands-on, you know, woodwork or metal work, things like that. . . . maybe fixing cars." She explained, "You know one of the things I'm noticing, too—a lot of them like to draw. . . . Maybe some kind of art class. . . . You know, graphic arts, to kind of channel these things that they do into something constructive." Disappointingly, none of these resources serve as electives or outlets for the youth at Hubert B.

There are times when some students enter the facility, and there is no certified teacher on staff to teach that particular course, or it's not a core course that is offered. Mary discussed what happens when a student enters the facility and needs to take a class for which there isn't a teacher. According to Mary, "We have two labs, Apex for them to do their coursework. . . . If he needs music appreciation, there ain't no music teacher, so he'll go to one of those labs, one of the Apex classes and . . . be put into his own [course]." Although Mary insists the youth should have the same resources as their counterparts on the *outs*, it is evident that there aren't the same level of resources that one might find within a traditional school setting.

There are computers at the facility, which potentially serve as a tremendous resource for students, but the teachers in my study do not allow the students to use these technological tools. Mary said, "Not during my class time." The computers for both the math and reading classes were removed. Mary would like to use these as resources but feels the juvenile justice staff do not efficiently help her monitor students who may wind up on inappropriate websites or damage the equipment.

Students are encouraged to serve as resources for each other in Mary's class. She explained, "Sometimes . . . I do allow them to work together. 'He's doing that if you want to help him. Can you help him, 'cause he's on the same thing?'" She uses this strategy particularly when several students have questions and she's not able to get to everyone that needs help. Mary expounded, "I'll be helping you with some questions . . . other people are waiting, and they get impatient but I'm only one person, so . . . I may ask somebody to help him with it. If not, they just have to wait 'til I get done." During my observations, some students took advantage of receiving help from their peers and most showed their appreciation of the one-on-one support they received from Mary by ending their session with "Thank you."

Mary believes the size of the class allows for students to receive better support. She shared, "The class I have now is so small, it's beautiful. You know, I mean, I can really try to help them, but I feel frustrated because people ask for my help, but I can't get to everybody." According to Mary, "They need one-on-one." And, she believes, "they need more resources in place to get the support they need." She divulged, "To tell you the truth, we need more help, more people, 'cause like for me, I can't always get to everybody, so I need to have somebody as a second help." Although Mary is happy about the size and requesting more assistance, during a class period with five students, only two students were on task and received support from the teacher.

Teachers provide books to students as a resource for the youth. Mary has books in her classroom for students to use but is unsuccessful with students returning the books. She stated, "I don't have a problem with them using the books, but they don't bring it back. You know, I don't mind. I'll let them check it out, but they don't bring it back." Students also have access to the books during their instructional time. For example, during math class, a student became frustrated as several students were making fun of his being in the red math book, indicating that he was on a lower level math than his peers. This taunting went on for some time until, finally, the youth returned the math book to the shelf, took a novel from another bookshelf, and sat down and read quietly. Although he did not complete any math work for the day, he took solace in reading a book of choice.

Accountability

The Florida Department of Juvenile Justice (FLDJJ) has requirements in place, including assessments and treatment team meetings, to hold the educators and the facility accountable. Mary shared, "When they come in here, they're pre-tested. They take a test and based on those scores . . . you do this set of assignments. . . . I give you the credit. It's a contract. It's an agreement. You do this, then you get that." This allows for there to be some form of record keeping that documents what the students were supposed to receive, in terms of instruction, and what they actually completed. Unfortunately, the only way the educators at this facility have devised a way to meet this requirement is by providing packets of work to the students, indicating the page numbers and required book assignments to complete. While there is merit in this, because documentation can be shown that the student completed or did not complete the work, this does not make room for any true hands-on learning and real-world experiences.

One additional accountability structure now in place is a new teacher evaluation system with an emphasis on merit pay. The teachers at this facility will be evaluated based on teacher observations and student data. Although it still remains unclear how these juvenile justice educators will be held accountable for the youth who they only have for a few months and who come from other counties, merit pay is in place as an attempt to hold the educators accountable for providing a high-quality education for their youth. Perplexed, Mary stated,

> I'm looking at this across the country. How is this supposed to work? How can you pay a teacher based on performance? I don't mind they check on me, see what I'm doing, make sure I'm doing what, but there's three people involved in this. You have the student—he's got to pull his weight, and where are the parents? It's not all on the teacher. . . . I don't understand how this is supposed to work.

Karen

Karen teaches reading at Hubert B. She has 12 years' teaching experience as a reading and English as a second language (ESL) teacher. However, this is her first experience teaching incarcerated youth, and she is in her second year at this site. Karen expressed some disequilibrium between the educators and the juvenile justice staff. Moreover, she hadn't yet forged positive relationships with many of her students. She believes she is doing the best she can while fulfilling her requirement to "teach" and leaves it up to the students to "learn." Karen also believes there are appropriate accountability measures in place.

Relationships

Karen recognizes a lack of relationship between the juvenile justice leader and the educators. She discussed what occurred when they had the youth write in journals to express themselves, as a form of therapy. According to Karen, "Once, we were keeping journals, and then the head of the facility, he stopped it. He said it's not working. . . . He didn't give us any particular reason. . . . He didn't give us any details but . . . he didn't like it."

Despite this perhaps stymied relationship, Karen stated that the educational staff works closely with the students and their case managers (juvenile justice staff) as needed. If there is an issue with a student, the teacher is able to get in touch with his case manager. "We work with the case managers, and that's very effective. If we have issues with the kids in class, you know, we talk to the case managers," cited Karen. She elaborated,

> We do incident reports and the case managers would now interview that student and do some counseling, you know. So, that's another thing that works. . . . When we do the writeup or the incident report on the student, we come in, we give them a copy so they know up front what's going on, so they address it.

While this seems plausible, this isn't always the case. During one of my observations, Karen chose not to write up a student who was being extremely defiant throughout her classroom lesson. At the end of class, she told me, "I'm not going to write him up. There's so much to fill out and then you have to send a copy to everybody, and who knows if anything will happen. [Juvenile Justice] staff was in here and did nothing."

Relationships between Karen and her students were also lacking. Principal Patrick believes teachers must establish relationships with students; Karen, however, did not know many of the students' names and stood behind her desk for the majority of the reading lessons. She only came around her desk during one class period to show students their grades as she carried her laptop to each student's desk.

Expectations

Karen expects that she will provide high-interest topics for her students in order to motivate them as learners. Karen explained, "[I provide] high-interest topics that the student will be motivated to read and assimilate and discuss, 'cause we do a lot of discussion before we write so they can share ideas. And, we work cooperatively and collaboratively." Although Karen uses round-robin reading, arguably an ineffective teaching strategy, particularly for students who are reading and comprehending at varying levels, she further expects herself to help students build their comprehension. She stated, "While reading, I always stop and monitor their comprehension. I ask questions, make sure that they're understanding. . . . They love to take turns to read. . . . I introduce all these activities that I think will build their comprehension."

Karen believes that when she teaches, she reaches every student. According to Karen, "I teach to the student and not to the grade level. When I teach I make sure that I reach every student." Unfortunately, this was not the case during the classroom observations. The highest percentage of students in any of her classes who completed their work or remained on task during her lesson was 50%, even when there were only eight students in the classroom.

Despite the lack of student engagement that was evident during the classroom observations, Karen sees "value in the student that they don't see in themselves a lot of the time" and expects to serve as a motivator and encourager for her students. She asserted,

> Some of them do really well. . . . Sometimes I ask them . . . "What school did you go to?" And some of them say, "Miss, I haven't been in school for years. Since sixth grade I dropped out." I said, "Well, you're doing extremely well. I think when you get out of here you need to go on, you know, go on learning, maybe go to college."
>
> I see a lot of potential in a lot of them that they don't see in themselves. Simple things like penmanship. Sometimes I see such beautiful writing and I say, "Who taught you to write like that?" This, I think is very encouraging for them. And I see good things can happen if we stay positive because when they leave some of them tell me, "You know Miss, I'll be going to college, you know, I'll continue getting my GED (General Educational Development). I didn't get it yet, but I'll sign up when I leave." You know, things like that.

Karen grades students based on their performance and participation. She insisted, "Every day I grade the student, okay. So, based on what we do, sometimes we may not do written work, but based on performance and participation, I grade them." She anticipates that she may have to help some students "every step of the way," even if this means they are copying her responses from the board for a grade. She explained,

> With the extended responses, I sometimes do it with them because I find if I have them do it on their own they just give me . . . two-word answers, you know (chuckles). And I feel most of the time I have to model it for them, and then sometimes they get really frustrated with it because they really don't know how to do it.
>
> So I discuss every question, and I do a lot of writing on the board. They copy the answers. Sometimes I say, "You don't have to copy it exactly as I have it. But you can change it around. Put more of your answers in. Make sure you agree with what I have before you copy." So I kind of help them with every step of the way.

She described this as a strategy she uses to also assist her ESE students. Karen shared, "I use so much modeling . . . writing on the board, because we have some ESE students as well and they have problems and just so that they don't get lost in the middle I do a lot of modeling." During one of the classes, a student had his head down for the majority of the lesson. But when it was time to do the work, he lifted his head, got a piece of paper and a pencil, and copied the following two sentences from the board:

> 14. I would like to be a _____ because _____. To acquire experience, I would work as an intern prior to starting my career.

> 15. I want to respond by attacking the person verbally and physically. I keep calm and walk away.

Once the student finished copying the two sentences, he turned in his paper to the teacher and returned to his desk to put his head down. Turning in this assignment guaranteed this student a favorable performance and participation grade for the day.

Karen insists only the "best and brightest" teachers are sent to this facility to teach and work with these students—a great contradiction to what Principal Patrick shared. Karen's perspective differs greatly as she explained her expectation of the principal, based on who he sends to this facility: "Our principal, he's very sharp. He knows who he can choose to teach these kids, you know (laughs). So, he knows that we are prepared."

She maintains this same belief for her students. "A lot depends on the student . . . 'cause a lot of this instruction that we do cannot be forced upon the kids," cited Karen. She continued, "They have issues going on, psychological and mental issues. . . . Sometimes they may get, you know, enraged, if, if you pressure them so we have to be—. They are very, very delicate situations to deal with, with these kids." Because of the needs the students have, Karen affirmed that the incarcerated youth should not be pressured into doing their work:

> They have more needs because they have more issues going on. They go to court. They are away from home. They are locked up. They don't get to see their family very often. Some of them, they don't get to see their family members at all, because they don't come to see them you know, for some strange reason. They miss their friends and they have a whole bunch of issues going on, so we have to be a little bit more understanding of that. Like, some days they may come and just not be in the mood to work, and you just can't pressure them. You just have to be very flexible with them.

Because of this expectation, during her reading classes, as few as 21%—3 out of 14—of students participated in the lesson. The highest participation was 50%, or 4 out of 8 students.

Karen believes the students need more than just what is provided for students' day-to-day instruction. She stated, "We need to get them prepared for jobs and/or college, you know, and with a lot of the lower-level people, we still have to focus on their basic skills curriculum." This highlights again this notion of basic skills, as if every student falls into this category.

Resources

The educators at Hubert B. serve as a resource for Karen. She insisted, "There was some teachers who were here before I came in and they give us a lot of support, a lot of tips, 'cause they've been here for a while and peer support is what we have."

Karen also appreciates the professional development opportunities she is afforded, although she did not receive any specific training for working with incarcerated youth prior to teaching at this facility. She confirmed, "[For] professional development we go to main campus and all the teachers from different campuses get together—DJJ plus main campus. We do it. It's a whole group thing, and we break up into groups."

In addition to the professional development sessions they have on the main campus, they have weekly staff meetings. Karen explained what occurs during these sessions: "Here, we have weekly meetings with our coordinator and our guidance counselor every Thursday at 12:30 and then we have a representative from [the facility] sitting at the meeting as well. . . . We discuss current issues and problems that we're having."

During my observation of the educational staff meeting, the lead teacher asked whether there were any educational concerns. They discussed transition paperwork for students who were going to be transitioning out from the facility. The teachers were also thanked for completing the paperwork for the treatment team meeting, even though they were two weeks behind on submitting the required paperwork. Mary volunteered to sort and organize the binder for the treatment team documents. And before the meeting ended, the teachers made a request for dry erase markers, pencils, lined paper, and file folders. When one of the teachers asked about the schedule that was going to be changing, the lead teacher responded, "Don't worry about the schedule. That's the AP's (assistant principal's) role. That's why they get paid the big bucks." Although the teachers' requests demonstrate a method for them to receive some basic materials needed in their classrooms, this last statement demonstrates perhaps the disconnect with hierarchical relationships at Hubert B.

Classroom observations serve as a promising source of support, but the teachers do not always receive feedback to potentially improve their practice. Karen shared, "Some of the walk-throughs, though, they're not meant to give feedback, but we are now being observed and it's online; and yes, those we get feedback for, the ones that are done online, because we are graded." She continued, "We have classroom walk-throughs at any time. . . . Our assistant principal, we have [our reading coach], she comes in. We have [our principal], he sometimes comes himself to visit. . . . We have—. It's ongoing, all year, classroom walk-throughs and observations."

Just as Karen views these classroom visits as a form of support for teachers, Karen also agreed with the need for a more hands-on approach with students. She shared, "[We should provide] more vocational [programs] . . . for the kids, because a lot of them are hands-on." Despite what the educators believe to be best teaching practices, however, none of the "hands-on" approaches to learning that was described is provided for the youth at this facility. There is clearly discord between what the educators believe students need and what students are actually being provided.

Karen believes Florida Virtual and Carmen County Virtual, two online programs, serve as a resource for the youth, particularly when a teacher might not be certified to teach a course that's needed. She explained its importance: "If the student needs a course towards their graduation that we don't have a certified teacher to give them, they can take it through Florida Virtual." Despite this resource, however, Karen further divulged, "I had some computers, but I asked for them to be removed because we just had, like, four. And it's very difficult for me to monitor the students on the computers while I work with the others." Again, Karen shares her wants and expectations with what's best for her students yet continues to feel and believe her hands are tied, that she doesn't have the resources needed to make this necessary learning tool available for her students.

Karen cited that the textbooks she uses with the students are very resourceful. She stated, "*Rewards* . . . has to do a lot with pronunciation and understanding . . . articulating . . . breaking up the words into syllables to help those who have problems with pronunciation. *Impact* . . . [has] very high interest topics . . . and the *Edge* [provides] a lot of reading passages, comprehension exercises." One resource currently in place is guest speakers. Karen elaborated, "Sometimes we have guest speakers. . . . For example, we had a speaker; he was incarcerated for like 40 years or so for a crime he said he didn't commit, and he came in and he spoke to the kids." The educators believe mentors coming in to work with students would also serve as tremendous resources for the youth. Karen shared, "Having mentors from the community coming in might be a good idea . . . people who are successful out there because they certainly look up to successful people." According to Karen, "They relate to other people with similar experiences . . . from the *outs*. The kids say the *outs*, from the outside (laughs)." She elaborated,

> They value connections a lot and connections, you know, they had all the wrong connections before they came here (laughs) so it would be a nice idea to have them get more positive connections. . . . You know, like the big brother, kind of, having someone to look up to. . . . Members of the community in high professions, you know, come in to work with them, spending voluntary time.

While Karen believes this is an added resource, none of the educators I interviewed could pinpoint even one mentor that has come in to work with a youth.

Accountability

Fortunately, there are a few accountability components in place for the educators and the youth at this facility. Students are assessed when they come in and assessed before leaving to determine what academic gains were made during the time they were at the facility. Karen explained, "When the student comes in, the student is tested . . . and when the student leaves, there is a post-test, so we try to see that there's some improvement in the grade . . . pretty much for the six months that they're here."

At the treatment team meetings, held every four weeks for each youth, the team determines whether a child moves up a level. This is used to determine early release for a student or to move him up or down a progression scale. Karen explained the procedure if they have an issue with a student: "If we have problems with that kid, if the kid isn't working, we note it as a comment so they don't get to be promoted to the next level if they're not doing well at school." She elaborated, "Each kid wants to be promoted, so if they messed up for one month and they didn't get promoted then, you know, they try and improve the next time." While this seems to be a viable accountability structure for the youth, during my visit, it was discovered that the teachers had not provided the education paperwork for two weeks. There also weren't any teachers at the meeting to provide insights on how the youths were doing academically or behaviorally in class. Therefore, students in the class who did not do what they were supposed to were not being held accountable; nor was anyone holding the educators accountable for not having the paperwork completed for the treatment team meetings.

Susan

Susan is the ESE support facilitator at Hubert B. This is her first year in this capacity and her first teaching experience. This is also her first DJJ assignment. Furthermore, her teaching internships to prepare her for her educational role were in suburban schools within her school district. She espoused positive working relationships, relatively low expectations, adequate resources, and appropriate accountability, but with the exception of low expectations, much of what she espoused was incongruent with what I observed.

Relationships

Although Principal Patrick and Karen expressed their desires for a more promising relationship with the juvenile justice staff, Susan shared a different perspective, including an appreciation for this perceived lack of relationship:

> I think they let us do what we need to do . . . They leave us alone. They don't say, "What are you doing?" I mean, and they have to

follow their guidelines, too, the things that they want and they don't want in the facility and we have to adhere to that, because we're the guests here. But for the most part, I think they leave us alone.

Susan believes the educators themselves have a much closer relationship and that they work together. The teachers have common planning time each day and, according to Susan, they use that time to communicate with one another, particularly to discuss issues they may be having with students. These sessions have the potential to strengthen the relationships among the teachers. Susan explained,

> We have planning, common planning where we talk to each other and feed off each other. You know, try to find out, if this student is doing this in class, this student is doing that, how can we work it to make it work for the next teacher; just collaboration with what's available and each other that makes it work. 'Cause every day, as you can see, when you get in that teacher's room they start talking about one student and the next teacher say, "Well in my class, the student does work but, you know, I do this, and it helps him with that." So you know, the teachers do feed off each other when they do talk about the student.

Susan also explained the conversations she has with her students to better assist them and to further establish a positive working relationship. According to Susan, "I also sit with them and ask them, 'Okay, what do you want to do?' And we start working towards that."

Expectations

Susan sees her role as a supporter, not as a teacher. She shared, "I don't really per se, teach, I support (laughs). . . . As far as me getting up doing a lesson, no." This was further evidenced during the classroom observations. When the teacher was up teaching the lesson, Susan sat off to the side. Once the teacher completed what she was teaching the students from the board and the students began their class work, Susan walked around to assist the youth.

Susan expects she will try to teach her students "something." There is no measurement of what this "something" is, as long as they've learned "something" more than they knew before they arrived. She explained, "I . . . just [try] to teach them (chuckles) . . . something. . . . Once they learn something . . ., 'cause they're deficient, too. . . . How much knowledge can you get to them? . . . From what's in their books, plus in their whole group, just expose them to as much as possible."

Susan focuses on providing more one-on-one with students and supporting the youth according to their abilities and at their own pace.
She believes that even with academic deficiencies, students should be
expected to complete the work at the same level of their peers. She
explained, "You tend to work more one-on-one with the students and
focus on their actual deficiencies." Susan elaborated, "[My] ESE students . . . I don't downgrade their academics. I may cut the assignment
in half and give it to them day by day, but they still are required to do
the same work as the other students."

Susan also expressed the challenges teachers in this environment
face when they encounter students who don't take learning seriously.
According to Susan, "If they're not willing to learn, they could make
it difficult in the classroom for the other students, because they can
have outbursts. They can curse you out. They can refuse. So, it's nothing
really you can do." Regardless of the students' levels of participation, the
educators expect students to be job ready when they leave the facility,
although there's not much that's done to prepare students to meet this
expectation. Susan shared, "I think they need to be job-ready." Yet currently no program exists, nor is one being proposed to help meet this
need for the students.

One negative expectation that Susan continues to maintain is that
students will continually be pulled out of their classrooms for non-educational purposes. Susan shared that the youths' "program come first;
education is second." She explained, "They're in and out of class, being
pulled in and out. . . . They could be in the middle of working and then
they're pulled out of class to go on transport." Susan elaborated,

If the kid have to go to court, it doesn't matter. Everything cease.
They go to court. If the kid have to go to the dentist, it doesn't matter.
If they have to close school for the day, it's closed (laughs).

Although Karen appreciates the separation between the juvenile justice
staff and the educators, as stated in the relationship section, she also
described this disconnect in a manner that she wishes would change.
Susan believes the educators should be kept in the loop when emer-
gencies occur rather than having to speculate about what is happening, particularly when the juvenile justice staff decide to close school.
Susan quipped, "If something emergency happen, they'll just say, 'Okay,
school is over.' And we may go around asking, like, 'What happened
(laughs)?'" She provided an example of a recent occurrence:

Like, two weeks ago, one of the staff lost their keys, so they just—, "School is over" (laughs). . . . So they shut everything down, 'cause they had to take the kids back and search them. So it was like, "Okay, everybody line up. School is over." And it's like, "Okay, where did that come from?" . . . And that was it for school that day, but we still have to stay and ask each other, "What happened?"

Resources

Susan explained how beneficial it would have been to have training in advance, particularly on "what to expect when you go in." She believes it would definitely serve as a resource to teachers. This is her first teaching experience, and her first year teaching in a juvenile facility. According to Susan,

Some teachers walk in and not really knowing the environment itself. You know, the youth, they can curse you out today, and tomorrow they're your best friend. The type of environment that they're walking into, the risk, the type of risk, it's not really per se, you're at risk for getting hurt, but anything can happen in these facilities. So, it's a type of risk that they would need to know beforehand; because, some teachers walk in blindly, never been in an alternative setting and . . . when they walk in, they're like, "I didn't expect this."

Because the professional development is not specific to incarcerated youth, Susan shared how she takes the information and "tailors" it to this unique setting. According to Susan, "There's no specific training when you go to professional development. . . . DJJ is a whole separate entity. You just take what you learn out there and you just tailor (laughter) it to the inside." She elaborated, "They teach you basic classroom management that's supposed to work for all, but it really don't work for all, 'cause your situation's so different. But it's no set training for this type of population."

Susan expounded on the ideal professional development that would be most useful in this setting. She recognizes the need for strong cohesiveness between the juvenile justice staff and the educators and believes training to address this need would serve as a significant resource:

And as far as what particular training that we would need (chuckles), actually I think it would be more, not really classroom management, it would be more of facility co-adhesive. 'Cause when you're inside a facility teaching, it's basically their rules follow and yours are second. So, it's more so—; you're like in opposition. So, it would be more training with the facility in which the school is housed, so everybody could be on the same page when it comes to the kids' education, basically.

Specific training for the teachers to better prepare them for their roles in this facility would be ideal and could serve as a tremendous resource, yet it is nonexistent and the educators commit themselves to "learn as [they] go." Susan quipped,

You're just in and you learn as you go (laughs). I hate to say it that way, but you actually just learn as you go and you pick up, you pick up different things from different people, from experienced teachers. That's basically the bottom line. I'm sorry.

Although Principal Patrick has an assistant principal who is also responsible for overseeing the educational services at this facility and several other facilities, Susan believes their hands-off approach and lack of demandingness serve as support. She explained, "It's not the breathing down your neck of, 'You got to get this done. You got to get this done.'" She elaborated, "You really can work on that—, hone in on that student. Like if I have a struggling reader, I can actually sit with that student and see progress of that student—progressing in reading . . . you know, taking that time."

Although Susan appears to appreciate not having too frequent contact with an administrator, she stated that the administrators "pop up on you any time." She described two divergent methods the administrators use to provide the teachers with feedback:

Depending on which administrator comes, it can be at that moment, you know, that same particular day or a later day when they set up a conference and say, "Okay, when I saw this—." Or, when we have our teachers meeting on Thursday it might be put out there that "[w]hen I went through a classroom—." It might not be a certain teacher (giggles). "I observed—." "We can't be—." And, if you were that teacher, you know, you will pick up on that (laughs). But if it's that important, they will pull you aside and they will correct you.

As an added resource, in addition to their core courses taught by classroom teachers, students have the option to recover credits through the courses online. Susan shared, "We have the option for the Apex. We have the options for the recovery packet. Apex is computer-based, where they get to go back and help them recover credits and help them move forward." She added, "The guidance counselor . . . talks with each student . . . looks up the record from their last schools, any records that we got from previous schools and then she would make a learning plan for that student and give to the teachers." For students who don't see graduating with a diploma as an option, they offer the GED (General Educational Development) examination.

Regardless of what's in place, Susan is adamant that the youth in this facility are receiving the same resources as youth who are not incarcerated. She asserted, "In actuality, they're getting everything what the basic schools are getting as far as technology is infused, as far as the curriculum and the test preparation." Students are eligible to take the SAT (Scholastic Assessment Test), but Susan explained that the students have to pay for this test. According to Susan, "They take the SAT if they close enough to graduate. They have that option, but they have to pay."

Susan said she provides books for students that serve as additional resources. She explained, "They are able to take it with them, but they can't keep transporting it back and forth. It has to stay on the unit . . . because that's considered contraband."

Susan also believes the structured learning environment serves as a resource for the youth. According to Susan, many of the youth pass the FCAT (Florida Comprehensive Achievement Test). She explained, "The majority of them do pass it, because I think the structured environment that they can finally sit down and say, 'Okay, I need to learn. I don't know how to read. I need to do this.'"

Last, Susan believes she also serves as a resource for her ESE students:

I may have a group, like, say, for instance, I'm in a reading class and I have six students in one class and she's doing a lesson and after she finish telling them what they want to do, I will go to them and say, "Well, I'm here," if they need help. And three or four of them may say, "Okay, can you read the story with us?" And we will just form a group and read.

Accountability

While time spent with each student or small groups of students is seen as a resource, this also demonstrates a lack of accountability for the services provided for the ESE students. There is no set schedule for Susan's role as the ESE support facilitator. She decides what classrooms she will go to, as well as when, and what students she will support. She explained how she spends her time. According to Susan, "One student could be 20 minutes. One student can be an hour. One student, it could be all day, so it depends what subject I'm working on, what work they need and . . . how low that student is."

With almost 50 ESE students at this facility, if the facility's sole ESE support facilitator spends an entire day with one student, there are 49 others who possibly would not have received the support outlined in their IEP. Susan, however, believes that she is held accountable for the services she provides. She asserted,

> My ESE specialist, she usually come out. . . . She have different sites that she go around. So she—, usually like the supervisors or the principals they come out and she'll just talk with the kids to make sure that they're meeting with me. Because you know, if you're not meeting with a kid, the first thing they'll say is, "Who is that (laughs)?" So you don't have to do much. They'll say, "Ms. [Susan]? Who's that? I don't know who you talking about." You know, they don't care. They don't have no filter. They just put it out there. "Oh, she only came and got me one time." You know (laughs). So, yeah, she comes out and she more or less talk with the kids to see, you know, if I'm doing what I'm supposed to be doing and meeting whatever needs they need as far as educationwise and ESE support.

Although Susan insists that she is held accountable for her role as ESE support facilitator, she believes there is a lack of accountability on the part of the facility as it relates to how students are disciplined. Susan surmised,

> Most time in these facilities, it's babysitting facilities, 'cause it's no hands-on. When I say hands-on, the kids have to be extremely endangering himself or someone, to actually put hands-on. So, it's more like babysitting. 'Cause some of these kids curse you out (laughs) and curse the staff, and all you can do, is, "Well, we gonna talk to your case manager. We gonna give you more time." But, and it's just a cycle and it's just—, and you see that more schools are closing and more of these facilities opening (laughter). It's more political than education.

Despite the lack of accountability that was evident for students' inappropriate behavior, fortunately, the students at Hubert B. are held accountable for taking the same assessments as students who are in traditional settings. Susan explained, "They take all the assessments that the regular school takes. They take the FCAT. Whatever assessments that the public school gives, they take also." Susan conveyed that the educators are expected to provide the same textbooks that are being used by the traditional schools within the school district. According to Susan, "Same as the regular, [Carmen] County School, whatever adopted books that they have, we have." Another teacher added, "First of all, we have to make sure the books are state-mandated. All our texts are mandated by the state of Florida." Although much more needs to be done to ensure students are exposed to a high-quality education, being accountable for minimally having state approved books is at least a start.

Discussion

There is an evident lack of much needed relationships with the educators at this facility. This deficiency affects the expectations they have for their students and the resources that are provided to ensure that youth are exposed to a high-quality education. Unfortunately, much-needed accountability mechanisms are also lacking.

Relationships

It is most unfortunate for the youth at the Hubert B. Juvenile Justice Residential Facility that the necessary relationships for them to receive a high-quality education are non-existent. Fortunately, there are some attempts for teacher–student relationships, with the way the teachers greet the students, know some of the students by name, and speak with and encourage the youth. The critical juvenile justice/education partnership, however, is absent. Particularly because they are the "guests," Principal Patrick recognizes the need for this relationship, yet one has not yet been cultivated.

During the interview, Karen stated the teachers receive support from the case managers when they have a problem with a student. She explained the process that occurs—writing the incident up and the juvenile justice case managers' following up with the students and teachers. However, when she was faced with a student demonstrating extremely deviant behavior, she chose not to write him up, stating that nothing will be done to correct the behavior. While this demonstrates clearly the cognitive dissonance at play in her own mind, the observations indicate that the relationships between the educators and the juvenile justice staff are not as strong as they need to be to ensure that every incarcerated youth is being exposed to a high-quality education.

Furthermore, relationships have not been properly established on multiple levels. The relationship with the principal and the facility director and the principal and the district are wanting, and that continues in a downward trajectory for the teachers at this facility, particularly because the teaching staff rotates every two years. Although Principal Patrick receives ample funding from the district to provide resources for his teachers and students, the monetary benefit seems to be the extent of the relationship. Because of this, Principal Patrick feels like he works in isolation. This feeling of isolation also appeared to permeate the teachers at this facility. Although the teachers have each other to talk to, and although mechanisms such as common planning time are in place to potentially foster positive working relationships among the teachers, often teachers did not know what other teachers taught and were uncertain of the roles of the ancillary staff.

Expectations

The low expectations Principal Patrick has for his teachers, knowing that he does not place his "best teachers" at this facility, are analogous to the low expectations the teachers have for their students. It is a disheartening reality. Teacher expectations of students are very low, ranging from wanting students to improve "one grade level" to "just learn something" during their period of incarceration. The educators also believe students should not be compelled to learn or participate in class, and this expectation allows many students to potentially lose out on learning critical skills. Students were allowed to keep their heads down on their desks for the entire lesson, and there appeared to be no consequences or a true expectation for their doing otherwise. The educators believe the students "have issues" and may possibly become violent if they force them to keep their heads up and to participate. Although the educators' expectations are posted, none of what's listed specifically addresses an expectation for students to be on task and keep their heads up during the lesson.

Even though Principal Patrick is responsible for an 1,100-student alternative school, other programs, and an additional four DJJ sites, he is compensated the same as a high school principal in his district whose sole responsibility is to oversee one high school. Principal Patrick expects to be compensated more equitably, based on the multiple facilities and programs for which he is responsible.

Furthermore, he believes that his teachers are not intrinsically motivated because he assigned them to teach at this facility. Regardless of how they end up teaching there, Principal Patrick expects that the teachers will establish positive relationships and also make learning relevant for their students. He expects that students need a highly effective teacher, yet he believes that the more effective teachers are at the alternative school. Mary concurred that it is difficult to be highly effective when teachers are moved from place to place every two years. Regardless of other people's opinions, however, Mary strives to be highly effective and expects that she must grade every question that the students answer to determine whether they understand the material and is adamant that her students must show their work.

The educators have become so accustomed to the students being brought to class late and pulled in and out of class that they believe there is not much they can do to change what is happening. Students were brought an average of 14 minutes late per class. Each class is 75 minutes in length, so on average, students missed 20% of their instructional time. That, coupled with having a disruption every 52.8 seconds, further lessens the opportunity for the youth to be exposed to a high-quality education. Furthermore, although the teachers believe they are reaching all their students, it was evident during the observations that this is not the case. The highest percentage of students on task in any observed class was 63% in math, even when there were only five or seven students in a classroom.

The educators at this facility believe that students should be provided with job training, yet no vocational program or job training is provided for the incarcerated youth. Despite this, students are expected and able to work at their own pace, whether they are moving slowly or want to advance themselves to earn additional credits toward graduation before returning home.

Finally, both Principal Patrick and Mary spoke about the conscious decisions they make to ensure that they are doing the best they can with the circumstances they find themselves in and with the resources they are provided. Although this is a laudable mission, it is important for these educators and the other educators at this facility to get out and experience successful juvenile justice educational programs. As human beings, we only know what we know. Even with the best of intentions and a moral compass, if we don't know how to effectively meet the needs of incarcerated youth, conscience alone will not provide what is necessary for the optimal learning environment for juvenile justice educators and students who are confined.

Resources

Principal Patrick acknowledges that he is not supported to the degree that he feels he needs to be from his school district, and that lack of support transfers to the educators at this facility. Although the district provides an abundance of funding for this facility, a result of the JJEEP quality assurance visits and feedback, the district's hands-off approach causes Principal Patrick to feel that he is working in isolation, lacking the support he needs to have a profound impact.

Moreover, he is conflicted about who he sends to this facility, because this facility is only one out of several sites for which he is responsible. His primary role is principal of an alternative school, a school to which he gives his full attention. While Principal Patrick is trying to run an 1,100-student alternative school, he is continually faced with competing interests and feels conflicted because of his responsibilities—finding teachers for students who appear to have a greater chance for success in the alternative setting versus teachers for students who are incarcerated and may not even live within the parameters of the county. Although highly skilled and qualified teachers who are able to motivate the youth at this facility could be a tremendous resource, this study revealed a lack of such educators. Principal Patrick believes students are not getting the best teachers possible, but he believes his hands are tied. Furthermore, the educators feel disempowered, yet they feel they are doing their best with the cards they've been dealt.

Principal Patrick rotates the teachers he assigns to this facility every two years, believing this will lessen the possibility of teacher burnout. However, this decision significantly decreases the educators' opportunity to cultivate high-quality, lasting relationships with the other educators and the juvenile justice staff in this facility. Particularly because the teachers are placed here, there's great risk that they will lack the motivation needed to inspire the youth with whom they work. Although Principal Patrick sees this as a response to not wanting teachers to burnout, other resources and mechanisms can be in place to support the teachers so that they can survive and thrive in this environment no matter how long they end up teaching at this facility.

It is interesting that, according to Principal Patrick, the funding is there, yet just as the resources appear lacking for the principal, the resources also appear lacking for the teachers and students. Meaningful training is needed, yet not provided, according to the teachers. None of the teachers interviewed received training before beginning their positions at this facility. And the training they receive during the school year does not specifically pertain to working with incarcerated youth.

Principal Patrick believes boys learn differently than girls and are more right-brained, and the teachers believe the students' learning should be more hands-on, yet specific professional development for the teachers on such critical topics have not been provided. Susan also strongly believes that training for facility cohesiveness is imperative because of their daily interactions with the juvenile justice staff. Although this could potentially serve as a tremendous resource, particularly because they are coming in to the juvenile justice facility as "guests" to provide the education to the incarcerated youth, such training is non-existent.

Although the teachers are provided with 1 hour and 15 minutes each day for their lunch and common planning time, Mary feels like she needs help with grading papers. It appears that much direction is needed, including resources and support, to help show the educators what tasks could be accomplished during their duty-free periods. During my time at the facility, the teachers appeared to be stressed, tense, and feeling unsupported. Because of this, some of the educators ended up working in isolation, and others spent their time complaining, venting, and consoling one another instead of using the planning time to complete tasks to minimize their workload or discuss strategies to further assist them and their students.

Online courses for credits, GED training, and testing serve as resources for the incarcerated youth, particularly for those who are over-age for high school with few or no credits. Treatment team meetings, students' helping one another, and books provided to read while in the classrooms also serve as resources for the youth. Unfortunately, job training and mentors, two major resources that the teachers believe are essential to the youths' success, are not offered.

Furthermore, although online courses are available for students to recover credits and to take courses that the facility may not have an educator to provide, the computers in the classrooms are not used during the school day, because the teachers don't believe they will be properly monitored.

Accountability

Although there are some mechanisms established to hold the facility and educators accountable, the current structure is not set up to ensure the facility meets or exceeds expectations for students to receive a high-quality education. Both a teacher at the facility and Principal Patrick made a statement about fragile programs "being out there on their own," citing the need for accountability. Yet very few mechanisms are in place to ensure this happens. Principal Patrick finds it difficult to hold this facility accountable because of the responsibilities he has overseeing multiple programs and DJJ sites, with his main role as principal of his 1,100-student alternative school.

Although it is evident that there is a need for accountability, there is little within the actual structure of the educational program that truly holds the educators accountable for providing the youth with a high-quality education. Susan, the ESE support facilitator, is able to create her own schedule and is able to work with one student for an entire day even though there are nearly 50 students requiring ESE support. In her mind, however, there is accountability because the ESE specialist and the administrators check in on her and her students and according to Susan, ask the students whether they receive ESE services.

There is a lack of accountability on how students are disciplined. Although there are expectations posted, little is being done to ensure that the youth are following those expectations or that there are consequences for their negative behavior. The educators, while adamant that they are providing the same resources to the youth here that any student in the district is able to receive, expressed different expectations with this facility because it is not in a traditional setting.

Mary expressed her concerns about merit pay. While merit pay is a response for more accountability across our nation to ensure that students have a highly effective teacher before them, it is equally imperative to have the necessary support structures in place for both teachers and students. It is important to explore all possible options for holding juvenile justice educators accountable.

Fortunately, the state of Florida mandates state adopted textbooks, and implementation of the Common Core State Standards, end-of-course exams, and FCAT. The FLDJJ also has its own requirements, which provide at least some standard for what the educational goals should be and for what components the educators and youth will be held accountable. One level of accountability for the youth is provided through the treatment team meetings.

Treatment team meetings are in place to provide students and their support team with feedback each month. Yet, lack of accountability allowed teachers to not submit their treatment team paperwork for two weeks, nor was there any educational representation at the meetings. At the educational staff meeting, however, as if everything was completed on time and appropriately, one of the ancillary staff members who took on the task of collecting the late forms thanked the teachers for submitting their treatment team paperwork. No additional feedback regarding the missing forms was provided.

While there is some evidence of emerging relationships and partnerships, the critical relationship between the educational staff and juvenile justice staff is lacking. Lack of relationships appears to lead to inconsistencies in expectations for teachers and students. It is very unfortunate that Principal Patrick feels like he works in isolation and that although he sends additional resources to this facility, the teachers seemed to feel unsupported as well. Lack of accountability is also an important part of the equation that must be further analyzed and addressed.

5

Gladys C. Juvenile Justice Academy[1]

Introduction

The Gladys C. Juvenile Justice Academy is a public facility, owned and operated by the Florida Department of Juvenile Justice. The state of Florida owns and operates 100% of its regional juvenile detention centers and approximately 5% of its residential programs. There are less than 50 youth housed in this level 6, moderate-risk facility. The majority of youth at this facility are children of color. Seventy percent are African American, 3% are Hispanic, and 25% are White. Forty percent of the youth are classified as Exceptional Student Education (ESE). During the 2008–2009 school year, the Gladys C. Juvenile Justice Academy was rated marginal satisfactory by the Juvenile Justice Educational Enhancement Program (JJEEP) for its educational services.

The Walter County Public Schools is responsible for providing a quality education to its more than 75,000 students, including the incarcerated youth housed at the Gladys C. Juvenile Justice Academy. The majority of students in the Walter County Public Schools are children of color, with approximately 45% African American, 10% Hispanic, and 40% White. Fifty-three percent of the students in the Walter County Public Schools qualify for Free or Reduced Price Meals (FRPM). During the 2008–2009 school year, the Walter County Public Schools was rated a B-grade school district by the Florida Department of Education for its student achievement.

The Gladys C. Juvenile Justice Academy is located in a remote residential area, at least two miles from a main road. Before I spotted the facility, I first noticed the fencing and bars that serve as security. As I approached the gate, I noticed a box with a speaker to the left. There was a keypad for an access code and a button to call. The only way to gain access to any part of the campus is to be buzzed in or to have an access code to enter. As I pressed the call button and waited for a response, I was asked to identify myself. After I informed the woman who I was, the gate slowly opened and I was able to drive into the lot and park.

The facility is located in a one-floor building on a property akin to a campground. I noticed many more fences and wires as I left my car to enter the main door. As I entered through the double glass doors, I was delighted to experience the open space of the reception area. There was a sign-in book for all visitors and a large self-standing metal detector off to the left. The area was well lit and photos of national leaders and the leaders within the organization, including President Barack Obama, Governor Rick Scott, the top DJJ leaders, and the facility's superintendent and assistant superintendent, were showcased. An employee of the month star was posted with a photo featuring the star employee, and a large white poster mounted on the wall included the facility's mission and vision statements and its five core values.

Once the main door was opened to the facility, I walked through a common area available for the youth that had tables and chairs and a pool table. I continued to walk down two hallways and made several turns before making my way back outside to the two trailers that serve as the learning environments for the youth. Each trailer has its own bathroom, office space for the teacher, and classroom space to comfortably hold approximately 12 students. The temperature within the trailer can be controlled by the thermostat located on the wall.

As I walked into the reading classroom, I noticed many resources for the students, including seven desktop computers, all lined in a row on the long tables in the back of the room, a dry-erase board, pulldown maps, and bookshelves with a plethora of books, including textbooks, GED (General Educational Development) exam preparation books, and novels. I also noticed a wall dedicated to posting student work. Upon further inspection, however, I saw that the student work posted was more than a year old, dated August 2011. Although the lighting is bright in the classroom, some of the linoleum-tiled floors had rust stains. There was a bathroom for students' use and an office for the teacher.

Within the math classroom, I noticed a small bookshelf off to the right with textbooks and practice test booklets. I also saw five computers lined up in the back of the room and another four computers on a round table in the far left of the classroom. There was a grading scale posted and a chart posted with the classroom rituals and routines: (1) Enter the classroom quietly. (2) Retrieve the textbooks you need. (3) Go to your desk. (4) Staff will bring you a pencil. (5) Look at the board for directions or wait for verbal directions from teacher. (6) Turn in all classwork in the basket for grading. There were CHAMPS (Conversation, Handout, Activity, Movement, Participation, Success) posters throughout the classroom, a poster with a Gandhi quote, and stars with various character traits posted on the wall. The teacher's office space was surrounded with glass windows and there was a bathroom for students.

Participants

Table 4   Gladys C. Juvenile Justice Academy participants

Juvenile Justice Educator	Position	Tenure at the Facility
Rae	Principal	1 year 2 months
Vicki	Math Teacher Science Teacher	1 year 2 months
Donna	Substitute Reading Teacher Social Studies Teacher	5 weeks

Educational Program

Each day, school begins at 7:30 a.m. and ends at 12:51 p.m. for the students. The following courses are taught each week: reading, intensive reading, social studies, science, math, and print shop. The students take three classes that last 1 hour and 45 minutes (105 minutes) each, for a total time of 315 minutes daily. Reading and social studies are taught by the same teacher, and math and science are taught by the same teacher. Sometimes, the teachers decide to teach only one subject each day. When this occurs, students receive their course instruction on a rotating schedule.

The teachers begin their day at 7:15 a.m. and end at 2:45 p.m. In addition to their 15-minute duty-free period before school, the teachers at this facility have 1 hour and 44 minutes each day for lunch and a common planning period. Their class sizes range from five to seven students.

Findings

Based on the four themes that emerged from this study, positive relationships were evident, yet there were disparate expectations and resources. There was also a lack of accountability.

The instructional methods used to work with the students at this facility were direct instruction, round-robin reading, and one-on-one instruction. Based on the 4 hours and 47 minutes spent observing the reading and math classes at this facility, the juvenile justice staff brought students an average 3.5 minutes late to class. The range of students on task at any given time during a reading lesson was as low as 40%, or 2 out of 5 students, and as high as 57%, or 4 out of 7 students. The range of students on task at any given time during a math lesson was as low as 16%, or 1 out of 6 students, to as high as 100%, or 7 out of 7 students. There were numerous disruptions observed during the instructional time, including student outbursts, singing, rapping, use of profanity, talking, getting up to use the bathroom, requesting hand sanitizer, laughing, throwing paper, entering and exiting the room after the lesson began, juvenile justice staff speaking with one another or with a student, and walkie-talkies transmitting. During the classroom observations, an average of 1 disruption occurred every 67 seconds.

Principal Rae

Rae is in her second year as principal at the Gladys C. Juvenile Justice Academy. She is also principal of an alternative middle school and is responsible for overseeing 11 additional programs, including additional DJJ sites, this facility, and youth development programs. Rae has three assistant principals who also provide administrative support to the facilities she oversees. She has prior teaching and administrative experience. Principal Rae recognizes the importance of relationships yet has mixed expectations, particularly for her teachers. At times, she believes adequate resources are provided for the educators and students, and she works on establishing varied forms of accountability.

Relationships

Principal Rae recognizes the importance of having positive relationships between the educational staff and the juvenile justice staff to better serve the incarcerated youth. She shared, "I think this is a very good facility in the fact that we have open communication with the facility side itself. Me and [the facility superintendent] talk often. Me and [the facility assistant superintendent], the direct care staff, we [are] usually on one accord." According to Principal Rae, "His staff has a role to play in ensuring our success. We have a role to play." She elaborated,

> If it's something they're going through—QA (quality assurance) or something special that he needs done, they have an advisory council. They'll call, "Can you come speak at this?" or "Can you do this?" We do that cause it's—. The relationship has been built and it runs well. That's not always the case. Sometimes it can be like you're a stranger

in someone else's house, because technically the facility is theirs, so I can't tell people they're going to work late. I can't say—. I bought SMART boards, I couldn't just say, "Well, we going to install these." Because at the end of the day, it's their facility.

So, if you don't have that working relationship, it becomes a tug-of-war. 'Cause I can say, "I'm the principal." And he can say, "Well, I'm the superintendent." And we can get tied up in that tug-of-war 'til, you know, as good as the day is long and it's not going to get results for students. And that happens in some places 'cause they feel, "You guys aren't going to do anything unless I say it's going to happen." So it just depends. Having the right personality, the right people at the table, is key; so some run smoother than others. It just depends on the nature of the leadership, because that trickles down.

Although two of the three teachers at this facility are relatively new, there is a relationship that coexisted between the principal and the facility's print shop teacher. Principal Rae shared, "I think he's been here at least 10 years. He worked at another school that I worked at as well. We were both at an alternative school." Although there is some history there, this seems to be an area that they are working to enhance. During my time at the facility, the teachers appeared to work in isolation, but I observed cordial conversations between the math and reading teacher, the math and print shop teacher, and the reading teacher and the paraprofessional whose primary function is handling the paperwork and ensuring that students are assessed.

Recognizing the importance of relationships, Principal Rae has fostered several relationships within her district to help ensure her teachers and students receive the support they need. Principal Rae disclosed, "So I am spread thin at most times, but I have a great leadership team [and] we stay concise and together, so it helps." She also has the support from her district since she once served as a teacher and administrator in Walter County. She shared,

When I came back to interview, I knew people in the district. Everybody that was on my interviewing panel, they were like, "Oh . . . we saw the name but we didn't know it was you." And they were like, "We have the perfect job for you (laughter). You got to take a look at this."

Unfortunately, they were not up front about the major issues that the Department of Juvenile Justice (DJJ) had with this facility and the fact that it was rated marginal satisfactory, let alone the possible reasons why it had that rating. Principal Rae recognizes this will be a slow process in establishing the necessary partnerships, as the district may be reluctant to trust that she is making the right changes for the organization. She divulged,

> When I came in with the corrective action plans and that had been going on [for years], there was some distrust. "I'm not going to give that principal or that program money, because things weren't happening the way that they should." And I understand that, so . . . I had to build that respect and to rebuild the name of the program and do some branding. And, no this is not where they just come and show movies all day and we don't do any academics. So, it's still changing that perception, and as we've done that, more and more people are coming on board.

Regardless of what happened in the past, Principal Rae continues to forge ahead with the partnerships she believes are necessary. She tries to educate her district on the challenges she faces. She described the meetings she had with the district's various departments: "I've had a meeting with human resources. I've had a meeting with our certification department, our legal team to say, 'Is there a different way that we can do business?'" Disappointingly, according to Principal Rae, they do not understand the issues she has in this very non-traditional setting and are unable to fully comprehend the challenges she faces and are therefore reluctant to seek out alternative solutions. A common response she receives is, "This is the way we've always done it."

Principal Rae has partnered with the Florida Department of Education and the Department of Juvenile Justice (DJJ), particularly when she found out there were several requests for corrective actions plans that formerly went unanswered. She affirmed, "[I] called the Department of Education and you know, we're great friends. Everybody knows my name. I know everybody up there. I had to call DJJ . . . to say, 'What is your monitoring process, and what is it that you expect?'"

Fortunately for her and her students, there is a partnership between the educational program at this facility and the Florida Department of Juvenile Justice. Specifically, they have joined together to begin the NCCER (National Center for Construction Education and Research) program at the Gladys C. Juvenile Justice Academy. Students will begin taking a vocational course this school year. Principal Rae commented, "I say masonry because that's the track we're thinking. . . . basically it's the core course and we're in partnership with the Department of Juvenile

Justice, because the actual instructor, he works for DJJ. . . . We're funding
the educational materials, paying for the training."

Unfortunately, attempts to build similar positive working relationships with other educational programs throughout the state of Florida's juvenile justice facilities have not been as successful. Principal Rae
cogitated,

> It's hard to say, "Well, who else is doing this work?" So you're in
> isolation. You're working in isolation. I'm sure there's other people
> doing it. It's just . . . not something that's public, that's out there.
> And, if I call other school districts, it's kind of hush, hush. "We're
> not going to tell you what we're doing, 'cause it might not be right."
> "But, this is what we're doing" type thing.
>
> Because I've reached out to several counties in Florida just to question
> how are they tackling the highly qualified and certified issue because if
> you have a facility where you only have funding for two teachers and
> your kids need five, six, seven subjects, how are you able to fulfill that?
> Well, some say, "We're doing Virtual School." So I'm saying, "Well, is
> that happening during the school day?" "Are you sharing the FTE (full
> time equivalent)?" [The] more questions I would ask, then I started to
> get shut down, so I don't really know what's happening.

Although Principal Rae has been faced with some roadblocks, she has
made several key partnerships for the students at this facility and building relationships remains "a passion" and a top priority. She expressed,
"A daily focus for me is advocating for my students and teachers. 'What
is it that they need, and who's the right ear that we need to get to?' And
some things, I haven't gotten to the right ear."

Expectations

Principal Rae expects herself to be a champion for those less fortunate;
and, because of the obstacles she faced coming into to this role as principal, she is much more empathetic to her teachers and believes she
must "act in integrity and try to be diligent on the behalf of kids." She
explained,

> I'm always a champion for the underdog or for the one that people
> say I don't know what else to do with them. And, I get parents all the
> time, "I've done all I know to do." And I believe that, and I believe
> people do what they know to do.

I don't profess to know everything. I could go to school and get two more doctorial degrees and I still would not come into it knowing it. . . . I just was baptized by fire, basically, but I can be more empathetic to the teachers and their struggles, 'cause I understand.

Pleased to offer the new vocational course to the youth at this facility, Principal Rae expects that she will continue to provide other learning opportunities for her students. She believes it's time for things to be done differently. She shared, "We can give them the traditional math, English, reading. They had that before. It didn't work for 'em. They need a different pathway. So . . . the extent that we can push out of the box, I'm trying to do that."

Because this facility houses fewer than 50 students, the budget is limited and thus the teachers have to be multi-certified. Principal Rae, however, believes a teacher cannot be highly qualified or certified in multiple areas. She asserted,

I may have a teacher who she really was a English major and loves English, but because this position requires her to now be the read-ing teacher, the social studies teacher, and she may can pass a test to say that she's those things, but at the end of the day you cannot be highly qualified and certified in every area. It's just not human. It's not natural to do that, but that is what the state is asking people to do.

Although Principal Rae believes the teachers should be certified, she recognizes the need for differentiation in expectations of certification for teachers who are teaching in a short-term capacity. According to Principal Rae, "They need to have certified teachers, but for the shorter stay, I don't think it's fair, personally. I just don't think it's fair to ask people at their own cost to go back to school." She provided an example:

The subject area exams are $200 apiece, so if I had two certifications luckily and I need four more, it's $200 for each subject area the first time I take it. Now if I fail it, or, I'm still trying to teach 'cause they give me a deadline of a year, so I've had a teacher who had 10. He was out of field for 10 subjects and they wanted by the end of the year for him to take each 10 of the tests, and I'm asking him to still teach, to still lesson plan, to still conference with kids, to still contact parents. So, at what point he was supposed to study and meet those accommodations? I don't know. So finally he just came down and broke down, "I really love this. I would love to find a way to continue to do this, but I gotta be smart about this 'cause I have a family to feed."

Principal Rae stated, "We're calling, we're calling you know, 'That's teaching. That's teaching in [Walter] County. That's the requirement.' We say that, but if you were in that seat, you know, wouldn't you want something different?" She has come to the conclusion that "the rules are the rules" and acknowledges that they lose talent and continually have teaching vacancies because of what she considers are unrealistic expectations.

Furthermore, Principal Rae expects teachers will continue to come and go based on the rigorous and, in her opinion, the unrealistic requirements placed on teachers to be multi-certified while still receiving the same pay as a general education teacher requiring only one certification. She spoke about one teacher who just left to join the law enforcement and believes Vicki will also be leaving shortly because "she has a law degree." She went on to say, "I can't fault anyone for that. Our salary steps are what they are. I couldn't give anyone a raise if I wanted to, so it's just the nature of it." Reflecting on this unique circumstance, Principal Rae reiterated, "All we can do is the best that we can do on behalf of kids." Unfortunately, there isn't a measure of "best."

Regardless of the teachers' credentials, Principal Rae expects her teachers to provide a high-quality education that includes differentiation for the youth. She expects the teachers at this facility to provide the level of instruction that is in the students' best interests. She cited an inappropriate approach:

> I haphazardly come in saying, "Everybody, turn to page 5. Write down these vocabulary words." And, that's English for today. That's not high-quality. . . . "It's just everybody gets this and that's what you get for coming into one of these types of facilities." To me, that's not the approach to take.

Yet, despite this expectation, that's exactly what happened during several math and ELA classes. After students entered their reading classroom, Donna began her lesson by asking, "Where did we leave off yesterday? What page are we on?" After they figured out the page, she asked a student to begin reading.

Fortunately, Principal Rae recognizes her teachers will need additional training in order to be highly effective. She divulged,

I'm not going to say that we got all high-quality, high-performing teachers. Many need to be coached up to that point. I don't expect a brand-new teacher to walk in and know how to differentiate instruction for four different grade levels, five different subject areas. That takes work. That takes time, and that's going to take some support.

She elaborated, "Just as . . . we do individualized plans for students to see what they need to progress, I'm attacking professional development for teachers and my administrators in the same way, because everybody's at a different level of experience."

In spite of her expectations, Principal Rae believes teachers don't need much to teach. They must know their subject area and be able to help students improve. She expounded,

I can do wonders with five textbooks and an actual person. . . . You can't get me a whole class set of books, I'm okay with that. You can't buy me five more computers, I'm okay with that but I can't replace human capital—a person who could really meet with small groups of students and who could really spend that intensive time to help a student get back on track to me is invaluable.

One of the main goals for Principal Rae is that her staff will ensure students are where they should be academically. She shared, "Our primary goal is to get their schedules or their academics as closely aligned to where they were before. . . . Each child ends up needing, you know, something different." In order to accomplish this, she described the expectation she has for her staff. According to Principal Rae, "So it's really gauge, trying to break down who they are, what it is that they need and what can we turn around in the . . . six months that they're here."

Resources
Although Principal Rae recognizes the importance of having resources in place, specifically for her as a leader, she admits this is a component that remains lacking. Her experience in this setting demonstrates the importance of preparation, coaching, and support to principals, particularly those working with unique populations. She confided,

Just as we're saying, it's hard to prescribe professional development for our teachers, same thing for me as principal. My job is not like any other job, any other principal in the district. So to say, "Well how do you handle this or where do you go?". . . . I couldn't have been prepared for what I walked into. I had no idea what the measures would be, what the matrix would be.

There's a significant amount of training that could have served as a tremendous resource for Principal Rae. Unfortunately, she doesn't recall any that has adequately prepared her for the role she's currently serving. Principal Rae explained, "So I got the pedagogy part, the theory part, but in terms of knowing how to work with specific students, I've yet to receive that." She continued, "Even at the highest level of doctorial degree, ed [educational] leadership. There's no course . . . like, 'How do you motivate a student who is disengaged in the learning process?'"

While the professional training is lacking, Principal Rae has been able to get some support from the district for advertising and hiring new teachers. She stated, "They advertise for the vacancy [on] the district website. . . . It's a form of what schools have vacancies and what the certifications are required. For my program specifically, they've done some special advertising. They've been going to career fairs." She described a greater level of support that was also provided this year:

> From May until probably about two weeks ago, there's a hiring freeze for the district. They weren't able to hire any teachers, because people were being surplused. Schools had to cut budgets, so they didn't have any place for them to go. So the district rule was, "You can't hire anybody. You're going to have to take someone from the list." But for me, they made provisions. "If you can find someone with the multiple certifications to fit your programs, we'll stand by, and we'll support that."

This support was also provided during her first year as principal. Principal Rae was able to hire Vicki, who was looking for a job and hoping to teach in one of Walter County's traditional public schools. Because of the hiring freeze for the traditional schools, Vicki accepted the math and science teaching position at this facility.

While Principal Rae appreciates the district's support, she still expressed her frustration with the difficulty of finding certified teachers. She shared, "That's been all well and good, but we haven't had anyone that's certified. . . . It's just hard to attract someone who's gonna be well versed in a number of subject areas."

There were very divergent views when the topic of resources and support for teachers was discussed. Principal Rae believed her teachers had everything they needed to be successful. She stated, "Teachers know that if they need something, we're here to support." Unfortunately, although both Vicki and Donna gave examples of some form of support provided, including classroom walkthroughs and feedback; they both laughed when I asked about support structures and felt that overall, there weren't any in place.

With the 12 facilities/programs Principal Rae is responsible for overseeing, she explained she isn't able to get to this facility as often as she'd like. According to Principal Rae, "I usually have a rotating schedule where [I go] at least twice a month because they do have an AP [assistant principal], so they're able to get some direct supervision." She believes this supervision ensures that the administrators are not "putting someone in there and just you know, letting them drown—to make sure we can ensure teaching and learning is happening to the best level it can."

Principal Rae explained how professional development opportunities are provided for her teachers: "If I'm teaching intensive reading and I feel like I need some more reading strategies for struggling readers, that's what I've noted, then we're looking, 'Well what opportunities do we have within the district?'" She described the resource in place for teachers to receive professional development: "We have this place called the [Teaching and Learning] Center . . . that's the main location for all of our district trainings. You can go online and register for different trainings. . . . We get them classroom coverage so . . . they can take advantage of that."

Principal Rae and her leadership team analyze the common themes they identify during their classroom observations to determine the professional development topics for their teachers. She believes this collaboration serves as yet another resource for the educators. She shared,

[We use] feedback on our teacher observations, so when we do, some me and the assistant principals do together; but they may observe a teacher and they got feedback from that end. We discuss it. I may have to observe five, six teachers and we can see a common theme. Everybody's struggling with pacing, class is not moving, they're staying too long in this workshop model, we're not getting the close, there's no summary happening.

Mentoring is another form of support for teachers. Principal Rae explained that their newest teachers in years 1 through 3 are assigned a mentor. Ideally, the new teachers have a mentor at their facility; but in reality, when the entire faculty is new, they are paired up with teachers from other schools in the district. Principal Rae cited, "We have a district cadre person as well. She comes out and does some mentor observations and will do some one-on-one with them to just kind of 'Do you need me to model lessons?' type thing."

In addition to the professional development trainings that are scheduled for the educators, Principal Rae purchased professional materials to further enhance their professional practice. She explained, "Charlotte Danielson's assessments [are] what they use, so since I was familiar with that, I was like, you know, *Teach Like a Champion* would be a great aid for them." She continued, "So that was something I went ahead and purchased for every teacher 'cause I knew that would be a valuable resource just from previous experience with the assessment."

Principal Rae also believes focus walks serve as an additional resource for her teachers. Focus walks are designed to provide additional data to inform teachers' practices. An instructional leader or team of educators decides on a focus for classroom observations, collect data during the focus walks, and uses that data to provide feedback, professional development, etc. She shared, "I also do focus observations. Sometimes, you've never seen it so you don't really know what the expectation—what it should look like." She seeks to provide hands-on experiences for her teachers because she recognizes that she "can tell you, 'Well, implement CHAMPS, and put it in your lesson plans and do this.' But until you're able to see it done effectively, you may not get that understanding."

Additionally, Principal Rae believes, "having best practices more readily available [is] valuable to all stakeholders." She recognizes more resources could be provided for her teachers especially if other juvenile justice programs were willing to share their best practices. She explained, "It's just not a whole lot of conversation about 'These are some resources for teachers' or 'This is what we're doing, and this is how we moved our program in the right direction.'" As she seeks out additional resources for her teachers, she also personally serves as a financial resource, particularly for those who could not afford to take the professional exams for teacher certification. She disclosed, "I've personally paid for people to take the subject area exams."

While Principal Rae believes the necessary resources are in place for her teachers, she indicated that this is lacking severely for students. She cited, "It's the students who need it the most, at a critical point, we're band-aiding it." She expects her students need educational options and incentives to further increase their motivation for learning. Principal Rae described the students placed in the brand-new vocational program offered to the youth at this facility:

We tried to identify students who behaviorally have reached a certain level as well as have some foundational reading skills so they can make it successfully through the course. We got one or two in there that they're borderline, but I think this may be the carrot for them. This, they can do some hands-on stuff. This may be what reengages them in the learning process so we're going to give them the opportunity to at least see how it goes.

There are systems in place after students arrive at the facility that also serve as a resource. Although they don't offer higher-level courses or classes such as physical education, Principal Rae stated that the guidance counselor at the facility is "doing credit checks to see what is it they have, what have they taken. We [are] having conversations. Our transitional team is meeting with them." Furthermore, to "start to devise a plan" to better assist the youth by providing the necessary resources, the educators ask students questions such as "What is it that you think you want to do? What are your future aspirations?" Principal Rae explained that she, the guidance counselor and teachers continually ask: "Where does this individual child want to end up, and if they don't know, how can we gear and help? What can we expose you to, to get you there?" And, they recognize, "for each child, it's a little different."

Regrettably, students who enter this facility on par with their peers in traditional settings are not provided with the adequate resources to help them to continue to receive their advanced level education. Principal Rae commented,

If you were a high-performing student who may have been in honors courses, AP (advanced placement) courses, prepared for college, and you made a mistake and you found yourself in a facility like this where all those things are gone; you won't be getting any fine arts, you won't get the foreign languages that you need in order to be able to graduate. It's going to be very limited in what we can offer.

In many cases it may be no course that we offer that you need, so you're basically, you've wasted a year because you can't take any of the higher-level courses till you get back to where you were. So the psyche of the student, "I'm wasting my time," and how do you engage a student in the learning process when that's really not what they need? That's not the level of service that they need so it is challenging. And it's, it's very limited in the resources.

Principal Rae discussed some out-of-the-box planning she's had to do for some of the youth who've entered the facility: "I have students who . . . may come in as juniors. . . . They're going to need five credits before they leave, so really focusing on how can we get you those five credits; and sometimes, it has to be thinking outside the box." For one student in this circumstance, Principal Rae informed me that she purchased a laptop for the youth to take classes on Virtual School, an online program. Demonstrating empathy for the youth, she stated, "There's no way we could offer what he needs, and it would not make sense for him to sit here for a year when all he needed was a couple courses to graduate."

Offering the TABE (Tests of Adult Basic Education) and the GED (General Educational Development) exam is a resource for the incarcerated youth, particularly for those who are overage for high school or who never viewed this as an option. Principal Rae talked about having students who are 18 years old and in the ninth grade, with no high school credits. She said she is focused on "really trying to get them the TABE test, the pre-GED support, seeing what do [they] really need that intensive support on to be successful on the GED test."

Read 180, a research-based reading program designed to improve students' reading and comprehension levels was once used as a resource for the youth at this facility, but it's no longer available. Principal Rae shared, "The district was using, it's called Read 180. . . . It's very expensive and to use it for a small program . . . that may or may not be there long term, they didn't see that as the best plan of action."

Principal Rae added, "Print shop is great, but you get no certification for that. It's just, at best, that might be a hobby that you can take up." Beginning the same week I was there to conduct this research, the students were starting their vocational class, in addition to the elective print shop course. Principal Rae described this added resource for the youth here at the Gladys C. Juvenile Justice Academy:

We just added a new vocational program. On Monday would have been their first time starting. This is in conjunction with the NCCER (National Center for Construction Education and Research). . . . Basically they're going to do the core course, and this core course can go into a variety of different industries. It's like the safety, the foundation course for plumbing, masonry, construction, electrical, what have you. Everyone has to have that foundational course, so the idea is we have students who come in 16, 17. . . . They haven't been in school when they got here, so they may have sat out of school two years. . . . And then, the likelihood of when they finish with us going back to a traditional education setting is slim to none, so we want to provide them with something that they could leave here and either go into a community college and finish up or possibly an apprenticeship . . .

So really moving towards trying to get some viable skills, where they can go out and find employment. So we're starting the masonry program. And they would get a little NCCER card so they can show to any construction company or community college that they go to: "I've had this course. I have this training." That they're hirable. . . . Not everybody's going to do it, but it wasn't even there before, so trying to fill the gap.

Although Principal Rae is pleased with the vocational program that's just starting for the students at this facility, she recognizes the limitation of this resource with only being able to provide masonry. She offered,

It would be nice to have a skill that you can take, but that becomes a challenge. What can you do for everyone? There's no, just, you know, one-stop shopping. So even [what] we're trying with the masonry program, maybe I want to do barbering. Maybe I want to open up, most people say barbering, detailing business is the hot topics, but maybe something different that I want to do.

Students who are low readers, as judged by their low scores on the Florida Comprehensive Achievement Test (FCAT), are not able to have an elective. They instead have an "intense reading" course provided by an outside vendor contracted with the educational program. Principal Rae explained, "If you are a level 1 or a level 2, they don't have [an] elective. . . . If it's a student who's a high-functioning student or they're on grade level, they would have their elective of [the] print shop class." Although the educators see the need for more hands-on instruction and job training for the youth at this facility, the students who would most benefit from such programs are not able to participate because of the intensive reading requirements. Principal Rae divulged,

The district itself has moved away from vocational programs. Just because you have a high number of students who are low-performing and the answer to that is, "They need more academic support, so . . . there won't be any graphic arts, there won't be any vocational wood-shop, home ec[onomics], all of that. We don't have time for that. We need to get to reading and writing." Right, wrong, or indifferent.

Outside resources, purchased through Title I funds, are used to provide small group instruction for students who are struggling readers. Principal Rae explained, "Our . . . low-level students on our standardized testing, we'll give an entrance exam to see what strategies or what strands that they're struggling in, and then the Catapult Learning teacher can support in small groups with those same strategies."

Principal Rae acknowledged the resources that should be made available to the incarcerated youth at this facility:

> I think the downside is the resources available. If I'm a struggling reader at [a local] high school, a comprehensive high school, I can be offered SAI [supplemental academic instruction] tutoring or tutoring after school. It can be a myriad of interventions and safety nets that can be provided to me within the facility. Once you come into a juvenile justice program, it's very limited.

Principal Rae also recognizes the importance for providing mentors for students and believes this can serve as a tremendous resource, but unfortunately there is no formal process in place for having mentors. She explained,

> If it's "We can hook you up with a mentor." . . . . It's no formal process on that. We're brainstorming. My transition specialist may call: "Hey, I got a kid, and he wants to work on auto mechanics. Do you know anyone?" "No, I don't know anyone. Let me call this person." And it's just trying to find, filter through what resource can we provide for that student.

Bringing in guest speakers is a resource Principal Rae would also like to provide. She shared, "Since you want to work in auto mechanics, can we get some speakers in to talk about what that's like, what the experiences, what are some things that you might need to have?"

Attempting to provide resources to students even once they exit the program is also something Principal Rae focuses on:

> Kids leave here, some parents have said, "This is it. You know, you got yourself into the situation, I'm done with you." And we had a student who came from out of county. He was here, but parents said he couldn't come back—was supposed to go back to [another county in Florida]. So, we're all calling around like, "He's gonna have to go to a homeless shelter." "Where's the men's shelter? How does this work?"

"He doesn't know the city. All he knows is he got transported here."
So, do you just leave him and say, "Well, you exited, baby, you not
my problem anymore?" or "What can we do now?" And it's, and you
know, you wake up with it and you take it to bed at night. Because,
I personally couldn't sleep well, knowing, well, we just put a student
on the street. What do we expect him to do? He's gonna have to eat.
He's gonna need shelter, and if we can't provide him an avenue, he's
gonna problem solve it his self and end up somewhere else.

Following up with students who transition out is an important
resource for the youth. Principal Rae shared some of the obstacles local
youth are faced with when they attempt to return to their home school,
including being discouraged from re-enrolling or being told they cannot return because of their offense or for not having the proper proof of
residency. According to Principal Rae, "We made ourselves responsible
for doing a year's worth of follow-up." She discussed what is in place to
help ensure that students are where they should be after they leave the
facility, and she explained how heavily she relies on her transition team:

Those who are in county—they go to another school—we're able to
do visits and follow-up. If they go out of county, it's contacting the
next transition specialist in whatever county to say, "What's going
on with this kid? Have you seen him? Have they been back in the
office?"

Although this is a much-needed resource for the youth as they transition out of the Gladys C. Juvenile Justice Academy, Principal Rae discussed the disproportionate ratio for providing this support: "When I
first stepped into this job, there was only one transition specialist, and
I had 800 kids that first year." According to Principal Rae, with the
800 caseload, it "was impossible to say that they would follow up," so
she "extended it and made two more," for a total of three transition
specialists.

Principal Rae recognizes that the resources and support needed for the
students to be successful extend beyond what they may be able to do for
them educationally. She surmised,

We can come, they get back on track, and their grades are up and the
attitude has changed, but we're releasing them back to the society
that broke 'em to begin with. So if we're not sending them home
with money for bus tickets to go and look for a job or food, we're still

doing a disservice. Why? That's not our job? If we're not attacking the whole child, we're going to be right back in the same situation, and I can have conversations with students, some of them are experiencing things and going through things that I've never in my life could imagine.

Accountability

Principal Rae believes that holding teachers accountable is important yet quite difficult particularly because of the amount of facilities and programs she oversees. She divulged,

> I can say that I don't have eyes everywhere. We have systems in place. I have administrators, I have coaches, I have guidance counselors where we try to all make sure that we're able to monitor instruction. . . . Everyone has to have a daily notebook. Everyone has to have lesson plans, to have some artifacts of that. But the reality is I'm not going to be everywhere, every time. So can I say 100% of the time differentiated instruction is happening, counseling is happening with students? I can't. I know that's not happening every day.

She collects the teachers' lesson plans every Thursday at 4:30 p.m. This is one way she attempts to hold the teachers accountable. She shared, "I'll get lesson plans for next week, so I have the weekend or whatever time at the end of the week to go through, provide feedback, and to see what they're gonna teach before it's actually taught." Despite her good intentions, the lessons I observed during the three days I spent at the facility were not represented in the plans the teachers provided.

Principal Rae recognizes that even when she sets her expectations in the beginning of the school year and has her administrators visit classrooms to see what's happening, there is still a chance that some students won't receive the high-quality education to which they are entitled. According to Principal Rae, "There's some people, if you get the opportunity, this is a movie day." To ensure that teachers are being held accountable, she believes there's a need for "being consistent and inspecting what I expect." She described one strategy she uses to accomplish this task: "So I may not tell you this is my scheduled visit. I'm just coming. I'm popping in and this is what I'm seeing, what I see, and I'm providing feedback on that."

Unfortunately, Principal Rae recognizes the harsh reality that "[r]ight now, there's not a standard of what well is." The Quality Assurance process established by the Juvenile Justice Educational Enhancement Program (JJEEP) was a form of accountability. This Quality Assurance process ended in 2010. Although JJEEP is no longer providing Quality Assurance reviews, Principal Rae still uses the quality assurance criteria to gauge whether or not they are providing a high-quality education for the incarcerated youth housed at this facility. She shared, "I'm currently still using the old QA standards, because no new, I guess, monitoring system has been in place, and I feel like if we're at least attacking those standards, we got some system in place." She elaborated, "If we need to tweak it or change it at least we have something, versus saying, 'Well, we won't do anything until they come back around.'"

The NCLB highly qualified teacher requirement is another accountability mechanism to ensure the incarcerated youth have a highly qualified teacher teaching each of their courses. Principal Rae, however, believes these mandates prohibit her from providing and retaining adequately certified and qualified teachers at this facility. She explained,

> Having to be highly qualified and certified in the state of Florida—. Say if you have one teacher in a facility, that teacher is supposed to be highly qualified and certified in every area for a child—in a program like this, sixth through 12th. So, to attract someone and say, "Hey, you need 25 certifications to fit this position" is not that appealing. "And, you're not going to get any additional pay or any additional allowances. You just got to do this for the love of kids." That's a challenge. So retaining quality talent is a struggle.
>
> If I look back in retrospect, the rules weren't what they are now. . . . They used to have that coding where you can do dropout prevention. You could teach whatever you needed to teach and they weren't flagged for out of field, anything like that. With the new highly qualified and No Child Left Behind and all those new initiatives, the rules are different.

Principal Rae also discussed the new evaluation system, which includes merit pay. Although she recognizes an accountability mechanism is needed to ensure that teachers are highly effective, she believes the quality of teachers are difficult to measure in this environment with such a transient population. She asserted,

> With the new evaluation system, 50% of it is tied to student achievement, and I don't really have a problem with that 'cause you want effective teachers; you want effective administrators to move students

along. But what data are you gonna look at? Because, in terms of standardized testing, we don't have students for the full year. So who we will have at the time of assessment? They weren't with us doing the preparation for it, but we will be the ones who get the end result; and I can't say that that's fair or any indication of what our teachers are performing.

Although merit pay attempts to hold the teachers accountable, the facility itself does not receive a school grade like a traditional public school in Florida. Because of the unique setting within this facility for incarcerated youth, Principal Rae is apt to take more risks than perhaps she would if the facility was a traditional public school. She described her thought process for a new reading program she recently implemented:

I had been asking different districts. I know [another county in Florida] used it. One of the turnaround schools here used it, and they were trying to keep it hush-hush just because they didn't know what data it was going to yield.

So not that I have nothing to lose, but I don't get a school grade. So I'm not under that accountability model. So I had a little more leeway to take a risk. So I did some research on it, and I said I really think this would be a viable program for us. So we've invested in that.

Despite the external accountability structures, it took many years and a new principal for the Florida Department of Juvenile Justice and the Department of Education to finally receive a response based on the quality assurance feedback and for the Walter County Public Schools to begin addressing the findings. Providing a clear example of the lack of accountability that existed prior to her taking on her principal role, and possibly while she is still serving as principal, Principal Rae disclosed,

Maybe a month in, I started getting these letters from the Department of Juvenile Justice and the Department of Education, and they're saying, "We really need to get in contact with you. We've been trying to contact the district, and the principal that was there was not responding." So I was like, "Okay, well I just got here." So I called and they said, "Well, you have five corrective action plans with the state and we're about to invoke sanctions on your district 'cause no one's been responding and these things have not been happening." So I was like, "Well, what are you talking about? What is a corrective action plan (chuckles)? What am I supposed to do about it?"

So I go to my boss, of course, and no one knows anything at this point. They're like, "Oh, we don't know." So I get [the corrective action plans] and it's just school after school . . . and just the minimum of things were not happening and . . . I could understand their frustration, 'cause it was year after year after year.

So it's like, "We told you year 1, and you signed off and said, 'Okay, we'll correct it. We're going to fix it.'" And year 2 they come back and the same things are out of compliance. So, I take it that had been going on for a period of years. So eventually, I was able to get to someone high enough in the district who could explain, "Yes, we knew about it, and that's why the other person is no longer there, but we need you to correct it."

Vicki

Vicki is responsible for teaching math and science at Gladys C. She has a J.D. degree and is in her second year at this facility. This is her first teaching experience with incarcerated youth. Before coming here, she taught in charter and traditional public schools for five years. Vicki has established positive relationships with her students and cordial relationships with her peers and juvenile justice staff. She has mixed expectations and feels as if much more could be done with her students if she had the right resources. She believes some of the accountability mechanisms in place at the facility restrict her from providing appropriate hands-on experiences for her students.

Relationships

Vicki greeted students as they entered the classroom with "Good morning (or afternoon), gentlemen." She had relatively low numbers in her classes, and after she finished teaching her lesson, she sat close to her students to provide assistance. At times, she had a student go and work out problems on the board. She also encouraged students to help one another, especially if she was busy providing assistance to another student.

I observed positive interactions among the teachers and between Vicki and the juvenile justice staff, particularly during the treatment team meetings, in which students are reviewed monthly to assess their progress in meeting the program requirements, moving up their levels, and determining when they might transition from the program.

Even while I interviewed her in her office, a student needed a calculator. I observed respectful interactions, including, "please," "thank you," and "you're welcome."

Expectations

Vicki expects she is doing all she can for her students and believes she must monitor her students' progress to ensure they are learning. According to Vicki, "I give assessments. Like, they have quizzes, they have tests, so that I can see if they are learning what the curriculum says they're supposed to be learning." She continued,

> I try to stay on curriculum, which isn't always possible here because we have so many students that are way below grade level. But I try to basically bring them up to where they should be . . . and teach according to the curriculum and . . . that's pretty much all I can do here (chuckles).

Treatment team meetings are held two days per month at this facility. On the education side, coverage is not provided for the teachers to go and sit in the meetings, so teachers leave the assignments for the students on the board in hopes that the juvenile justice staff will ensure that the youth complete the work. Vicki, however, explained what typically happens:

> Usually the kids don't have a teacher in here. They don't hire a sub to come in or whatever, so it's usually like a makeup day. And they'll make up work, but I know they're not in here doing work. . . . The direct care staff will probably show a movie or something like that, or they're on the computers playing games or whatever. . . . I usually leave an assignment on the board, but they don't usually do it. Once I'm gone, they don't do the lesson.

The educators expect the students to develop enough skills during their time in the facility to be productive after they leave. Vicki shared, "The primary goal would be they have enough skills that they can go back out into their regular school." The educators in this facility believe there needs to be a strong focus on job training skills for the youth. Vicki cited, "We have the type of students that they're so far below they need to like work on job skills." She asserted,

> A lot of them are not going to finish. You know, if I was to predict, a lot of them are not going to go back to high school. Some of them will tell you they're not going back. A lot of them are not going to get their GEDs even though that's their plan, because . . . you can tell just based on teaching them, working one-on-one, that they're not

going to pass anybody's GED test. . . . They're really skilled with their hands, so I think if we could provide like an elective, where like welding, or, I don't know, carpentry, plumbing, you know, that construction; those type skills, I think would be beneficial for them.

Vicki also believes students need to be motivated. She uses the computers to incentivize the youth. She stated that she uses the computers "as a motivational tool to get them to do their work; as a . . . kind of reward for them, you know, to be motivated to do their work and for some of them it takes that." She explained, "I use [the computers] to get them to do their assignments. . . . Even though they can't access, like, Google and different things, they would probably want to go on, they can still get on the computers and play games."

Resources

Unfortunately, the job skills that Vicki believes are so needed for students, and the additional resources needed for teachers, are lacking. There seems to be dissonance between what Principal Rae and the teachers constitute "support." Principal Rae believes that she provides ample resources and support for her teachers, but Vicki, when asked what support structures exist for the teachers at this facility, replied, "I would say there aren't any."

Vicki shared that the assistant principal "comes in several times a week and sometimes she'll sit in and she'll observe your class." She further explained the feedback she recently received from the assistant principal: "Just last week she came in and gave me a classroom walkthrough sheet where basically it had comments and checks . . . on things that she saw me doing in class, things that I did well; that sort of thing."

Despite the fact that this was Vicki's first teaching experience working with incarcerated youth, she did not receive any specific training for working with this unique population before beginning her teaching assignment at this facility. Fortunately, however, Vicki had some prior teaching experience, and she was also provided with a mentor. Vicki described the mentoring she received when she began teaching at this facility last year:

I came back into the district, so I was considered a new teacher to the district . . . and they basically come in and they help you with, like CHAMPS. . . . CHAMPS is like an acronym that basically allows a student to know what they're supposed to be doing in class like the conversation level, what they need to do if they want help, the activity that we're doing for the day, basically what the movement is. Can they move around? Do they need to remain seated? What participation looks like and success. So, that's CHAMPS. So they help you with like, learning CHAMPS if you don't already know how to do CHAMPS, and how that works; how it looks in a classroom. They help you with, I don't know, like, real basic things that, like, a first-year teacher would need help with, like lesson planning and stuff like that. . . . But you know, that's not, specific to a facility like this. They don't really have like a mentoring type thing for, for, DJJ schools or youth development program schools.

Although the mentoring program provided some support, Vicki doesn't believe it addressed the needs she had as a juvenile justice educator—an unfortunate missed opportunity for her and her students.

Vicki added, "We have professional development days on early release . . . so this Wednesday would be an early release day. . . . But that's not targeted directly to dealing with troubled youth." Vicki described the other professional development opportunities provided as resources for the educators:

You can take like different classes, workshops, seminars, webinars, through the [Teaching and Learning Center]. . . . They offer, like, professional development courses, workshops, seminars for teachers to, I guess, develop skills, to learn different things that they may be deficient on, to learn new things that would help or tools, give them, basically, tools that they can integrate into their classrooms to better be able to educate students.

Vicki believes training specific to teaching in this juvenile justice setting where multiple math levels are taught in one period is much needed. According to Vicki, "I have to teach so many subjects, I would have liked to receive some type of training on how to go about teaching all those subjects within one class period." Vicki divulged, "It's something that I kind of had to learn through trial and error." She provided the following example:

I have to teach geometry, algebra, and algebra II in one class period and then some days, let's say, a student gets in trouble and . . . is caus-ing a problem or they can't be with certain youth because they've fought them. Then, they'll separate them. So, I may have a mid-dle-school kid in with the high-schoolers and then I have to teach middle-grade math also in that class period. So that was difficult to adjust to. I kind of didn't really know how to go about doing it and doing it effectively, and I would have liked to receive some type of training in that.

While there is tremendous potential for professional development sessions to serve as a resource for the educators here, this is not being fully realized. The educators have regularly scheduled professional development sessions every other Wednesday. On the early release Wednesday I spent at this facility, there were two main trainings being provided for the teachers: literacy training for a new computerized program they were beginning to launch for their students at designated facilities—the Gladys C. Juvenile Justice Academy being one of the designated sites— and training for the new teachers. Vicki and the print shop teacher informed me that they were told earlier that Wednesday morning that they could stay at their site because no pertinent training was planned for them or going to be provided—another missed opportunity.

What could serve as an additional resource for the educators has been sitting in boxes for more than a year. Vicki chuckled, "We have smartboards, but they're right there (points to them and laughs). They're not up. We've been waiting for those to be put up for a couple of years now." She elaborated,

> Since I've been here, they were sitting in boxes and this is my second year and they haven't been put up yet. . . . We have some great stuff, but it just hasn't been put up yet. . . . We put in an order ticket for it, and they came and tagged it. We heard that they were coming to put it up, but it just never happened.

This provides yet another example of how resources are there for teachers and students; and yet are not being fully utilized.

Furthermore, while Vicki believes the youth at this facility are able to take the same courses as their counterparts in traditional public schools, she shared the tremendous discrepancy that exists with their resources. She divulged, "We have, like, the same courses that they would take at a traditional school, so I think that they have most of the same opportunities; however, they don't have the same resources." According to Vicki, "We don't have some of the newer books, but I think this year they worked really hard to get a lot of the same books they're using at traditional schools, but still, we don't have all of them." She elaborated,

They don't have the workbooks. . . . We don't have access, like now, to the Internet, and because we don't have access to the Internet, we don't have access to Compass Odyssey a lot of times. Compass Odyssey is like a Internet-based program where they can go on and do extra work with, like, on math problems, or reading problems, science, whatever subject it is, if they're having problems.

I think we're last on the list for everything, so I don't even think that deals with the money, I just think that deals with we're just always last on the list to get, like, new, the new books that come out and, yeah, just last.

The teachers shared the skills/strategies that should be used with the students to further provide them with appropriate resources. Although Vicki believes that the educators "try to provide" the youth with an education at "the same level that the district offers," she also feels that she is limited in the resources she can provide her students. Vicki explained, "I can't really differentiate too much. Like, at a traditional school you can have students on the computers, you know if they needed extra assistance with different things. You have a lot more resources. . . . You don't really have those [here]."

Vicki believes having more ports for Internet access and up-to-date computers would serve as additional resources for the youth. She expressed the need for the proper equipment "that would allow the kids to be able to access [the] Internet . . . because I know a lot of them learn that way. . . . [We need] better computers, 'cause those are so ancient (laughter). It takes forever, you know, to get to anything."

Although Vicki's classroom has enough computers for a one-to-one student to computer ratio, she believes she's not able to use the computers as a resource for her students. She feels the students could benefit tremendously from using computers with Internet access, but is frustrated that only three to six computers have such access and thus does not make use of them for instructional purposes. She explained,

Over there [the classroom next door], they have several computers that are connected to the Internet, so you know, she could use technology more if she wanted to; but, I don't have that same luxury in this class. . . . When the Internet is up, all of those computers have Internet access, so she could, you know, do some lessons with the Internet if she wanted to. Here, the kids just don't have access to the Internet [on all the computers] in this class. . . .

I don't have enough ports to be able to hook them all up. I mean that would be useful. Then, I could really, you know, differentiate the learning.

During my classroom observations, the youth used the computers to play non-educational games such as solitaire and pinball when they completed their math assignments. Within the 105 minutes of class time designated for math, the youth had almost 50 minutes for their math work and 50 minutes to play on the computer.

Another concern Vicki has with the computers are the safety measures placed to ensure that the youth are limited in what sites they can access. She shared, "A lot of times, you know if I know I have to work with other students, I don't want them in under my login, because who knows what they're going to be getting into." Despite her hesitation, however, she disclosed that she sometimes logs in with her administrative username and password and allows students to explore sites that they would typically be banned from visiting:

Because of the facility that they're in, they have firewalls. And so those firewalls prohibit them from being able to access anything except for the [Walter] County website. So they can't even, you know, unless I log them in under mine, and then I have to watch them like a hawk (laughter). . . . I like my job (laughter). I like being able to pay my bills; so, you know I really don't want to log them in under mine, so that presents a problem, you know, when they can only access, you know the [district] website.

Print shop, an elective course, also serves as a resource for the students. Although this is not a certificated course, all three educators mentioned that the youth tend to enjoy making items in this class. Vicki explained, "They learn how to make like cards. I think they're learning how to like, make T-shirts, like print things on a T-shirt."

Some outside organizations are brought in to provide resources for students. Vicki shared, "Work Source comes to help, but they help them with like writing résumés and cover letters, and I think they try to help find them jobs once they leave." She acknowledged that a much better effort could be given to develop students' "resumé writing skills and how to write a cover letter, basic job skills, how to go out and find a job, what to say once somebody does call you—how to interview with the person."

Tutoring could serve as a resource for students, but they have not provided such services at this facility. Vicki said, "They talked about . . . that last year, but that never came to fruition. It was going to be after school, and I think they have like some interns or . . . some students from . . . some of the surrounding schools that are like education majors." She continued, "They were supposed to come in and, like, do some tutoring or something like that, but that never happened."

The Treatment Team meetings, a requirement on the juvenile justice side, serve as a valuable resource for students. Vicki described the process that occurs:

> We submit our paperwork to them, and they put together like this whole compilation like from the educational, education department, from direct care staff, from mental health. Everybody submits information to the social service counselors and then when a student comes into the treatment team, we're able to basically see how they're doing . . . with each department. . . . And . . . basically we assess how they're doing and that determines whether or not they make their level.

During my observations of the treatment team meetings, the juvenile justice staff had the progress reports for each youth who was being reviewed for the day. Vicki and the print shop teacher sat in on the meetings to provide additional details that may not have been included in the paperwork they submitted. A parent was there to learn first-hand about his son's progress, and the educators were able to respond directly to parents' questions.

Accountability

The Florida Department of Juvenile Justice's treatment team meetings, designed to review the youths' progress, serve as a form of accountability. The educators are responsible for submitting the appropriate paperwork for each of their students and attending the meetings to discuss the youths' academic and behavioral achievements. During my visit, all the appropriate paperwork was submitted, and the educators participated in the treatment team meetings to provide additional feedback about each youth who was presented.

The teachers at this facility are afforded a tremendous amount of autonomy and decide on their own what they will teach and when they will teach their assigned courses. Vicki is responsible for teaching math and science, and Donna is responsible for teaching reading and social studies. They have 1 hour and 45 minutes, or 105 minutes, of instructional time that could easily be divided into two ideal periods per class. This would allow students to have a 50-minute block of math, science, reading, and social studies each day. Instead of this design, however, the teachers only focus on one subject area per period per day, rotating days. During the math classes I observed, within the first 45 minutes of class, most of the students were finished working and spent the remaining 50 to 60 minutes at the computers playing solitaire, pinball, and other non-academic games.

For safety and security reasons, the educators are held accountable by the juvenile justice staff to ensure that they are not bringing items into the facility that could be perceived as contraband. Vicki feels limited because of these safety requirements placed on the teachers and students. She expressed that she is not able to conduct some of the hands-on lessons she believes would benefit her students. According to Vicki, "You're not allowed to bring in certain things into the classroom." She explained, "Like, for science, you have to get special permission to bring in like different items for labs and then you may ask, but they may say no, because certain items are considered contraband."

The youth at this facility are also required to take the state's end-of-course exams. Vicki described how this requirement poses a challenge to her and her students. She believes the youth are academically too deficient to pass this exam that is designed to measure students' mastery of grade-level standards:

> The fact that they come in so low. . . . sometimes it's hard to stay with the curriculum, you know, stay on schedule, because you have to go back and do so much remediation. And, that makes it difficult if they have to take an end-of-course exam . . . 'cause if I have to go back and remediate, then you can't possibly be learning what the district expects for you to learn, but you're still required to know it on . . . the end-of-course exam. So I think that's a challenge, and if they don't pass the end-of-course exam, they can't pass the class. So I think that's a big challenge.

In addition to the state tests that must be administered to the youth, the youth are also responsible for taking pre- and post-tests at the facility, a Department of Juvenile Justice requirement. Vicki acknowledged, the students are "tested once and then they're retested . . . before they get ready to leave." It is expected that the youth will show some academic progress from the time they entered to when they are released.

Donna

Donna is a substitute teacher in her first year at Gladys C. She is responsible for teaching reading and social studies. This is her first experience working with incarcerated youth. She has served as a substitute teacher in various school districts throughout the United States for the past 12 years. She also recently earned an Ed.D. degree. Donna recognizes the importance of establishing positive relationships. She expects that she is providing resources and support to her students that many hadn't received prior to her being at Gladys C. She wishes there were more accountability mechanisms in place, particularly among the juvenile justice staff and for the students.

Relationships

The teachers knew students by their names and generally greeted them when they entered their classroom with "Good morning" or "Good afternoon." Donna described how she attempts to build relationships with her students. According to Donna, "I watch these kids and I ask them questions and I cater to their response. And they love sports, and so I have a sport Friday." Because of the youths' interest in sports, she allows the youth to read about sports or to watch sports on the television. Donna stated, "Everything that we're doing is academically inclined."

She continually has conversations with the youth to encourage them and these discussions also help foster the relationships she attempts to build with the youth. She described a conversation she had with one of her students:

> I says, "I know you're in trouble. I know you're here because you thought the life of crime might work for you, but you see it doesn't. And you know, you can make lemonade out of lemons. . . . Why don't you take this situation as something like a . . . [retreat]?. . . . And you know, he says, "You know what . . . I thought about it like that." I says, "Yeah, use it that way. You know, you're here, you might as well just think about all the positive things that are happening to you right now, and what have you, and what you're getting out of this. Turn this into a positive situation."

Donna further divulged how much she values this partnership between her and her students. She explained, "I believe they're teaching me how to teach them and I'm just listening. Yeah, I'm just listening, and I'm moving forward."

While Donna is very conscientious about the relationships she establishes with her students, she has also established cordial working relationships with her colleagues and with some of the juvenile justice staff. Donna had only been teaching at this facility and within this school district for five weeks before my visit. She hasn't yet established relationships within the local school district or outside entities relative to meeting the needs of the incarcerated youth, but she owns a for-profit company and hopes to eventually have components of her physical training and fitness programs incorporated into the juvenile justice facilities and local communities. For this reason, she began reaching out to the local Police Athletic League (PAL), an action that can potentially foster a relationship between the local PAL and this facility.

Expectations

Donna believes that in her role as substitute teacher, she must come to class aware and prepared. She professed, "Because I do believe in education. . . . I am prepared for them whether the instructor leaves a lesson plan or not. I'm gonna come in with a lesson plan, just as I did this juvenile justice situation." Donna recognized the difference between this setting and a traditional public school setting and expected that she had to find other strategies to ensure students completed their work. She averred,

> What I notice is that based on my attitude when I come into the classroom will determine if whether or not they're going to participate. With the public school system, the main school system, the students know that there is a grade and that they do have a permanent teacher that will respond to whatever information I leave behind, regarding them doing the work or not—helps them to really be on point. In the juvenile justice program, my coming in to this situation, where they know that they don't have a permanent teacher, it took a tad bit more to get them to do the work although their behavior was compliant.

Donna explained, "I think for the most part it's the behaviors that you have to deal with before you can teach, before they will trust you to learn from you." She shared how confident she is with teaching and how she anticipated she would have to approach this teaching assignment:

> [I] feel very, very confident in teaching with them. I think being an athlete, one, is not being afraid, you know, facing my fears, knowing that there's some competition. And you do have to compete with their past and gain their trust. And with me having so many different

areas of degrees, I pretty much understand how to reach them and as long as there are books around, I pretty much understand the system of teaching.

Donna believes that she had to build relationships with the students before she could truly reach the youth. Because the students are academically behind, she believes she must teach students on a lower level. Donna elaborated, "I understand the issues of troubled youth, and it's not, I mean, of course, a lot of troubled youth are not on their grade level, so basically you go to [an] elementary form of teaching." To better meet the academic needs of her students, Donna creates her own forms "to give it to them very layman and in chunks" because she believes "they have to go to the basics . . . to understand what a noun, a pronoun, a verb, an adverb, an adjective. They have no idea of what those elements are to writing to speaking." Donna believes this approach is successful: "I find that repetition with these different elements help them to understand. And I see it working. I see the difference in their work and I see the difference in their behavior."

Donna is committed to providing other learning materials for her students. After they read aloud round-robin style, they were given a Bloom's taxonomy worksheet she created. Bloom's taxonomy was designed to develop and enhance students' higher-order thinking skills and is made up of six components: knowledge, comprehension, application, analysis, synthesis, and evaluation. She urged, "I would caution anyone to come into this classroom with this diverse classroom setting in youth expecting the books to be the end all, the be all, end all in them learning." Unfortunately, too often in education we focus on those deficiencies and don't expose struggling students to higher-order thinking skills because we are so stuck on their need for the basics. Based on my observations in the various juvenile settings, there are ranges of demonstrated abilities, and, again, teachers tend to focus on the deficiencies. In Donna's classroom, students appeared to be accustomed to completing the teacher-developed worksheet, but, again, filling in the blank, putting a few words or sentences does not enhance any teacher's capacity to truly determine or assess students' capabilities.

Donna expects to engage students in discussions to further strengthen their knowledge and understanding and uses the elements of Bloom's Taxonomy to assess their comprehension. She shared,

> My goal is to give them information and let them know what the
> expectations are. . . . You have to show me you know it . . . and that

you comprehend it . . . apply it, analyze it, synthesize it, evaluate it, and if you could do those things, you know, verbally, if you can't even write it, then I understand that you understand it, and that's value to me.

She believes it's important for her to help students see the connections between reading, writing, and real life. She attempts to tie in what students are learning in their elective print shop course with what she is teaching them for reading and social studies. She explained,

One of the things that I recognized when I came in is that they really like . . . printing and so they're learning how to print and they come in and they're tracing things and what have you and they weren't paying attention to the subject. This is the first week, and so I had to find a way without being hard with them, but being firm with them as to, "Put that down."

. . .

So I was able to take this class and relate it to their printing class and they put that other work, you know, down, to pay attention. . . . I don't believe that you can be in one class and talk about that one subject matter without bringing in the other aspects of life.

Donna expects that teachers will recognize that "this is more than just a job." She implores educators to use materials other than just textbooks for students to increase their learning. She declared, "Supplemental materials [are] important. I bring that in, and I think that makes a difference." She elaborated,

I don't know what they were doing beforehand. I think they were reading the books, and what have you. I don't think that's enough. I think an instructor has to come in, look at what is before them and create a schematic, something to help them bridge what they don't know and help them as quickly as possible through that. Back to the basics, you know.

Donna believes the teachers lack the much needed expertise and passion to be effective for the youth at this facility. She commented, "I have a passion . . . for these kids and where they come from . . . but they're not going to get anybody in here like me. I don't think teachers even like teaching any more. I'm not saying the whole gamut of them." She detailed,

If you don't love what you're doing; if you don't have a passion; if you don't care then this is just a holding tank and they're just making money. And from the stories that I've been told about those that have been here, that have come here to teach to these kids—they don't like these kids.

Donna believes the educators need additional training "to be able to manage the classroom and also to be able to bring up the confidence level of these kids." She recognizes this importance, because "a lot of them haven't been to school in years, and when they trust you, when you're giving . . . information related to the subject matter . . . this is also a life skills component when you're working with youth in this population." Donna stated, "I think it's incumbent of the instructor that comes here that knows it's more than just a job. Know that they're working with a population that they have an opportunity to make a difference with." She continued,

So I've heard stories of instructors coming in and just writing on the board and they go in and literally put their feet up on the desk . . . get on the computer and . . . of course the kids, they see that, and so they're not going to learn from you. They're going to throw chairs in here, and they're going to have to have those guards restrain them. And, it's a zoo, and it's only because of the instructors—this position, when they walk in.

To combat this apparent lack of caring and inefficiency, Donna urged that the school leaders need to "train these educators to understand that they're not teaching kids in the public school system. They're teaching a whole different population of youth that don't think about education and don't even see the value in education." Donna believes educators must "bring in other aspects of life" and cited the following example:

If we're reading a story and we're talking about a child that was smoking weed and his environment was full of drugs and violence and sex, and what have you, we have to pull that into the curriculum, you know, because examples that doesn't relate to that will not relate to them, and they won't see the value in the material that they're reading.

Although this is Donna's expectation, it's important to note that during one of her classes, while reading a book about drug and alcohol use, one student yelled out, "I don't want to hear about kids smoking crack."

Donna expects that the youth should be exposed to multiple arenas with which they could be certified and that the youth ought to be able to leave this facility with some form of certificate so that they will be employable. Donna affirmed, "You can come out of school, take that certified personal training test, become a personal trainer . . . even if you don't get your high-school diploma . . . even if you don't get a GED." She expects this certificate will help more youth leave the facility with the ability to earn an honest living and expand their horizon for what they may be interested in and able to accomplish. She believes becoming certified as a trainer and getting a job in a gym "is a great option."

She also has expectations for the juvenile justice staff to have a better handle on the youth within the facility. Donna believes the juvenile justice staff are too lenient with the youth and don't take an authoritative enough stance. She believes they must work together for students to get the most out of the educational program provided for them at Gladys C. Donna chided, "This system might be a little—, a tad bit too easy. Guards may not deal with them the way they need to deal with them." She elaborated,

> When they were bringing in paper and they were doodling, I said, "This—. We can't—. This is not going to happen here." I said, "This is going to have to go." And I had to challenge a guard. "My job is to teach them. Your job is that they are in their seats; they have nothing in front of them." It's that they enforce the rules, you know. "That's your job."

Donna discussed how important it is for the juvenile justice staff to take their roles seriously while in the classroom. According to Donna, "I see one guard that doesn't get the respect, and, and it's too much play, and I don't like that, because that makes an impact at how serious they are when they come into the classroom." She disclosed,

> I don't necessarily like to see a student joking back and forth with a guard, you know. I don't necessarily like to see a guard relaxed among these students. Some of these students are on medication. A lot of them have a history of violence, and I've seen a fight break out myself. So if they're going to take you seriously, you can't play with them. And I know that you're with them. I know that you assist and that they see you every day and what have you, but when you walk through that door, it's showtime, and you have to maintain that disposition in order to get the respect.

Resources

When asked what support structures are in place for teachers, Donna chuckled,

> There isn't, and I get that, because the instructors have confided in me. They've confided and there is no support, and when they ask for support, there is no support. And they're felt like they're being made to feel like they should not have [asked] that. And, it's like the cartoon character on the piece of paper, "You asked for it when?" And they start laughing. It's one of those things. They're not getting what they need and because they're not getting what they need, these kids are not going to get what they need.

Despite Donna's disbelief, she did share some examples of support provided for teachers and students. Teachers receive feedback based on what is observed. Donna recalled the note she recently received from the assistant principal assigned to this facility: "Friday, I received . . . a little note that was on my desk. . . . I sure would like you to read it because it really made me smile." Donna believes it was written with empathy. She disclosed,

> I've witnessed [the assistant principal] being insulted by the kids and how she felt . . . how she ran out. . . . So I'm sure she's concerned about me and if whether or not I'm able to facilitate . . . teaching so that they will learn here, and based on her note, she's seen them turn around with their behavior.

Donna also had some previous substituting experience, and she received some guidance from the substitute-staffing agency that helped to place her at this facility. Although the training wasn't specific to working with incarcerated youth, Donna believes the packet she received during the orientation serves as a resource. According to Donna, "[The packet] talk[ed] about some of the behaviors that may go wrong. It did give information about what to do when there isn't a lesson plan, and to be honest with you, I believe I am using those skills."

Although there is an early release day every other Wednesday specifically designed for professional development, Donna informed me that as a substitute teacher, she is not included in the trainings, even though these take place within the contracted time of the school day.

Donna replied, "I've witnessed them leaving early and going to training." What a missed opportunity! Principal Rae recently implemented a new online reading program at Gladys C. On the Wednesday that I was there, training was provided for the reading teachers for the various sites the program was going to be implemented. Donna was not included in the training, even though as a substitute, she will need to ensure that her students are successfully participating in the program.

Donna believes that the educators' abilities to threaten the youth serve as a resource for them at this facility. Even though this has a negative connotation, she believes that threats increase the likelihood that the youth will stay on task. Because of this aspect, she feels comfortable teaching in this environment and believes that the incarcerated youth also serve as a resource for her, as a substitute teacher. Donna shared, "I plan to go into the collegiate system and teach on the sports management . . . in that arena. But I have a passion for these kids and . . . to be honest with you, it also helps me with my oratory." She disclosed, "I'm getting training by just being able to come in here and to do this, so I'm really benefiting from that."

Donna uses supplemental materials with her students that she believes serve as a resource for the youth. She explained, "I use supplemental materials . . . that would reach the different grade levels, and being that a lot of these students have not been in school for some time . . . chose a way of presenting the information in a layman way." She emphasized that the deficiencies of the students are "the reason why the supplemental materials are so important."

Upon entry into the facility, the students complete a career interest survey that has the potential to serve as a resource for them if the survey is used. Donna offered, "Here they have an assessment in terms of what careers might be suitable for you based on your interest in answering these questions." If resources are aligned to match students' career interests, this can be very beneficial to the youth.

Donna believes consultants should be brought to work with the youth based on the areas students are interested in, like auto body mechanics or personal trainers. Donna recalled, "Sometimes, they have those kids in that one little common area running and doing pushups, sit-ups, and doing the circuit training, and you should see the looks and the participation on these kids." Because of the youths' desire to train, Donna suggested that someone should be brought in to "talk to them about becoming a personal trainer."

She provides one-on-one support for her students and stated, "Basically, these students will tell you, 'I don't get this.' And they'll get mad. . . . You'll hear things like, 'Oh, you're dumb.'. . . . I will go to certain ones that I see are having problems, and I will . . . help them through the lesson." Donna shared that she is sensitive to some of this taunting and developed a resource to assist those who may be academically behind:

> I have a diagram that I use, and it is for those who may need it to be broken down just a tad bit, and I'll focus on that, but it's the same page, so they don't feel like they are below level of the other students. So, that's the mind game—I wouldn't call it a mind game, but I will, because they are on different levels. But, it's how you present it to them and if you can do it where their neighbor doesn't see that it might be a little, you know, on a lower level, then they're open and then when they can express themselves about it . . . they're able to discuss and they have an opinion, and they feel good about learning.

In addition to the educational resources, Donna acknowledges the resources the students are provided from the juvenile justice side. She explained, "These youth are probably getting something that they've never gotten before, and that is a therapist, a counselor, a social worker, mentors come in and talking to them."

Accountability

According to Donna, there is nothing in place that holds the students accountable for completing their schoolwork and doing so successfully. Donna acknowledges that the only form of accountability they may have with their students is threats. She shared, "From what I gather, they don't have to do the work, you know. They can come in and after so many months, they have to leave anyway whether they did the work or not." Although the idea of posing threats may have a very negative connotation, she explained "threats" help to hold the students accountable, because "when it comes to the classroom, they really don't have to learn."

Donna believes the juvenile justice staff could provide better assistance them to ensure the youth are held accountable to behave appropriately and complete their assignments. She discussed the need for "the guards . . . [to] maintain that 'guard' . . . that type of demeanor. Moreover, "There is that person that interacts with them, okay, they don't need to be that person." She continued, "The superintendent, the assistant superintendent . . . [needs to] make sure that these guards are compliant and that the instructors have what they need in order to instruct." Emphasizing the need for accountability, she expounded, "Everything starts from the top down. If they realize that there's going to be some consequences, then they may heed; but if not, they could be lackadaisical."

Donna referenced the importance of using the Florida Sunshine State Standards as she plans lessons for her students. She believes she holds herself accountable to provide directions for her students and to ensure the youth complete the work they have been given. Specifically, however, she believes that work must be "related to the standards set by the Florida benchmarks." She also acknowledges the importance for the youth to be ready for the Florida Comprehensive Achievement Test (FCAT). She shared how she plans to prepare her students: "I said, 'Okay, this is what they're looking for, whether or not they have the knowledge, the comprehension, the analyzing'. . . . And, I put [that] . . . as their lesson tools. . . . So, now they know . . . how to answer, you know, those type of things."

Discussion

Although this facility was rated marginal satisfactory, Principal Rae is making strides to improve the quality of the educational program as she continues in her second year as principal. She recognizes the importance of having relationships but struggles to accept the expectations the state and district have for teachers and students. She also feels unsupported, partly because she feels that her district's support personnel do not fully understand the unique challenges she faces in this setting and partly because of the lack of juvenile justice educators within Florida who are willing to share their best practices.

Relationships

Principal Rae understands the importance of relationships and is continuing to build relationships with stakeholders at all levels. Recognizing that it is "their facility," she works hard to ensure that she maintains a positive relationship with the juvenile justice facility's superintendent and assistant superintendent. The relationship she has established with the juvenile justice leaders and educational staff is evident as there are shared expectations for what will take place in the classroom setting, including the juvenile justice staff's role in passing out and collecting pencils.

Furthermore, Principal Rae finds it difficult to staff the positions at this facility, particularly because of its small size, which requires teachers to have multiple certifications. Although she gets some support from her school district, like marketing for teaching positions, Principal Rae still believes that she works in isolation. Although it appears that there is a positive working relationship between her and her district, from the comments Principal Rae made, its scope is uncertain, as SMART boards sitting off to the side had not yet been installed for the teachers and students—SMART boards that have been there for more than a year.

Although the print shop teacher and teaching assistant have been at this facility for several years, Vicki is in her second year and Donna had only been in place a few weeks, still in need of developing working relationships with each other for their and their students' benefit. Fortunately, the teachers knew and called their students by name and held conversations with students, adding a personal connection to the youths' learning experiences.

The teachers hadn't established relationships with other educators in their district or with outside entities. Vicki shared that she took this job because the district had a hiring freeze and Principal Rae was the only school leader who was able to hire new teachers. Because of this circumstance under which Vicki was hired, and because she has her J. D. degree, Principal Rae doesn't believe Vicki will be teaching at this facility much longer. Donna divulged that she is hopeful that her for-profit business, focused on physical training and fitness programs, will eventually make its way into facilities like this or within the surrounding communities. While she was setting up meetings to discuss her programs with the local Police Athletic League (PAL), it is hopeful that this potential relationship could also be used to benefit the educators and youth at this facility.

Principal Rae wants to establish positive relationships with other juvenile justice principals. Disappointingly, however, when she has reached out to other juvenile justice facilities throughout the state, she has found very few juvenile justice educators who are willing to share effective strategies and practices.

Expectations

The Walter County Public Schools' expectations of Principal Rae seem unrealistic for her to be effective in her role as principal. It is very difficult for her to provide the time and energy focused specifically on the educators and youth at this facility when she must also fill the role of principal of an alternative middle school and oversee 10 additional facilities and programs within the district. Moreover, the principals in her district are paid salaries based on the number of youth who qualify for Free and Reduced Price Meals (FRPM). Because this data is not calculated for incarcerated youth, Principal Rae disclosed that she is the lowest-paid principal in her district.

Principal Rae expressed empathy for the teachers working in this environment and also believes students should receive hands-on training. She expected that the youth would benefit tremendously from a vocational program and worked closely with the Department of Juvenile Justice and the superintendent of the facility to help implement the facility's first vocational program for its incarcerated youth.

Donna believes it is important to gain students' trust, particularly the youth in this environment. She speaks with them often, solicits input from them, and gives them advice to help them make better choices. Both Vicki and Donna remained in close proximity to their students during the observed lessons.

Principal Rae struggles to find appropriately certified and highly qualified teachers required by the No Child Left Behind Act to teach in her facilities, and this causes her to feel frustrated and question whether or not this expectation can ever be realized. While she expects her students to receive a quality education, she believes the expectations for multi-certified and highly qualified teachers in this setting are too unrealistic.

Principal Rae also believes the most basic materials can be used to effectively teach youth. She expects classes won't begin with "Everybody turn to page 5." Unfortunately, however, this is exactly how Donna began one of her reading classes. Additionally, the educators spoke a lot about providing just "the basics" to students because they are so deficient. The expectation is that lessons will be differentiated and Donna prides herself on using Bloom's taxonomy with her students but expects that students must be taught using a very basic approach. Aligned with Donna's expectations, the youth were only required to provide one- or two-word responses on a "supplemental form" she created.

The educators also communicated that they expect the juvenile justice staff to be effective in their roles. They expect the juvenile justice staff to not joke around with the students and to help ensure that students complete their work when the teacher is attending monthly treatment team meetings. Donna is also adamant that the juvenile justice staff must provide better assistance in maintaining order in the classroom.

Resources

Principal Rae believes she receives support from the district when she needs to hire teachers, especially when the district was in a hiring freeze. However, she appears to have to continually seek guidance and support from her district in hopes that they will better understand the challenges she faces. Despite the support she receives, she mentioned several times that she feels as if she works in isolation.

There were also conflicting views of resources for teachers. Principal Rae believes she has provided the necessary supports for her teachers, including classroom visits and feedback from the assistant principal, professional development opportunities, and resources for them to enhance their classroom instruction. Although this may be true, the teachers shared that they do not feel supported. Both teachers acknowledged written feedback they received from an informal observation conducted by the assistant principal assigned to this facility. Yet they believe there are additional supports needed for them to be successful, including relevant professional development and full use of updated technology for the youth.

There were several observed examples of the conflict at play between the support structures Principal Rae believes are offered versus what is actually provided and teachers' impression that "there is no support." During my visit, the literacy training being provided was for a new computerized reading/literacy program that was going to be implemented at several sites, including Donna's classroom. Donna, however, was not included in this or any professional development sessions, because she is a substitute teacher, even though she is there on a long-term assignment, responsible for effectively teaching reading.

The other training offered on the early release day, during my visit, was for new teachers. Even though Vicki really wants to learn strategies to effectively teach multiple levels of math within the same classroom, this was, again, a missed opportunity. During a professional development day that should have been designed for Vicki and other math and science juvenile justice teachers to be further developed, she was notified the morning of the early release day that no professional development was planned for juvenile justice math teachers. Training was only for those who were implementing the new online reading/literacy program and for new teachers.

Furthermore, the educators also discussed the need for mentors. Specifically, the educators expressed a need for teacher mentors who work in similar settings and who have an understanding of this unique context and have experience with teaching in juvenile justice facilities.

Resources for students are available, but are also not being appropriately or fully used. Vicki pointed to the SMART boards that had been in her classroom office for at least the past year. Also, although computers are in the classrooms, Vicki said she feels limited because only a few of the computers are in working condition and have Internet access.

Therefore, she only allows students to use the computers as incentives for completing their work. It is interesting to note that monies were just spent on a new online reading/literacy program, and yet the teachers talked about the difficulties of regularly accessing the Internet. It will be interesting to see whether and how the teachers and students will be able to fully use this program. Hopefully, it will serve as a resource for the teachers and students, unlike the SMART boards that have been sitting in boxes collecting dust.

The GED exam is provided for the youth, particularly for those who are overage for high school and have little or no credits toward earning a high school diploma. On some occasions, additional resources, such as a laptop, were provided for students who needed more time to complete online courses for credits.

On one hand, the educators state that they believe they are providing the same resources as those provided in the traditional public schools; on the other hand, Principal Rae points out the additional resources that would be afforded a youth who was in a traditional setting, such as higher-level courses and after-school tutoring, which are not offered to the incarcerated youth at this facility. If a student was taking honors classes prior to his adjudication, he won't receive the higher-level courses at this facility, because the educators only provide basic core courses.

The educators believe a great resource that should be added for the youth at this facility would be guest speakers, mentors, and consultants from specific fields who could come in and work closely with the youth. Hopefully, the educators will work to ensure such resources are in place for their students.

Accountability

Principal Rae has established some measures of accountability, but this area must be further strengthened for the youth to continually be exposed to a high-quality education. She proudly stated that she reviews lesson plans the week before the teachers execute the lessons, yet the lessons that were taught during my observations were not the lessons indicated on the lesson plan sheets. Because her time is so limited between 12 facilities and programs, Principal Rae must decide which of her efforts will help ensure that students are being exposed to a high-quality education each day.

There also appears to be some cognitive dissonance, perhaps because of the need to always defend what one is doing. One example of this is when Principal Rae stated that this facility was not a place where "movies are shown all day." However, when speaking about how she can hold her teachers accountable, she candidly disclosed that she is not able "to be everywhere" all the time, that it is possible that teachers are showing movies. Although she is trying to change the perception that this facility is not a place where movies are shown all day, her focus on so many sites and programs doesn't allow her to hold people accountable to the degree she feels necessary.

Furthermore, the teachers decide how much time they allocate for each course. With 1 hour and 45 minutes each day for math/science and reading/social studies, each course could be offered in a 50-minute period except when experiments or other aspects of a lesson would require longer blocks of time. During the observed math classes, most students completed their work within the first 45 minutes of class and were allowed to play non-instructional games such as solitaire and pinball on the computer. This is not making full use of the students' instruction time to ensure every moment is of high quality.

Fortunately, the teachers at the facility are held accountable for participating in treatment team meetings, and the youth must take the FCAT and the state's end-of-course exams. Because of the size of the facility, treatment team meetings are held only twice a month. Instead of arranging for a substitute for the teacher to participate, the teachers just leave an assignment for the youth to complete while the juvenile justice staff monitor the youth. Vicki clearly stated that this is ineffective, yet nothing is in place to ensure that this time is maximized.

Merit pay is designed to ensure there is a highly effective teacher in every classroom. Although Principal Rae believes in its importance, she doesn't believe the matrix used to measure effectiveness is fair. With the transient nature of the incarcerated youth, and because they come from all over the state, she believes it will be difficult to determine a juvenile justice educator's true effectiveness.

During the time when the Juvenile Justice Educational Enhancement Program (JJEEP) was conducting quality assurance visits to assess the educational programs at each of Florida's juvenile facilities, there were many negative findings at this facility, and the school district was required to implement corrective action plans. According to Principal Rae, the corrective action plans were to be addressed years before she arrived, yet many of the issues had not been corrected. Although the quality assurance is needed, there must be other mechanisms in place to ensure the facilities are, minimally, rated satisfactory, or there must be harsh sanctions. Unfortunately, the 2009–2010 school year was JJEEP's last year providing quality assurance, as the state of Florida did not renew the discretionary grant for the services. Without this accountability structure in place, there is no way of determining whether this facility is providing a high-quality education, as mandated by Florida statute, or whether the school district is being held accountable. The incarcerated youth at this facility deserve much more than this uncertainty.

Although there were some positive elements found within the four themes, much work is needed at this facility to ensure that all students are exposed to and in fact receiving a high-quality education.

6
Philip I. Juvenile Justice Residential Center[1]

Introduction

The Philip I. Juvenile Justice Residential Center is owned and operated by a for-profit security organization that has been in operation for more than 15 years. The organization owns and operate many facilities throughout the United States as well as overseas. There are more than 100 youth housed in this level 6, moderate-risk facility. Fifty-five percent of the youth are children of color. Thirty-five percent are African American, 20% Hispanic, and 45% White. Forty-five percent of the youth are classified as Exceptional Student Education. During the 2008–2009 school year, the Philip I. Juvenile Justice Residential Center was rated superior, the highest rating possible, by the Juvenile Justice Educational Enhancement Program (JJEEP), for its educational services.

The Joyce County Public Schools is responsible for providing a high-quality education to its more than 75,000 students, including the incarcerated youth housed at the Philip I. Juvenile Justice Residential Center. The majority of students in the Joyce County Public Schools are children of color, approximately 22% African American, 31% Hispanic, and 40% White. Fifty-four percent of the district's students qualify for Free or Reduced Price Meals (FRPM). During the 2008–2009 school year, the Joyce County Public Schools was rated an A-grade school district by the Florida Department of Education for its high level of student achievement.

The Philip I. Juvenile Justice Residential Center is located in a mixed residential and business area. There is no indication from the outside that this is a facility housing incarcerated youth. As I drove onto the premises, I noticed some signs indicating drug awareness month and other important messages to youth and adults about the negative effects of drugs. As I approached the double glass entry doors, I was able to see someone at the security desk through the glass windows on the left while I waited to be buzzed into the facility. After being granted access into the facility, I noticed the open waiting area and the large poster with the facility's mission and vision statements, values, and expectations. I also noticed a trophy case featuring awards received and pictures posted of the juvenile justice staff, Governor Rick Scott, and Secretary Wansley Walters. The large walkthrough metal detector and the security wand were also nearby. Upon signing in, I was required to leave my keys at the security desk; I retrieved them when I exited. The cold air certainly made me wish I brought my sweater or jacket.

While walking through the hallway to find the classrooms, I noticed photos of the students and staff and several sayings on the walls for the youth as a means to keep them motivated. Because of the large number of incarcerated youth housed at this facility, two floors are used to better manage the youth. Four classes are taught each day on each floor.

In the reading classroom, there were myriad books on shelves and in bins for the students. Current student work was displayed all over the classroom. There were also photos of the teacher with some of her students posted on the wall. There were two computers on a back wall and an LCD projector and screen. A closet with a padlock was also there for the teacher's use.

The math classroom had teaching charts and posters on the walls, along with 5- by 7-inch cards that had math terms and definitions. The teacher's desk looked like one you would find in a traditional classroom—bins for student work, a computer, printer, paperwork, stapler, tape dispenser, and so forth.

Within each classroom, I also noticed a large poster with the following expectations listed for students' behavior: (1) Enter quietly. (2) Use appropriate language. (3) Heads up at all times and stay awake. (4) Remain actively engaged. (5) Remain seated. (6) Raise your hand to answer/ask a question. (7) Show respect. I also took note of another chart indicating the following: Earn 1 point per day for meeting ALL of the expectations. Earn ALL points for the month and be entered into a drawing for the monthly reward. And, a third chart read: Any student who did not earn 1 point for a day can earn ½ point for the following items: serve as the class assistant; serve as a peer helper; clean up the classroom (if needed). You may only earn back 1 point per week.

There was a bathroom in each classroom and a hand sanitizer dispenser on the wall just outside the bathroom door. The carpet in each classroom had about a 1.5-inch gap between two pieces of shabby carpet and was rather filthy with dust and bits of paper.

Participants

Table 5   Philip I. Juvenile Justice Residential Center participants

Juvenile Justice Educator	Position	Tenure at the Facility
Richard	Principal	2 years, 4 months
James	ESE	4 years
Israel	Substitute Math Teacher	1 month
Juanita	Reading Teacher	5 years

Educational Program

Each school day begins at 7:30 a.m. and ends at 2:15 p.m. for the students. The following courses are taught each week: reading, social studies, science, math, careers, physical education, driver's education, and personal career school development. Additionally, some students are able to participate in a Home Builders program, computer mentoring program, and a program that allows them to work closely with dogs. Students take four classes daily that last 1 hour and 15 minutes (75 minutes) each, for a total time of 300 minutes each day. Every semester, or approximately every nine weeks, students' schedules alternate so that the youth can receive the other four courses.

The teachers begin their day at 7:15 a.m. and end at 2:30 p.m. In addition to their two 15-minute duty-free periods before and after school, the teachers at this facility have 1 hour and 35 minutes each day for lunch and a common planning period. Class sizes range from 14 to 19 students.

Findings

Based on the four themes that emerged from this study, there appeared to be positive relationships, high expectations, appropriate resources, and effective accountability. The instructional methods used to work with the students at this facility were: direct instruction, guided practice, assessment (check for understanding), self-selection of texts, and two-on-one and one-on-one instruction. Positive rewards were used to incentivize students. Based on the 6 hours and 18 minutes spent observing the classes at this facility, the juvenile justice staff brought the students an average 5.8 minutes late to class. The range of students on task at any given time during a reading lesson was as low as 84%, or 16 out of 19 students, and as high as 100%, or 19 out of 19 students. The range of students on task at any given time during a math lesson was as low as 83%, or 15 out of 18 students, to as high as 100%, or 14 out of 14 and 18 out of 18 students. There were disruptions that occurred during each lesson, including student outbursts, singing, rapping, laughing, use of profanity, talking, getting up to use the bathroom, entering and exiting the room after the lesson began, juvenile justice staff speaking with one another or with a student, and walkie-talkies transmitting. An average of 1 disruption occurred every 170.52 seconds, or every 2 minutes and 50.52 seconds.

Principal Richard

Richard serves as the principal of the Philip I. Juvenile Justice Residential Center. He is also responsible for overseeing 10 other programs, including several additional DJJ sites. Three assistant principals provide administrative support to the facilities he oversees. Richard is in his third year as principal. He has been at this facility in other support and administrative capacities and within this school district for more than 12 years. Principal Richard espouses positive relationships and high expectations and believes that he provides the appropriate level of resources and accountability for the educational program to be successful.

Relationships

Principal Richard recognizes the importance of the relationship between the juvenile justice staff and the educational staff. The two work hand-in-hand to ensure that students receive what they need to be successful while they are incarcerated. According to Principal Richard,

> We have a very strong partnership with the executive director at this program [facility] because typically it is their program [facility]. We just provide the educational services, and that's not always the case; but, but I'm happy to say, this is a strong partnership.

This partnership is further evidenced as Principal Richard described the meetings that were held with the educational staff, the juvenile justice staff, and Home Builders to establish a vocational program for the older youth housed at this facility. He shared, "It really was a partnership. It truly, if you want to break it down to bare bones, it was the facility and Home Builders, but we were a part of the meetings."

I was able to observe firsthand the positive working relationships that exist amongst the educators. Principal Richard asked his assistant principal to sit in on the interview with him, and they conducted the interview as a team. Principal Richard said, "[My assistant principal] will chime in. We'll kind of just tag team the answers to the questions." This team spirit also occurs when they interview potential teaching candidates. Principal Richard stated, "[We do a] committee interview because it really gets buy-in from your staff." He discussed the process he has in place:

> Usually whoever the assistant principal is for that particular site, I'll sit down with that person. We'll review the resumés and then we'll come up with a final list of people to interview. At that time, we do the committee interview, which it would be myself, the assistant principal and possibly a couple teachers from that respective site.

The positive relationships were further reflected in the camaraderie witnessed amongst and expressed by the teachers within the facility. During the PLC (Professional Learning Community) meeting, it was evident that the educators have a healthy relationship with one another. They entered the classroom, where the meeting was held, in a jovial spirit. And, as they were discussing how they use a particular graphic organizer for their students as an extra academic support, each teacher was engaged in the discussion. There were 12 teachers present, including two substitute teachers. All but one substitute teacher participated in the discussion.

The educators at this facility have a partnership with their local school district and with outside entities. Recognizing the unique context of the eleven facilities he oversees, Principal Richard explained the waiver his school district granted regarding early release days for professional development:

> Our district, every Monday is an early release day, so it's a one-hour early release day. That doesn't help me, because it'll take an hour for some of my people to get to me. So what we did is, we wrote a waiver and we actually take those one hour a week and we combine 'em to four hours. So, once a month we're able to all come under one roof for training and team building, all 11 sites.

He also described the additional partnerships they have that allow them to provide more resources for the youth at the Philip I. Juvenile Justice Residential Center. Principal Richard affirmed, "We have a partnership with Project Promise, formerly Neglected and Delinquent. . . . They have in the past, provided tutors, after-school tutors. They also provide funding for our kids where guest speakers, our computer mentors will come into the program [facility]."

During my visit, one teacher also talked about the partnership they have with a local fast food restaurant that donates 10 sandwiches each month. A drawing is held, and sandwiches are provided to recognize and celebrate students who consistently exhibit the expected behaviors.

Expectations

The administrators expect the educators who teach at this facility are here because this is where they want to teach. While it is protocol for the school district to have an employee assigned to any one of its schools as an administrative placement, Principal Richard doesn't have anyone at this facility who meets that criterion. He shared that all the teachers here are teachers who interviewed for the position and chose to teach in this facility. He recognizes that the best teachers for his students are those who want to be here and are qualified in the subject areas they teach. Principal Richard asserted, "The single most important thing in that classroom is the teacher. So it starts with the teacher and I'm proud to say that all of our teachers here . . . are first certified and . . . every one of 'em is highly qualified too." He elaborated,

> It always starts with the teacher. . . . It's the strength of the teachers that they are certified, they are highly qualified, and you know, that, without motivation, means nothing; so they have that ingredient, too. They're motivated, and they want to be here. . . . They weren't placed here. We didn't go out and solicit them. They wanted to work with this population. That's very important.

Principal Richard expects that the educators will provide "relevant and rigorous academics as well as workplace readiness skills" for their students. He discussed his belief that it is incumbent upon the educators within the facility to appropriately provide the resources students need to be successful. He concluded,

> Today's society, first of all, is we're in that technological boom. And the jobs that we prepared kids for a decade ago are not the jobs that are available today. So, with that being said, some of the kids when they leave have no intentions of going back to school. . . . That's why we really try to prepare them, these kids that can get their GED and stuff so those, those work-ready or workplace readiness skills are definitely important.

Principal Richard expects that what they offer their students is exactly the same as what the students are afforded at their local schools. He stated, "It really is the same as a traditional school, but what we do is we try to tailor not the instruction, not the curriculum, but meeting the needs of the respective child."

While Principal Richard hopes the youth will take full advantage of the educational opportunities provided for them at this facility, he believes it is a matter of choice. He averred,

> A 16-year-old—they're still in those formative years. . . . So it's really our job to provide them the skills. What they do with them is their personal responsibility and a personal choice, but we feel good at the end of the day that we gave them the skills necessary to be success-ful or at the very least go to the next level of education and possibly vocational.

Resources

One extremely valuable resource for Principal Richard in his role as prin-cipal is the fact that he has been working with these facilities for more than 12 years, and his former principal appropriately groomed him for his current position. He explained, "I was promoted to assistant princi-pal. The former principal was my mentor, so when she retired, I took her position. I think she really prepared me for this position."

Additionally, the teachers at this facility have access to a multitude of resources and support including access to and participation in profes-sional development sessions, and they work closely with other teachers at this facility, mentors, and the juvenile justice staff.

Professional development sessions for the teachers serve as essential resources. Principal Richard shared, "The training's ongoing, and we are very . . . proactive in providing training to our staff." He described the types of trainings they offer their teachers:

> Some of the trainings we're doing this year are single-gender training, infectious disease training, gang awareness training, so it is definitely ongoing and thorough. . . . I have several employees that are aspiring administrators, so it's good opportunities for them to take leadership roles and to solicit those organizations for trainings.

Principal Richard talked about another resource, the district trainings that are also ongoing for his teachers. In addition to the site-based train-ings, his teachers are able to participate in a "slew of district trainings, some mandated and a lot on a volunteer basis." Moreover, he shared, "We have subject area leaders who meet with their particular disciplines on at least a quarterly basis. So, all the math teachers for my 11 sites will come under one roof and just train on math."

Principal Richard affirmed, "We really overhauled how we do business and how we support our teachers so every teacher in this program is assigned a peer or mentor depending on how many years they have in service and that's district wide." He detailed what this support looks like:

So the peer comes in. They observe them. They meet with the teacher. They talk about what was good in the lesson. They talk about, you know, areas that could have improved, where learning could have been better. So that's set in place. Not to mention, my APs [assistant principals] work with them; of course, I work with them.

The educational office/staff lounge also serves as a resource for the teachers. There are two paraprofessionals whose desks are located in this space, but there is still plenty of space for a copying machine, desktop computers, printers, and so forth. There is a restroom there and a bulletin board with updates.

Much like the support structures in place for teachers, Principal Richard also spoke proudly about the resources they provide for their students. He acknowledged,

A lot of our kids are significantly behind grade level so it's not uncommon for a 17-year old kid to come here and be in the eighth grade or the ninth grade with 3 or 4 credits. When they leave, the chances of them receiving a high-school diploma are very slim so we will identify those students and try to put them on a path for GED . . . our goal is to identify that kid that GED is a viable option, 'cause it's not a viable option for every kid, and make sure that they take the test while they're with us. . . . It's really tailoring the instruction to the individual needs of every child.

The school calendar is also designed to serve as a resource for the incarcerated youth. Principal Richard explained, "Our school is year-round, and kids have the opportunity to earn credits year-round while they're with us." He quipped, "I don't want that to be an incentive for them to come to us, but it is a good thing when they are here, because they are so far behind."

There are a host of additional resources for the students. "All our textbooks are current adoptions. We have computers in some rooms . . .

most of the classrooms have a LCD projector and an ELMO (document reader) and it's part of the instruction. . . . Some kids are using the computers to complete ready-to-work," stated Principal Richard. The assistant principal also chimed in:

> We use MP3 players for reading classes so they can hear the fluency and things like that that they need. The ELMO (document reader), the projector, PowerPoints are shown. Our language arts, reading teacher is great with using like a five-minute, seven-minute clip and then show a relationship, so . . . it just brings in real life stuff for them.

The PCS (personal career school development) class serves as a tremendous resource for students, particularly for those who won't be returning to school when they leave. Principal Richard described this class: "We offer the PCS, which is really a workplace readiness class and we do things like interviewing, finance, how to, you know, fill out a checkbook, how to open up a savings account."

Principal Richard discussed other programs that serve as tremendous resources for the students as well. The facility partnered with Home Builders and implemented a new after-school program this year. He explained, "They identify those kids that are 16 and above and they actually build stuff in the facility; lay tile, put walls up, so . . . it's construction [and building], and electrical."

The assistant principal also described another program they offer the youth at this facility. She shared, "They bring in different animals, dogs, so the boys learn to care for them. . . . It's been in place for a while, and it still is, because it's been great." She detailed what occurs: "They bring in dogs, and the boys actually do the care for grooming, training, discipline, feeding. They learn everything about it, so it gives them a real responsibility, and they come in twice a week, I believe, with them." The assistant principal elaborated:

> The same boy has the same dog every week, so they get the bonding experience and. . . . It really teaches them the responsibility and the love and care for that bonding, that . . . a lot of them do tend to miss, and then those dogs are then sent to homes that need them, want them. And so when they go, the boys are sad. They're happy because they've done their job, but they're sad, too, because now the dog is gone.

The incarcerated youth at this facility also have access to computer mentors. The assistant principal described this program as an additional resource for the youth. She explained, "Computer mentors comes in. The boys actually [complete] . . . I believe it's 60 hours on the computer, and they have to get different certifications. Then when they leave, they actually get to take a computer home with them."

Additionally, the students receive physical education and driver's education courses each week by a teacher certified in these fields. These are courses not typically provided by certified teachers within Florida's juvenile justice facilities. Principal Richard proudly declared, "We offer PE. We have a certified PE teacher. . . . In addition to that, we offer driver's ed, which is a first. We've never offered that before, 'cause we have, that same teacher is certified in driver's ed." Although the youth switch classes every nine weeks, Principal Richard allows the youth to switch floors each week for physical education and driver's education so "both groups of kids have the opportunity to go outside."

Principal Richard also shared that the youth at this facility are able "to earn ready to work credentials which are signed by the governor. So, if a kid leaves, they walk onto a job site they have that filled out—. . . . It's basic skills that the kids are provided."

He added, "And we also develop an IAP, an individualized academic plan, for every student to meet their needs with goals and objectives." Principal Richard continued,

> They come in and they take the common assessment that the state requires that we do, so we get a baseline math and reading score on them. Then they also take a learning styles inventory when they first come in. They take a career interest when they first come in. That's done with our assistant teachers in the office. . . . Then each individual teacher also gives different assessments once they enter their classrooms just like a traditional school.

Accountability

Although Principal Richard is responsible for overseeing 11 programs, he assigns his three assistant principals to provide hands-on, daily support to these facilities. Philip I. houses one assistant principal, including office space and an administrative assistant. Having an administrator in the building helps to hold the educators accountable. Lead teachers are also developed to assume leadership roles and provided to support and hold their peers accountable.

James

James is the ESE support facilitator at Philip I. He is shared between two facilities and has been at this facility for four years. He has more than 10 years' teaching experience in traditional and charter schools. James believes the educators at Philip I. have established the necessary relationships to be successful. He espouses high expectations for himself, his peers, and his students. He also believes that they have the necessary resources and levels of accountability to provide a high-quality educational program for students.

Relationships

James recognizes the importance of the education/juvenile justice relationship and was eager to explain how the partnership works. According to James, "The facility provides us with what we need to teach: classrooms, time to teach, time to do special activities, and so on. So I think the combination works together." He expounded,

> Their staff are the ones that monitor the students. So if the students talk out in class, you know, we correct them, and the staff picks up from that. Says, "Okay, obviously the teacher doesn't want you talking, so stop talking, or you're gonna get written up." Things of that nature. So they provide the safety and security of the facilities, and we maintain ourselves as being professional and learning, and continually learn.

James described the partnership he has with the teachers he works with when he goes into their classrooms as the ESE support facilitator. He recognizes the importance of and appreciates the open communication he has with his colleagues, particularly because he is between two sites. He explained, "Sometimes my planning is on the phone, through text, through email. . . . 'Where did you leave off? What are we doing?' And . . . then I know what I need to bring in, what I need to do."

Expectations

James expects that he is prepared for his role as an ESE support facilitator. He also feels comfortable receiving feedback from his colleagues to further improve his teaching practice. He shared, "As far as me finding somebody to help me out, it's basically me working with the older teachers here and saying, 'What do I do about this, or what do I do about that?'" He averred,

I think the preparation is all on me, so I am completely prepared to teach whatever the curriculum is . . . whatever class I'm in . . . I'm in the science class. I'm in the social studies class. And I love both of those subjects. And as I told you, I'm certified in those areas. . . . Some ESE teachers are thrown in the class. They're like, "I'm here for my kids, but don't ask me a question about the material."

James also expects that he will motivate his students. He asserted, "You don't need a lot of stuff to teach. All you need is to care and to have some knowledge of the material and to enjoy what you're doing." He expects that with even the most basic materials—his teaching experience, caring attitude, and ability to motivate the youth—are enough to provide his students with a quality education. He elaborated, "As far as resources: paper, pencil, books, and the ability to motivate a young man that might not really care. . . . I think when you make whatever you're learning relevant to them, their motivation increases, 'cause of course, their knowledge increases."

James believes he is prepared to support any student to be successful, whether the youth is a general education student or ESE. He affirmed,

I don't just work with [ESE]. . . . I work with the whole entire group, because we don't do pullouts here. They get their support in class, and they're not identified in the class. For example, in a class full of 23 people, 23 youth, you would not know which one—. If you walked in, you wouldn't see me just working with the ones that are ESE. . . . I don't single out. If any youth has a question . . . I assist them.

The expectation of the educators in this facility is not only that they will stay for at least several years to provide continuity of the educational programs for the youth, but also that they will maintain themselves as professionals. James shared,

There's two entities in the facility. There's the facility and then, there's the teachers. . . . We do our part for providing a high-quality education, by again, maintaining you know professionalism, taking coursework, keeping up with our PLCs [Professional Learning Communities], of course maintaining our certifications.

The high expectations they have for teachers are also evident in how the educators dress. One visit with them and you will think you are in a business meeting on Wall Street. Women are in professional attire, and the men have on dress pants, dress shirts tucked in, some with a tie and dress shoes.

James is adamant that "the teachers have to be certified." He believes having highly certified teachers is non-negotiable. "I think that's important even though you have some certified teachers that are horrible and some non-certified teachers that are great. But I think that's a starting point," said James. He emphasized,

> You can't teach these youth unless you're certified, and everybody here is highly certified, highly qualified. You have to provide them with the academic instruction that's going to help them with transition. When they go back to wherever they go, they . . . have to be on the same level as everybody else. My biology student here . . . has to have been taught the exact same material as a biology student at [the local] high school. Because if they're not, when they assimilate back into the real world, "the outs," if they're still far behind, then I'm doing them a disservice.

James believes so strongly in being multi-certified, even though he holds ESE and multiple subject area certifications, that he plans to obtain at least one additional certificate. Recognizing the importance of "keeping up on the latest teaching practices and research," James shared, "I'm in a science class, and I know I'm middle school science certified, but I want to be specific, okay, biology, and so on and so forth."

James believes the juvenile justice staff could do a better job monitoring students while they are on the computer. He stated, "I don't like having computers in the classroom. They're not monitored well enough by staff." He also shared his belief that "some of the [juvenile justice] staff haven't bought into the whole education thing." According to James, "In the past, we had some [juvenile justice] staff that . . . pretty much, did things counter to education. [The juvenile justice staff] thought they were better teachers than us; meanwhile a lot of people barely had their high school diploma." Fortunately, he said, "It's better now than it has been."

James also acknowledges the need for motivating students: "We find motivational strategies that are gonna help them sit there learn about, you know, cell division, meiosis and mitosis (chuckles). We provide the excitement somehow to get them to sit there and find interest in that." James also believes the youth need to be taught in a manner that makes learning relevant. He shared, "We have to find things, ways of making it relevant to the students so that's on us as teachers. That's what we really do." He expects students learn better when he taps into their senses and provides hands-on experiences for the youth to truly understand the material he presents. He explained,

> I try to get them involved—you know, using all their senses. I want them to hear it, not just from me but from a professor. . . . I might show a video with some college professor that says the exact same thing and it's just a different mode. I like movement. . . . I like to build things, okay. I can tell you about DNA or you can construct a DNA model or draw one. I think you'll learn better if you get more involved. . . . You know, if you're getting all the senses involved, it's not just listening to me talk. You're reading, you're writing, you're moving around the classroom.

Although James recognizes learning should be hands-on for students, he expects students to be exposed to more than just a vocational program. He asserted, "We have to give these kids a chance to further their education. . . . We have to provide these kids with an education that's going to help them, not close them off." He cautioned,

> A lot of vocational type programs, job training kind of programs teaches them to do menial tasks. Now those tasks are important, but give them the opportunity, the option, to choose. That . . . vocational type program . . . that should be just one of their classes, not their program, you know, 'cause, it closes them off.

James expects students will make connections with what they are learning and apply it to improve their lives. According to James, "It's not just 'Can you learn these definitions out of a book? You've learned this, what are you going to do with it? How's it gonna affect your life, today, tomorrow?'"

James also believes that these are the same students that he taught when he was a traditional public school teacher. He stated, "They are the same kids that were in my [high school] classroom. They're the same kids, but they just got in trouble or got caught and got locked up."

James also believes that these youth should have the tools they need when they leave the facility so they no longer have to live a criminal life. He explained, "When they leave here, they should have what they need so that a life of crime should not be an option to them. That should not be their goal." James expects the youth will take advantage of the resources in place for them at this facility. He affirmed,

We're on block schedule, so we can get a year's worth of work done in six months. So, if you were behind on your credits, you can get some credits. If you're very far behind, you can get your GED, and then you can get on to some community college and things of that nature. . . . When those kids walk out of this door on their last day, they are a teenage boy with options. They don't have to go back to the street corner, start selling, start using. They have options, and hopefully in the time that they were here, their body—'cause it's a drug treatment facility for the most part—the ones that were users in their six months to a year they were here, hopefully their body has been weaned off of at least the physical desire for that, if not the emotional and mental desire for that as well.

Resources

James believes ample resources are provided for the teachers and students. Professional development is one resource that he values greatly. He offered,

There's some youth services specific trainings and PLCs [Professional Learning Communities] that we go through and we specifically talk strategies for behavior, strategies for academics. We specifically have PLCs based on that. We have . . . county wide in-service opportunities that we go to that you are with other teachers in other different schools . . . and we get to choose them, either teacherwide or specifically for our discipline. . . . They're available. Any teacher that wants to see what's out there, they can.

James appreciates the variety of professional development opportunities and the freedom he has to take advantage of these sessions. He shared,

Anything that's available on the PDS [Professional Development System] system I can sign up for and go on my leisure. I can go anytime I want, what's available. So we have things that are in-house . . . PLCs that are just here and we have anything that we can sign up for, if you have time for.

James believes the peer mentors are helpful based on feedback he has received in the past and his observations of the interaction between a peer mentor and a second-year science teacher. James recalled feedback he received from his peer mentor: "He said that I do a good job of taking something that might be a little bit dry or mundane and making it relevant." James also shared, "Now the second-year teacher that works downstairs, he has a mentor that comes in quite often, actually she's here a lot, and gives him pointers and observes him on a more regular basis."

The teachers in this facility who typically have more than three years' experience rely on each other for support. According to James, "If your evaluations were below a certain level; you're supposed to get somebody to come in to observe you and give you pointers. That hasn't happened yet. . . . For us veteran teachers, there's nothing, really, aside from each other." In his role as ESE support facilitator, James receives input from his colleagues frequently. He shared, "I got another certified teacher in there with me, so they might say something to me like, 'Okay, let's do this; let's not do that.'"

James also plans collaboratively with the teachers he works with to provide students with a quality education. He explained, "We'll sit down, 'I'm doing this and this, okay.' Well then I might go get a video . . . some supplemental materials based on what he's doing, or just some general activities that will contribute to the lesson." James talked about how much their common planning serves as a resource. He described the benefits of having the time together before class starts in the morning, their lunch time and the common planning time in the afternoon: "We have some time to sit and talk . . . get materials, and things that we need. So there's plenty of time for us to collaborate."

Feedback from administrators also serves as support to the educators at this facility. James said he receives informal feedback on a regular basis from his assistant principal. According to James, "She's always giving pointers or saying whatever it is she has on her mind." He elaborated, "I feel I'm prepared. I think my administration, especially [the assistant principal], she does a great job of making sure I got what I need to teach my class." James's prior background working with ESE youth also serves as a resource. He disclosed,

> I was an SED [severely emotionally disturbed students] teacher, so obviously there was lots and lots of trainings. I took some . . . coursework at USF (University of South Florida). There were so many in-services that I had to take; one because they were required, two because I had to get 'em if I wanted to be successful. . . . I've learned lots of strategies in working with troubled youth.

According to James, one of the greatest resources the students have here are the teachers. He shared, "I would definitely say it's the teachers.

I think you got some people here that truly put their heart into it; that truly care." He elaborated, "I mean, [these teachers] they really care about seeing their students do well, and I think that's by far the greatest strength; more than the curriculum, more than the classrooms, more than anything else, it's my coworkers."

James believes the teachers serve as a resource for students because they provide them with assistance as needed and are committed to ensuring the students have what they need to be successful when they leave the facility. He insisted, "I think the fact that we have such a staff here that from teachers to teachers . . . all they do is make sure they are prepared academically when they get out of here, they have all the stuff that they need." He cited a specific example of the support he was presently providing to one of the youth: "I'm actually helping one student with his [community college] application. He wants to get into [the local community college]. . . . He's got his GED. I'm just getting him the information that he needs so he knows where to apply."

James told me the youth have access to the same courses they would if they were in their local high school. He explained, "The students here are in regular courses. The courses they take here are the exact same courses they would take at [the local high schools] . . . or . . . whatever middle school that they're in . . . the exact same classes, exact same textbooks." He continued, "Whatever a student can get at any school in this county, or really in Florida, 'cause these are statewide courses, they can get here."

James also confirmed that there was after-school tutoring that began around 3:30 or 4:00 p.m. since he began teaching at this facility; however, tutoring may have ended due to lack of funding. He explained, "For the years that I've been here, there was tutoring all along. . . . I think it might have been cancelled, budget cuts, I think. 'Cause I know some teachers that did it are not doing it."

James described how his method of teaching supports his students. He believes using PowerPoint allows his students to experience learning in a more effective way. James said, "You can lecture something or you can do the exact same lecture with the PowerPoint behind you, and the kids will pay attention if the PowerPoint is on." He also shared how he and the other educators incorporate videos to ensure that the students' learning is more authentic. He divulged,

> We can't access YouTube here, but I can save the videos on my thumb drive and bring 'em in and show the videos. That, that helps them learn some things or see experiments that they can't do here.

You know I could tell you, "If you do this, this and this, this will happen, but here's a video with the exact same thing."

Furthermore, James explained how incorporating music helps his students:

All the kids think that they're the best rappers in the history of rap, and they think they could make Little Wayne retire tomorrow. So once in a while I'll do a project or an assignment where whatever the topic is, write a rap song about that topic. Whatever the vocabulary is, take five of those words and include those five words in a rap song; any beat you want. You don't have to get up and perform it, just write it out. So that kind of helps them. . . . We've done it a couple times.

Because of the limitation placed on materials being brought into the facility, the educators found a creative way to still make learning engaging and hands-on for their students. James described the way they use Gizmos:

Gizmos are some experiments that are digital that you can kind of manipulate. Oh, if you're doing a plant-growing Gizmo; "Well, what if I gave this plant extra nitrogen?" "Oh, it's very green." "What if I gave it extra phosphorous?" "Oh, lots of flowers." "What if I didn't water it for two weeks?" "Oh wow, it's wilting." "What if I didn't water it for three weeks?" "Oh, it's almost dead." "What about if I flooded it now?" "Wow, it didn't come back." You know, so just—, there's different ways to manipulate variables online and you can project it out to the class and have the class participate.

Accountability

James believes accountability is a necessary tool to ensure that students receive the services they deserve, even while in the incarcerated setting. He shared, "We don't get a pass for this being a DJJ facility. They have to pass their county exam, or else they don't get their credit, and then we look horrible." James described the assessments the students at this facility are held accountable for passing. According to James, "They've got to pass FCAT, or else we look horrible, so we don't get a pass for the DJJ kids, 'Oh don't worry about them.' So we do whatever strategies it takes to get 'em to pass."

There is a master schedule that includes each of the teachers' and the ESE support facilitators' day, time, course, and location. Furthermore, the assistant principal and her secretary both have offices in this facility, which also allow for a continual administrative presence.

James wishes more could be done to keep better track of the students or to follow up with them once they leave. He divulged, "I know the [juvenile justice] staff tracks 'em; but education, once we send our stuff off to their new school or their new district, or their returning district, they're kind of out of my hands." He went on further to explain why this would be ideal:

> I know that's extra work for us. But I have no way of making sure that, like, the student I'm helping with getting his paperwork for [the local community college], I have no way of finding out if he's done it unless he decides to visit or whatever, or email.

The teachers at this facility ensure students' IEPs are followed, another form of accountability. James described what this process looks like:

> For ESE students, they have an Individual Education Plan. . . . We as teachers provide the . . . instruction that's tailored to that particular student. Now, they still have to do . . . what the county says . . . they still have to follow the state benchmarks, but we tailor our education to what their goals are and what their objectives are, and we have to make sure that they're meeting their objectives.

The educators are also responsible for submitting paperwork for treatment team meetings. Treatment team meetings are held monthly for the youth. The youths' case manager, an administrator from the facility, therapist and medical assistant sat in on the meetings I observed. The case manager contacted the youths' parents, and they participated in the meeting via phone. The educators are responsible for submitting progress reports for each youth, in advance. During my observations of these meetings, none of the educators were present, but the case manager who facilitated the meetings shared detailed notes she received from the teachers regarding the youths' academic and behavioral challenges and accomplishments.

Israel

Israel is the math substitute teacher at Philip I. He had been serving in this capacity for about four weeks, replacing a longtime educator who recently retired. He has been a substitute in various schools throughout this school district for four-and-a-half years and was serving as a reading substitute teacher at Philip I. before accepting the math teaching position. Israel recognizes the importance of maintaining positive relationships. He has high expectations for educators, juvenile justice staff, and students in this setting. He wishes there were more resources in place to help the students experience greater academic success. Israel has become accustomed to some of the accountability tools in place, including across-the-board assessments for the youth.

Relationships

Israel told me that the reason he decided to accept the math substitute position was because of the relationship he had with the math teacher who was retiring. According to Israel, "I've made friends with some people here." He was initially covering for a reading teacher who was on leave. Israel shared,

> Previously, I was assigned to reading. . . . I knew the math teacher who was here, and he said he was retiring, and he asked me, you know, "Would you take the class?" Because I think the students had liked me, or whatever the reason, and I said, "Sure. Why not?" He has been in the teaching business, I think he said about thirty something years. He had a master's in math—very nice fellow. He and I became very good friends.

The teachers also expressed the comfort they have for approaching their colleagues for suggestions and to discuss students' progress. Israel provided an example of these conversations: "'You have so and so in your class?' You know, 'I've got a lot of problem with them. What do you think about it?' And, the conversation starts about him and just keeps on going about other students too."

These positive conversations and partnerships were also observed through Israel's interactions with his students. He greeted them with "Good morning" and "Good afternoon." He referred to many by their names and others by "gentlemen." Some students greeted him with a handshake and others with a pound—or fist pump, as some refer to this form of greeting. He had a gentle manner with them and effectively used humor to further solidify his connections and relationships with his students.

Expectations

Israel believes teachers are born rather than developed: "In a way I feel that sometime teachers are born rather than you could actually make a teacher. You know, if you got it, you got it. If you don't have it, you just don't have it." He further discussed his expectation that all the teachers at this facility understand the population they are working with and are dedicated. Israel affirmed, "Understanding some of the issues that may come with students coming into your classroom might give you a better handle to communicate with them." He continued,

> A lot of these kids coming here, they're on drugs, and sometime it's no fault of their own. It's from the environment they're coming from, and you have to understand that. And you've got to be a little patient with them.
>
> Some of the teachers seem to be a bit dedicated, you know. This could be a very rough environment compared to the regular school, because you could never tell when one of these kids may just lose it, and it could be dangerous, too. So to work in this facility, you really have to be a little dedicated, because in other environments, it could be a lot more cleaner, a lot more fancy, you got better equipment, and so forth. And the kids, you're dealing with, the manners are a little better, compared to this environment.

Israel believes the learning should be relevant for the students he teaches. "I picked some topics I think that they probably could use help with and from the questions they ask and I base my daily work on that," cited Israel. He explained how he expects himself to know what students are able to do and determine in what areas additional support is needed. Israel averred, "Sometimes, [I] invite the students to come on the board to see if they could do the problems, then I know if they really understand or they don't understand based on that." This was evident as Israel worked closely with two students who were having difficulty solving algebraic equations. He had the two students go to the board and allowed them to use the dry erase markers and work through the problems while he stood closely offering feedback.

Israel believes the students should be receiving an education "comparable to the regular school." However, he urged that many students may not be working to their full potential because of the obstacles they face. Israel said, "There are a lot of issues that are holding back students. It could be social issues, it could be physical issues and you have to be aware of those things, especially the physical issues."

While Israel believes students should receive a comparable education, he always cites the need for students to be exposed to a basic education and be trained for jobs. He shared, "A lot of them are between the age of, let's say, 11 to 18, around that group, so there's still an opportunity for education outside, a free education." He expounded,

> In today's society, it is so competitive, I think you have to train them for jobs. Number one, they've got to express what their interest might be. It's no point training them for something that they don't have an interest in. And number two, you have to get them a bit motivated at the same time. You've got to explain to them, "This is for your benefit." A lot of them don't understand that. They came from that society, "It's a dog eat dog world."

Israel expects that students will learn important life skills while they are incarcerated to help them make a smoother transition back into society upon exiting the facility. He advises the youth: "When you come into a facility, you don't try to steal, or you don't try to criticize the superior people, you know, because that's the way you're used to it." Israel said this advice is important, because "some of these kids, they bring their gang attitude in here and you try to mold them to fit into society that [they'll] be a little more productive."

Israel expects the juvenile justice staff to dedicate more time to students' learning beyond their instructional day. He believes the time he has with them in the classroom is not enough to provide the youth with all the academic supports needed for them to be successful. Because most items are considered contraband, the students are neither assigned homework nor allowed to take learning materials outside the classroom. Israel shared,

> The 50 minutes or one hour that you got, you really can't do it within that period of time. Like I said, if they miss class, you know, you can't make up for it. They don't have the books. You can't take a book to the pod to read. And I think they're at a disadvantage there. . . . Give them a little chance, not just to look at television, or to be in the gym, but also to spend some time reading or doing an assignment— homework. . . . Because the brain . . . after a while you don't put it to use, you forget about it, so they need to be able to do a little assignment after school.

Resources

During my time in this facility, there were two juvenile justice staff who were in the classroom with the students and teacher to provide support as needed. Israel explained how the juvenile justice staff members serve as a tremendous resource:

> I feel very comfortable for the simple reason there is a staff member, sort of like an officer, in the classroom. In case you got discipline problem, you know, that person would be able to handle it, and you don't have to focus on that. . . . So I think in a way, discipline here is a lot better compared to high school.

The support from the juvenile justice staff also helped the students stay engaged and on task. Even with up to 18 students in the classroom, the least amount of students who were on task was 83%, and the highest percentage of students who were on task was 100%.

Israel believes the courses students are enrolled in also serve as resources, particularly their PCS (personal career school development) class. According to Israel, "They teach them a little about how do you operate if you're on your own, what a budget is all about, what income is all about, what expenses is all about . . . how you go about doing a job interview." Additionally, Israel shared, "There are some trainings for putting together résumés. They talk about job skills, how to develop those job skills. Sometimes you have guest speakers coming in."

Israel described the additional resource students are looking for but the inability to provide it due to the constraints within the facility: "Some students are begging for [tutoring]; because of budget constraint they weren't able to do it." He divulged,

> I have volunteered, you know, to help some, because some of these students are really crying, and some of them, they could use it, and some, they're pretty good students, it's just they happen to be in the wrong environment, whatever the situation might be. I volunteered my time, but because of the, how to put it, the staff constraint, they don't have staff to be with the students all the time. And, I guess it's mandatory [on the DJJ side], you have to account for the students all the time, which makes it a little impossible. . . . But we have a meeting today, and that is going to come up again, because these students really begging, and it would be to all our benefit to help these students in the long run.

While Israel intends to ensure that the youth have additional instructional resources outside the regular school hours, he also attempts to find topics that are universal so that regardless of what level of math students are at, they can increase their knowledge of mathematical concepts while they are in his classroom. He shared, "I started a topic today that cross all boundary lines. It cross algebra, geometry, trigonometry, precalculus. Pythagoras theorem, simple thing as that. So you teach that, and everybody . . . would be using it in the future."

Unfortunately, although Israel has been a long-term substitute, he's not included in any of the professional development sessions, even though these take place during the contracted teachers day. Although Israel shared that no administrator had been to his classroom in the four weeks since he started as the math substitute, he does, however, attend the weekly PLCs facilitated by the lead teacher at the facility each week. During the weekly professional learning community [PLC] meeting I observed, the TABE and GED testing was one of the topics discussed. Data, provided by the lead teacher, revealed that the students who recently took the TABE did not score high enough to be eligible to take the GED. As Israel mentioned earlier, the concerns that students are not able to receive the additional tutoring after school that they once had led the educators into conversations about what should happen to ensure that students receive the support they need. The lead teacher said that he would discuss this with the administrators and said that he could probably go through Project Promise, another partnership for student resources and support, to get the funding and support needed.

According to Israel, students are asking for more support. He shared, "There was some program previously, and some kids have begged for assistance, especially in math. They're so far behind. But they beg, "Could you help me, you know, to get up to speed?" Israel described a program that was in place to provide additional academic support to the youth, but believes it was cut due to a lack of funding. He, however, emphasized the need for these resources to be reinstated: "There was some programs, I think in the afternoon, but I think because of financial reason, it was cut off. So, they really can't get that one-to-one attention as they really deserve."

Accountability

The educators at Philip I. are committed to working with students to ensure that they pass the assessments for which the students are held accountable. Israel discussed the other forms of testing at this facility. He shared, "Based on the testing that they do. They've got the FCAT, which is Florida's test, and then they've got some county test or state test or something; a number of tests that goes on, just like the regular school." According to Israel, "The past few weeks I've been here. . . . I was working basically on those worksheets or those test papers just to get them prepared for this [end-of-course] test so they could do good when time comes around."

Juanita

Juanita teaches reading at Philip I. and has been teaching at this facility for more than five years. She has prior experience as a classroom teacher and librarian in another school district in Florida. Juanita espouses positive relationships among the educators and with her students. She maintains high expectations and uses the resources placed in her classroom for her students' benefit. Juanita wants her students to do well on their assessments and believes she should be held accountable for their success.

Relationships

I observed many positive interactions between Juanita and her colleagues. They appeared to work as a team, just as Principal Richard modeled with his assistant principal. This was further evidenced during my visit when the lead teacher entered Juanita's classroom to discuss a student's performance:

> Lead Teacher: *How's [student]? He doin' any work for you? [The teacher]*
> *upstairs tells me he's not doing anything upstairs.*
> Juanita: *Well, this is a former student of mine, so I'm getting him to work.*

The conversations about the educational leaders were also positive. Juanita spoke highly of the previous and current administrators at this facility. She stated, "She was a very good principal, and at that time Mr. [Richard] was the assistant principal. So it's been wonderful working with them."

In every classroom I observed, the teachers knew each student by name. There was an evident respect that was shared between teachers and students. Each class began with a "Good morning, gentlemen" or "Afternoon, gentlemen." Students were acknowledged when their hands were raised, and the teachers provided them with feedback throughout the class periods.

The teachers shared that they also continually check in with students to ensure that the youth feel they are being taught with the teaching strategies that best suit their needs. Juanita discussed a conversation that one of the ESE support facilitators had with her students after they completed a learning styles inventory. According to Juanita, "[The ESE support facilitator] told the youth: 'Now that you know what your strengths are, you know, maybe better, you can help us as teachers, you know. Let your teachers know that you learn best this way.'"

Juanita also places a heavy emphasis on building relationships with students. She stressed the importance of letting students know that she cares about them and often facilitates discussions with the youth and shares personal stories to further connect with the youth. She indicated, "They need people who can kind of relate to them, and you might have heard the quote that 'Nobody cares how much you know until they know how much you care.'" One way Juanita shows her students that she cares is by spraying the classroom with potpourri well before they are lined up outside her classroom door so that when they enter the classroom, they walk into a pleasantly scented learning environment. She also begins each of her classes with a quote and uses various forms of media to use as springboards for rich discourse on real issues faced by her students. Juanita believes these conversations draw her closer to her students. She elaborated,

> I found out through the discussion that many of my students have been homeless, and they don't really want to talk about it, but one student who was brave enough to share with us: "Ms. [J] I wouldn't want that for anybody, you know, I was cold, I didn't have a place . . ."

Juanita also shares personal stories with her students including stories about her oldest brother, who is currently serving two life sentences. She explained, "He dropped out of school at the age of 17. And I tell my students we all came from the same mom and dad, okay, it was all about a matter of you know, choice that he made."

The established relationships lead students to leave behind some of their cherished work for the teachers. Juanita described a gift she received from one of her students who left the facility: "I mean, when he left, he left me with a booklet of poems that he had written. I'm like, 'Sweetheart, you have enough poems here to publish them. Publish your book of poetry.'"

Expectations

The educators expect one of their primary functions is to serve as a motivator for their students. Juanita shared, "I've always been with at-risk students and want to encourage and motivate. . . . By encouraging them to want to learn, by motivating them, I spend a lot of time in discussion . . . I kind of try to touch their heart." She has a quote written on the board, and that's what she uses to motivate her students each day. Juanita explained,

> Former President Theodore Roosevelt had a quote, and when I heard this quote, I loved it so much that I had one of my boys to do it in

graffiti writing, and I have it on my wall. . . . I had it posted to the ceiling, so if anybody walks in, they look up, they could still read it (chuckles). And it says . . . to educate a person in mind only and not in morals . . . you'll create a menace to society...And I said, "Guys, what does that mean?" "Okay, 'cause I can stand here and try, you know, and teach you strategies and how to comprehend and vocabulary development and so forth, but . . . it's not making you whole. So, I'm not here just to educate your mind."

Juanita believes she must find additional ways to motivate her students and recognizes the importance of understanding how boys' and girls' learning styles may differ. She stated, "I find that the single-sex classroom works best, because boys do learn differently than girls and mostly in the public school system, we teach to how we as females learn." She continued,

Boys . . . have other factors, that they, you know, sexual attraction and all that other stuff plays in the classroom. . . . So, when you take that out of the picture, you know, then you can kind of, like, find out exactly where they're at or what it is that you can do; you know, since they don't have those other distractions, what you can do to kind of like, motivate them. A lot of times, they've lost their motivation, their enthusiasm for education.

She strongly believes the personal career school development (PCS) class is a perfect opportunity to motivate students, particularly because so many of the youth are "business-minded." She divulged, "Truth be told, I really wanted to be a PCS (laughs) teacher, because I'm business-minded and I know that we can really use that to capitalize and really motivate them to want to excel."

The educators further expect themselves to be prepared to provide what is needed for the students to be successful. Juanita believes that she must "provide them reading opportunities to increase their skills in the area of comprehension and vocabulary." She expects that she will provide the necessary resources for her students regardless of their divergent academic levels. Juanita indicated,

I have different reading levels, like intensive reading 1, 2, 3, 4, a, b, c, and so forth, but it's basically all the same, 'cause you teach to the reading skills, the strategies (chuckles) that they need. And then if they're advanced, I like to use the computer to, kind of, where they can go on to get the advanced learning that they need. And I do have some materials, printed materials that they can use, too, in terms of building their critical thinking skills.

This was evidenced as Juanita made use of the two computers in her classroom and allowed students to work on programs to increase their reading comprehension and other pertinent literacy skills.

Juanita expects that the educators are at this facility because they want to be here to make a difference in the lives of the youth. She echoed Principal Richard's sentiments:

> The teachers who are here are teachers who want to be here . . . and . . . most of the teachers have been here over three years. So, you know, when teachers transition out, it's just like even in the public school . . . especially in a ESE class, you have all that change. It's not good for students, 'cause students feel nobody doesn't care.

Juanita began as a substitute teacher in this facility and was hopeful her substituting would lead her to a permanent teaching position. She explained,

> So I substituted, and so in substituting, I guess one of the teachers here . . . she was our language arts teacher, and she was out for a week, I believe. And so I picked up that assignment, and she just heard rave reviews, and then when they found out they had a reading position open, they asked me would I want it. I said, "Yes!" (screams with excitement) So, I've been here for five years and interviewing with the principal, I remember she asked me, she said, "Ms. [Juan-ita], can you give me five years?" And I—, "Yes, yes, I can give you— (laughs).". . . . And this is going on my sixth year.

The educators at this facility also expect they will focus on students' strengths and meet the needs of each student. According to Juanita, "And so we found that if many of the teachers, you know, capitalize on the strengths of their students, you know, be it verbal, visual, whatever the case may be, it'll . . . help them process."

The expectations the educators have for students are explicitly posted in each classroom on large poster paper. This is evident as soon as you walk into the classrooms. Adjacent to the expectations poster is another poster explaining how students are able to earn a point each day for their behavior and how those points qualify them for a monthly reward.

These expectations and the learning environment Juanita established helped to ensure that most of her students were engaged in their learning. With up to 19 students in her reading classes, the lowest percentage of students who were on task was 84%, and the highest percentage of students on task was 100%.

The educators expect students will strive to excel with the proper incentives and motivators. They believe that posting current student work with teacher feedback and celebrating students for their academic and behavioral progress will encourage students to continue to exhibit the expected behaviors. The educators also established a character award to recognize those youth who display commendable character traits, such as honesty and respect. Although they didn't restart this recognition program yet this school year, Juanita explained the benefits from when they incorporated this in the past:

> We used to have a character award, character development for students you know. Because, a lot of times, most of our boys, they don't respect authority. . . . That's their biggest downfall. They don't respect authority. With the [character] development . . . we choose one student per class who has shown that character trait for the month. So for the month of January, maybe respect. The next month, it may be . . . determination, you know, the different traits and we reward them, okay. So each teacher gets to choose a student and, and at the end of the month . . . the ones who were chosen receive a certificate and we do like an ice cream social celebration for them.

According to Juanita, "Our mission is to make sure that every student is educated to the best of their potential and make them productive citizens." The educators believe they are making a difference in the lives of their students and expect the youth to do well once they leave the facility. Principal Richard ensures every facility he oversees is kept informed of the youths' progress. Juanita shared,

> One of the things that we do for all of the facilities, we send out a bullet point you know, when students have gotten their GED. With the high school diploma, it's a much more lengthier process. I've had two students who just left, okay, and we received notice on those two students—one who's been in school for ten days . . . and he was one of my best students, too (smiles). I was very proud when I got that email. And then another one, he has a A in Biology and a B in Math . . . So he was doing good.

Juanita believes her students are highly intelligent and business-minded, and she regularly encourages them to come up with business plans. She said, "I was telling my students here that I don't see them working for anyone, because they don't have that mindset to be on anybody's job. . . . They're business owners. They're entrepreneurs . . . because that's what they're doing on the streets. . . . They're hustling." Juanita expects her students are "A" students who made poor choices when they engaged in criminal activity. Juanita affirmed, "They're smart students, just made wrong choices." She elaborated,

It's not that these kids are not educated. They are. Okay, it's just that they (chuckles) probably got caught up with the wrong type of friends, made poor choices, and just, you know, just dropped out of school for whatever reason. A lot of times, you know, they're supporting their families you know and selling drugs or whatever the case may be. But I find that they're "A" students and some will say, "Ms. [J], this is the first time I've gotten all A's in my classes (laughs)."

Resources

One of the great resources Juanita so proudly shared has much to do about the educators themselves. Juanita celebrated, "We work together."

Juanita also agrees that the professional development sessions serve as important resources and support for the teachers. She explained, "Well, we definitely have the professional development; staff development after school and during school hours, you know, if the system can afford you to go during class time. . . . We do get the training that we need." Juanita elaborated, "We have training, staff training, every first Friday . . . Mr. [R.] (principal) will bring in guests who will come in to do the training. . . . I think we're going to have a gang awareness training next month." Juanita shared that, "[Principal Richard] did a survey at the end of the school year, of what things that we as teachers want to see that we feel that will help us in the classroom." Juanita said she requested gang awareness training because the youth do "things that we don't think [are gang-related] and sometimes that's what leads to their problems on the zone. There [are] gangs, and they don't do it during our class time. Sometimes they may, and we don't pick it up."

Juanita really appreciates the single-gender training they received in a recent professional development session, as this helps her to better understand and be better prepared to work with her male students. According to Juanita, "When the young lady came in to do the training, she was showing us how girls learn different as opposed to boys.

And because most of our facilities . . . are boys. . . . Knowing how the boys operate [is important]." Although she appreciates these training sessions, Juanita wishes she had been exposed to much of the information and helpful strategies she's learned before she began working with this population.

Describing a recent training the educators received in hopes of learning more about the population they are working with, Juanita said, "They brought in the young lady who taught about . . . the brain, and . . . we attend the dropout prevention conference, but it's not made available to everybody, and it should [be]."

In addition to the professional development sessions, the teachers at this facility are also assigned a peer mentor. Peer mentors work specifically with first- and second-year teachers and possibly other teachers, depending on their needs. Juanita mentioned that along with the principal, there is a peer mentor who "comes in and evaluates us. . . . This person is from the district. . . . Every new teacher gets a mentor, and so, even in our facility, and he knows about our facility, so he mentors all of us."

The teachers also receive a stipend each year to purchase extra materials they might need. Funds are set aside for the classroom teachers, ESE support facilitators and the teaching assistants. The amounts are identified in advance and provided for the educators in the annual handbook they receive at the beginning of each school year. Juanita described how she uses this resource:

> We have the curriculum, we have the materials and so forth, it may not be the very best that we would want (laughs) . . . some a little outdated perhaps. . . . I do have supply monies. . . . I think we get $300 for the year, and I think someone was going to try to get me some MP3 players. 'Cause I told them I just want to go to Office Depot and just get the little cheap— . . . because, if they tear it up anyway, at least to have something. . . . I have enough supplies, so no need to spend money on supplies. So I spend my money on technology.

Juanita also described the resources the students were once able to access; however, because of the lack of funding on the education side and the lack of coverage on the juvenile justice side, the youths' access to those resources ended. Although the teachers are willing to work with the students, even when there is no funding, they must ensure that there are enough juvenile justice staff to help supervise the youth. She talked about the partnership they have with Project Promise and the funds they used to receive for after-school clubs and tutorial groups. Juanita shared, "I used to do after-school clubs with the students . . . it was an Art Club and a Games Club where they could you know, come in and use their creative abilities just to draw and so forth, create pictures—." Unfortunately, mentioned Juanita, these funds were cut.

Juanita and one of the ESE support facilitators administered a multiple intelligence assessment that serves as a resource to the teacher and students. They know what is needed and can provide the appropriate support to the youth. Juanita averred, "We found that in doing a multiple intelligences test with them, that most of the students are kinesthetic learners and being that they're kinesthetic learners, they have to have movement." Because of this finding and the training they received, Juanita believes students shouldn't have to be seated and quiet for the entire class, and she tries to ensure students have mobility and a voice during the instructional time. She explained, "We find out most of these boys who are like that, they're the ones that get in trouble in the regular schools 'cause they can't sit, you know, or they need some hands-on activities."

Fortunately for the students at this facility, resources for students extend beyond their grade level curriculum. Juanita provides reading materials for the youth that she believes they enjoy because they can relate to the experiences they are reading. She uses books like the *Chicken Soup* series, *Tough Times*, and *Prisoner's Soul*. She believes these serve as resources to them because, "they can hear, you know from some of the prisoners and how they're dealing with what they're going through and how it'll kind of help them change their mindset."

Juanita provides high-interest books and allows students to self-select the texts they are interested in reading. Students are expected to read and respond to questions. She said, "We have Plugged into Reading. That is a new system that we've used for the last three years and it's a group of books basically to—, books that most young people would enjoy reading." She also believes her encouragement and finding the right materials serve as resources for her students. She learned from her students that they enjoy reading books that have stories similar to their lives. When she first started teaching, she had difficulty getting the students engaged with the books they were supposed to be reading. Juanita shared this conversation she had with her students: "'Ms. [Juanita], you don't have any books that I want to read.' 'Okay, come on, tell me what it is you want to read. What is it that you like?'" Juanita further disclosed, "I have books on cassettes, and I found . . . that many of them want to listen to the books on cassette, and that kind of perked up their reading." This was evidenced during my observations. Some students selected to listen to a personal CD player with headphones while reading along with the accompanied text.

Juanita also described the use of the TABE test for any student who wants to get their GED; another resource provided to the youth at this facility:

> I also use the TABE for those who are interested in getting their GED. Those students who are like two, they have to be basically two grades behind, I believe, and maintain like a C average in all of their educational classes, and they can take the TABE test. And after they take the TABE, they qualify for the GED.

The juvenile justice facility itself also provides resources to the students. Juanita described the added resources students receive during the time they're incarcerated, from the juvenile justice side. She shared, "Every child has a case manager and a therapist, where they do group sessions. . . . As I said before, they do come in needy, and . . . the counseling is the biggest thing."

One support Juanita hopes to establish for the youth is a student council, similar to one found in a traditional school setting. She believes this would serve as a great resource for the youth to "voice their opinions on what they feel that could help improve their situation here, while they're here for the six or nine months." She explained how she broached this subject with her students:

> "Guys, they're not going to listen to you, you know, profanity and . . . the way you're speaking." I said, "How many of you would be interested in, in, in being on a council that you would get a chance to speak to [the executive director of the facility]?" "We'll have the principal, the assistant principal, whoever, to voice your opinions about how the facility should be run, or what you feel will improve the situation."

Accountability

The outside accountability mechanisms for the educators at this facility come primarily in the form of assessments. The Department of Juvenile Justice requires students to be assessed when they enter and exit the facility. Juanita explained, "Every student when they come in, they are tested, okay. I think we're using the STAR test now, and they're tested in reading and math." Juanita works hard to ensure each of her students improve their educational level during the time they are in her educational program.

Discussion

The educational program at this facility demonstrates strength in the four themes that emerged from this study. To ensure that incarcerated youth have the possibility for a high-quality education, positive relationships exist, and high expectations are maintained for the educators and students. Furthermore, adequate and effective resources and accountability measures are in place for each stakeholder.

Relationships

There is a strong relationship between the educational leaders and the juvenile justice leader. This is evident as the educators are included in meetings with the facility director to discuss programs, like Home Builders, that are beneficial for the incarcerated youth. Principal Richard and the teachers recognize how critical this relationship is and are in agreement that although there may have been issues in the past with the juvenile justice staff, the current leadership of this juvenile justice facility ensures that matters are addressed immediately. This allows the relationship to be strengthened and greatly appreciated. Using this positive relationship, the educators should have a discussion with the juvenile justice leader to emphasize the importance of having the youth brought to class on time each day. The youth were an average 5.8 minutes late to each 75-minute class, which resulted in a loss of 8% of their instructional time.

The relationships between the educators allow them to work well together and provide an ideal learning environment for their students. The collegial relationships were evident during the principal and assistant principal's "tag-team" interview and during my observations of the classroom interactions between the classroom teachers and the ESE support facilitators. This was also evident as teachers approached one another with questions and suggestions and used humor during my observation of the PLC. Additionally, during the interviews, the teachers spoke highly of their administrators and peers, and the administrators spoke highly of their teaching staff. The additional observed interactions were that the educators were jovial and appeared to genuinely care for one another. Several of the teachers I spoke with have been teaching at this facility for six or more years, ample time to establish collaborative relationships.

The educators' positive relationships with each other transfer to their positive relationships with their students. Photos of students and Juanita are posted on her classroom walls as outward displays of the positive relationships she has with her students. Moreover, an inordinate amount of student work is posted in her classroom, which demonstrates their partnership—they complete the work; she displays it for all to see. Juanita also shares personal stories with her students and uses quotes to help students share more about their experiences. This allows for rich discourse on topics relevant to their lives and further strengthens the teacher–student relationship. The educators also knew and called each student by his name and greeted each student when he entered the classroom.

They have established a positive relationship within their district and were able to receive a waiver to adequately ensure the professional development time for the juvenile justice teachers is being fully maximized. Their partnership with Project Promise has also been fruitful, but Juanita indicated—and James concurred—that the funding was no longer provided for tutorial services for the youth. During the PLC, as the teachers were discussing the data they had recently received—that none of the 12 students who recently took the TABE passed—the lead teacher facilitating the PLC mentioned that they could put a plan together and "probably reach out to Project Promise." Because of the great work they are doing for youth, it seems as if they should have many more partnerships or sponsors they can call upon for assistance.

Expectations

Relationships are sound, and the leaders' expectations for the teachers are explicit, which further transfer to the teachers' expectations of their students. The administrators expect there will be continuity and consistency of their teachers to further ensure that there is a stable learning environment for the youth. That is evident in Juanita's description of the principal's question, when Principal Richard was an assistant principal, whether she would be willing to give them five years. She is now in her sixth year—evidence that longevity is both expected and valued.

The teachers seem to be very clear about what is expected of them and that positively impacts the teacher's expectations for their students. One of the most important expectations listed for students is that they will keep their heads up all at times. Throughout the observed classrooms, up to 100% of the youth met this expectation.

Juanita believes the educators must touch the hearts of the youth here as much as their minds. The educators also believe that they are well prepared for their roles as juvenile justice teachers, and James expects that he can use a bare minimum of materials and still be an effective teacher for his students.

In addition to the expectations, the teachers recognize that students may need incentives to be motivated. Expectations for students are made explicit and are posted in each classroom along with the rewards for following the expectations. Even with as many as 19 students in the class, up to 100% of students were on task. The educators expect that students need to be motivated, and they celebrate students with a monthly drawing for the youth, who earn one point each day during their class time for meeting the expectations. They also provided character development ice cream socials to further reward and encourage the youth for displaying important character traits.

The educators believe that boys learn differently from girls and that the single-gender setting helps the boys focus without distractions. Because of these differences, Principal Richard ensures that professional development for single-gender education is provided to his juvenile justice teachers with the expectation that they will provide the necessary resources and support for their students to be successful.

Principal Richard believes the teachers are intrinsically motivated to be there with a desire to make a difference in the lives of the incarcerated youth. Aside from the posting of the job opening, no staff member was solicited to be there, and all the teachers chose to work in this facility. The educators also believe that their peers are certified, highly qualified, committed to being there, motivated, and able to motivate their students. Many of the educators have been there for six years. They believe that they must continually improve and be developed to benefit their students. Although certified in ESE, history, and middle school science, James also seeks to be certified in a specific science to provide greater support to his students.

They believe they provide ample opportunities for the youth to be successful including a relevant and rigorous curriculum, GED preparation and testing, and workplace readiness skills. They also believe that it's up to the students to take advantage of the opportunities provided.

The educators expect the juvenile justice staff to properly monitor the students. In one math class I observed, the first student who entered the math classroom decided to stand on two chairs; one foot on each seat, as the rest of the class was entering the classroom. As soon as the juvenile justice staff member saw the youth, the youth was told to sit down. With very few exceptions during my visit, the students appeared to be appropriately monitored.

The juvenile justice educators also communicated an expectation that the juvenile justice staff would understand the importance of education and allow students to complete work or assignments after school. The juvenile justice educators appeared to value education during my observations, as they were assisting students who needed help with their math problems.

The educators believe that the youth should receive hands-on training. However, they believe that they should have more options for vocational programs—not just Home Builders, offered to the youth who are 16 years or older, who have their GED. Once a student has his GED, he is no longer able to receive the school district's educational services, as the GED now affords him the right to join the work force or continue his education at a community college.

The educators at this facility expect that myriad support structures must continue to be in place for them and their students to be successful.

Resources

Longevity and being trained and mentored in his role as an assistant principal proved to be a helpful resource for Principal Richard, his teachers, and their students. These support structures help Principal Richard to be both comfortable and confident in his position.

Furthermore, the teachers chose to teach at this facility, and they believe that they receive the necessary resources and support to help them and their students achieve. The relationships and expectations that exist certainly serve as tremendous resources for the students. In both the reading and math classes, up to 100% of the youth were on task and actively engaged during the observed lessons.

The teachers made use of the LCD projector; even with only two computers in Juanita's classroom, she made certain that students were on the computers during each class, working on a reading program to improve their phonics and comprehension skills. Additionally, CD players were made available for the students to listen to the text being read to them while they followed along in the books. Israel allowed the students to talk him through some of the problems he was working out on the board and worked with one or two students at a time, allowing them to work out the problems on the board and explain their methods for solving the equations. There were two juvenile justice staff members in most of the classrooms, and during my observations of the math classrooms, both juvenile justice staff members were working one-on-one with students who needed support with their math problems.

The educators also have the support of the juvenile justice staff to help with discipline, although Israel voiced his concerns that this could be an area they develop further. James indicated that the juvenile justice staff's support in this area has improved.

Specific professional development for the juvenile justice educators is provided to assist them in their roles. They receive training in single-gender education, gang awareness, and both left-brain and right-brain learners. Additionally, aspiring administrators are provided with opportunities to take on leadership roles by facilitating the PLC meetings and scheduling some of the professional development sessions. Unfortunately, however, the substitute math teacher is not included in these professional development sessions even though he is on long-term assignment until a permanent teacher is identified. The half-day monthly professional development sessions take place during the substitute teachers' contracted time, so, particularly for long-term substitutes such as Israel, substitutes should be included in the trainings.

The school district provides ample professional development opportunities in addition to the professional development Principal Richard provides for his 11 sites and the weekly PLC meetings held. Additionally, the district provides a peer mentor to further contribute to the teachers' development. The teachers believe that they are fully equipped to provide the youth with a high-quality education.

Common planning time is used as a resource for the teachers. The ESE support facilitator is able to plan with his cooperating teachers for the upcoming classes they have together, and the teachers are able to share best practices and discuss their students' needs to ensure that they are holding students accountable for completing their work.

Principal Richard ensures teachers have funding and autonomy each school year to purchase materials they believe will be most helpful in assisting them and their students. Teachers are allocated $300 annually, and ESE support facilitators and teaching assistants also have a dollar amount; this information is provided to the juvenile justice educators each year in the staff handbook. Because of this, and the additional support they receive, the educators feel they have enough money for supplies.

The teachers serve as a resource for the youth at this facility. They offer GED courses and testing and the "same courses as the local schools." Because of the certification of a newly hired teacher, this facility is also able to provide youth with physical education and driver's education, not courses typically available to incarcerated youth.

The use of technology is extensive at this facility, offering the incarcerated youth more resources to be academically successful. MP3 players, books on CDs, videos, and Gizmos are used to provide as much hands-on learning as possible. PowerPoint presentations are used, and Juanita typed her students' responses on the computer and used the LCD projector to display their responses during a class discussion.

As students were reviewing for an upcoming test, they were creating PowerPoint slides as a review; as an incentive, the teacher told the students that if he uses any of their slides, they will earn a piece of candy. Although some traditional schools within the United States have banned the distribution of candy to students for health reasons, it is a much-anticipated treat, particularly for youth who have been incarcerated for six months. Additional programs such as Home Builders, dog care and therapy, and computer mentoring also serve as resources for the youth, as do treatment team meetings, counseling from case managers, therapists—what the facility provides.

Books are also provided for the youth, particularly in Juanita's classroom, where she provides an extensive array of high-interest literature for the youth to read. In other classrooms, teachers also bring in books they purchased from book sales at the library or garage sales. Some include magazines, but teachers must remove the staples from magazines before making them available for the youth. Like many items, staples are considered contraband in the facility.

Unfortunately, there is a lack of funds for the one-on-one and small-group tutoring needed for the youth. The educators are committed to working with Project Promise and other sources to ensure that they can restart a tutorial program in the near future.

Accountability

The educators want to be at this facility, and they expressed how much they enjoy what they do. For this reason, there is a high level of self-efficacy and accountability on the part of the educators that further facilitates their desire to excel. There are also mechanisms in place to hold the educators accountable. One example of this is the master schedule posted on the wall in the educational staff room. Every teacher, including the ESE support facilitators, is listed with the corresponding teaching schedule.

The assistant principal provides another level of accountability for the educators at this facility. Although she has three additional sites, she has an office within the facility, and her secretary has an office to provide an administrative presence.

James wishes, on the educational side, that there was a way to hold students accountable or follow up with them after they've left the facility to ensure that they are continuing with the plans they communicated during their time of incarceration.

The educators are conscientious about and committed to meeting or exceeding the standards established by the Florida Department of Juvenile Justice, the Department of Education, and Joyce County. These expectations hold the educators accountable, and the teachers and principal work hard to ensure they meet the required mandates. The educators expect their students to pass the state's end-of-course exams and FCAT. They also believe that their ESE students should receive appropriate accommodations.

The juvenile justice caseworkers also appropriately hold the educators accountable for ensuring that the students' progress reports are submitted on time. This information is pertinent, as it is provided to the youths' parents, therapists, juvenile justice administrators, medical doctors, and the youths themselves. These meetings are used to discuss whether a youth is making adequate progress and the additional services that are needed for the youth to be successful.

During my classroom observations, an average of 1 disruption occurred every 2 minutes and 50.52 seconds. Although additional strategies should be implemented to further decrease the disruptions in this learning environment, it is important to recognize there could have easily been many more disruptions had it not been for the positive relationships, high expectations, appropriate resources, and level of accountability in place. At the Philip I. Juvenile Justice Residential Center, these necessary components are evident, and there is a strong possibility that as these elements are strengthened, the quality of education for the incarcerated youth will further improve.

7
Cross-Facility Discussion

There were similarities and distinct differences among the four facilities and the educators at each site.

Relationships Cross-Case Discussion

According to Witmer, "If educators are focused on making learning meaningful and fostering student achievement, strong relationships among all the stakeholders in education are imperative."[1] In education, we tend to think of these relationships occurring between the teacher, student, and parent. Based on my research, however, I believe that four crucial relationships must be established to provide a high-quality education for incarcerated youth—the relationship between the educational staff and juvenile justice staff, the relationship between and among the educators, the relationship between the educators and the student, and the relationship between the educators and other employees within the local school district and with outside entities.

Although the necessity for these relationships may seem obvious, particularly when speaking about its importance in an educational setting, the context for this is unique. After a youth has been adjudicated, the judge decides what facility is best suited for the youth. Furthermore, the youth is recognized as a ward of the state and the Department of Juvenile Justice is considered in loco parentis—Latin for *in place of the parent*. In traditional settings, we know the importance of fostering positive relationships between the educators and the parents. In the juvenile justice settings, one of the most important relationships that must be established is between the educators and the juvenile justice staff. For the students' benefit, this relationship is a critical one and is probably the most important in relation to students' instruction.

Principal Alexander and the educators at Greta Olive recognize that the success they have in this facility has much to do with the relationship they have with the juvenile justice leader. They understand the importance of reciprocity and do what is needed to ensure that their students have greater access to resources, particularly as relates to their hands-on vocational program. The relationships Principal Alexander cultivated when he was an administrator at one of the district's high schools have proven effective, as many of the guards working with the youth are some of his former students.

The educators at Hubert B. clearly recognize how critical it is for them to have a positive relationship with the juvenile justice staff. Unfortunately, however, merely believing in this does not ensure that the proper relationships are established. Principal Patrick recognizes this importance, yet he does not have a strong relationship with the juvenile justice leader, nor do his teachers have positive working relationships with the juvenile justice staff. This is evident as students were brought to their classes an average of 14 minutes late, and there were far more disruptions during the instructional time than at the other facilities, where relationships were stronger. When teachers sought help with youth who were disrupting the learning environment, instead of providing assistance, the teachers were often told: "Just write him up."

Principal Rae understands the importance of having this relationship and has been working on building her partnerships with the juvenile justice leader since she began her role as principal at Gladys C. This proves fruitful, because their relationship allowed them to work collaboratively to develop shared expectations for the juvenile justice staff and establish a new vocational program for the youth. Written expectations including the staff's roles in handing out the pencils are posted in the classroom, and the youth are being exposed to a vocational program for the first time at this facility.

At Philip I., Principal Richard is thrilled that he and his teachers have a great working relationship with the juvenile justice staff. They believe that if they do have any issues, after those issues are brought to the juvenile justice leader's attention, the matters will be handled promptly and appropriately. Moreover, during my observations, the teachers appeared to have cordial working relationships with the juvenile justice staff, greeting each other by name and working together to ensure that the youth were on task. In each of the math classes, the juvenile justice staff also provided assistance to youth who were in need of academic support. This proved fruitful, as the least number of students on task in any observed class was 83%, and that was in a class of 18 students. Most of the time, however, 100% of the students were on task, even when there were 19 students in the classroom. Furthermore, the classes in this facility experienced 2.5 to 3.25 fewer disruptions than the classes at Gladys C. and Hubert B. experienced respectively.

Both Principal Alexander (Greta Olive) and Principal Rae (Gladys C.) shared the importance of the relationships between the educators and the juvenile justice staff, particularly when the facilities are going through the quality assurance process. This partnership is needed because the quality assurance review focuses on the educational programs housed within the juvenile justice facilities. Although a formal quality assurance process is no longer in place, this was one way these two school leaders ensured that they were working closely with the facility leader.

The educators within the facilities also recognize and appreciate when there are positive working relationships among the educational staff. It was evident that the educators at Greta Olive and Philip I. genuinely appreciate and admire their peers. Kyle (Greta Olive) freely shared the accolades he and his colleagues have received over the years demonstrating their excellence in education. The teachers at Philip I. also appeared to enjoy one another. Many of them have been working together for years at the facility, and they have established a bond over time. This was quite evident during my time in the facility, particularly observing their interactions at their PLC meeting. These partnerships serve as extra support systems for the educators and help students receive additional assistance, as evidenced when the educators at these facilities spoke about finding out students' reading levels, students' reading interests, students' learning styles, etc.

Although there were pleasant conversations amongst the educators at Hubert B. and Gladys C., this is an area that they will need to further develop. The educators at Hubert B. often didn't know what the other teachers or ancillary staff members were doing or what their roles were. Although Principal Patrick (Hubert B.) believes that transferring his teachers every two years decreases teacher burnout, this strategy negatively affects the necessary relationships the teachers must form with one another to be more effective. Principal Rae and Vicki were both in their second year and Donna had only been at Gladys C. five weeks when this study was conducted. During my time in Gladys C., I witnessed positive interactions between these teachers and the print shop teacher and teaching assistant, but much more time and a concerted focus in this area is needed to ensure that these relationships are further developed.

Positive teacher–student relationships were evident during my visits to the three facilities where observations occurred. At Philip I., the teachers knew and called each student by name and greeted them with

"Good afternoon, gentlemen" or "Good morning, gentlemen." Juanita's classroom demonstrated this mutual partnership. As students complete the work she expects, she celebrates the youths' accomplishments by posting their work. In another classroom, one teacher called a student up to his desk, whispered something to the youth and allowed him to choose a regular-sized chocolate bar. It turns out it was his birthday. What a sight it was to see this student return to his seat, bow his head to make a wish, and enjoy the Kit-Kat bar he selected. This is another example that demonstrates their genuine care for the youth, and this act of kindness certainly strengthens the teacher/student relationship.

The teachers at Gladys C. also knew their students by name and greeted them when they entered the classroom. Vicki appeared to be very comfortable around her students, particularly when she was working one-on-one with the youth. According to Donna, incarcerated youth are dealing with a lot of trust issues, and she takes pride in establishing strong relationships, even though she is in a substitute capacity for a teaching position that had yet to be filled.

At Hubert B., although some of the teachers knew the students by name, and although Mary often greeted the youth with "Good morning" or "Good afternoon," it was evident that the necessary relationships were not established. Particularly, the students in Karen's class often challenged what she was saying and often demonstrated disrespectful and uncooperative behaviors. Karen stood behind her desk during most of the lessons that were observed. This lack of connection also contributed to most of her students being disengaged.

The educators at Greta Olive appear to be supported the most by their district and outside entities. They have a wealth of partnerships with other educators within the district, and this equates to exchanging favors and receiving extra funds. Principal Alexander also shared two examples of how mentors played important roles in the lives of the incarcerated youth at his facility, which might not have occurred if there weren't strong partnerships.

The educators at Philip I. feel supported by their district and believe they have a strong partnership because of the waiver they received to conduct their professional development. Instead of one hour each week, Principal Richard is able to have a four-hour professional development session each month with the educators from his 11 sites. The educators also shared how helpful Project Promise has been as they have received different resources for their youth. Because of the many positive aspects found at Philip I., the educators should be certain to spread the word about what they are doing to draw more outside partnerships.

Principal Rae (Gladys C.) believes that she has a good working relationship with her district and outside entities. She returned to this district and accepted this position after having served as a teacher and administrator in previous years. She appreciates the help she's received, particularly when the district had a hiring freeze. She was still able to hire candidates who had the certifications needed to teach at her sites. However, Principal Rae feels frustrated at times, because she believes that her district doesn't have a true understanding of the challenges she faces. Principal Rae believes they could do much more to assist her; perhaps the relationship isn't as strong as she needs it to be. She cited numerous times that she works in isolation. This is most unfortunate for her, for her staff, and for the students for whom they are responsible.

Principal Patrick (Hubert B.) also does not feel supported in any way. He believes his district's only solution when he encounters a challenge is to make sure he has enough funds. This is most unfortunate, because he, his teachers, and their students need so much more support. Frustrated with the lack of relationship, Principal Patrick also shared his feelings of working in isolation. To a large extent, one could conclude that this isolation may cause a sense of disempowerment. And, this feeling certainly affects the educators within Hubert B. So often, when things are not the way they should be—high teacher turnover rate, low student achievement, people respond, "If we just had more money. . . ." Principal Patrick's dilemma demonstrates that the answer is not found within a fund balance, but rather in a relationship balance, if you will. Rather than feeling completely isolated, if he was able to feel connected in some way to his district, he could further build relationships and unity to ensure that his teachers and students had what they need to be successful.

Overall, there was evidence of extremely strong relationships found in the two superior-rated facilities, the Greta Olive Juvenile Justice Academy and the Philip I. Juvenile Justice Residential Center. These positive relationships fostered high expectations and helped to provide more resources and support to the educators and their students.

Expectations Cross-Case Discussion

Rubie-Davies, Peterson, Irving, Widdowson, and Dixon recalled a theory that has been around for decades: "[W]hen teachers expected their students to do well they interacted with them in ways that led to their expectations being fulfilled."[2] It was evident that the educators within each facility held different expectations of themselves, their peers, the juvenile justice staff and their students. Expectations ranged from David's goal to see a student improve three to four grade levels during the six months at Greta Olive to Susan's hope that the youth will "learn something" during their time at Hubert B. In the facilities with higher expectations for students, the educators recognized the need to also incorporate incentives to further motivate the youth. In the classrooms where expectations were explicit, students spent more time on task and fewer disruptions ensued.

The administrators and teachers at Greta Olive and Philip I. expected the teachers were there because they wanted to work with this specific population. They also expect the educators to be experienced and intrinsically motivated. The teachers at these facilities applied to teach there and went through a formal process to be hired. Continuity of program is valued at each of these facilities and is evident as most teachers have been there for at least 10 and 4 years, respectively. These teachers expressed their passion for working in this setting. And, much like my research on juvenile justice education, when you have a passion for something, you joyfully put forth your effort to pursue your passion. When students are around teachers who love what they do and demonstrate a desire to work specifically with this population, students feel connected and seek to meet or exceed the stated expectations. Particularly in this setting, where most of the outside distractions have been removed, it behooves us to focus on ensuring that incarcerated youth have experienced and intrinsically motivated teachers who are able to motivate their students while maintaining high expectations and continually celebrating their progress.

Principal Rae is struggling to find this type of dedication along with qualified educators who can fill the teaching positions at Gladys C. She recognizes that Vicki has her J. D. degree and believes she will not be teaching there much longer. Vicki also shared with me that she was initially planning to teach in a traditional school within Walter County Public Schools, but when they had a hiring freeze, she applied to work with Principal Rae because she "needed a job." Donna was teaching in a substituting capacity with no intent to apply for a full-time position. She has an Ed.D. degree with intentions to teach at the collegiate level in the near future.

Unfortunately, at Hubert B., Principal Patrick's strategy for rotating teachers every two years, reasoning that they will burn out otherwise, does not provide a similar level of motivation and experience embodied at Greta Olive and Philip I. Furthermore, because the teachers don't have a choice about whether to be there, the likelihood is further decreased that the students are getting the very best education possible. Hubert B.'s classrooms had the least percentage of students on task and the highest percentage of classroom disruptions.

Different from the every two-year turnover at Hubert B. and lack of stability at the Gladys C., the educators at Greta Olive and Philip I. want to be there and have multiple years of teaching experience. This allows them to feel empowered, and they revealed a strong sense of pride and passion. One example of this is with James (Philip I.), the ESE support facilitator stating he wants to get an additional certification for his own edification; yet, Principal Rae (Gladys C.) complained that she is unable to find teachers who are multi-certified and believes that having multiple certifications is an unrealistic expectation.

Principal Patrick believes that he has too many responsibilities to truly be effective. In addition to overseeing Hubert B., he is principal of an 1,100-student alternative middle/high school and is also responsible for multiple programs, including four additional juvenile justice sites. Although each of these sites should be getting the best possible resources available, he shared the conflict that arises when he looks for what teachers he should place at what facilities. He continually decides to place who he believes are his best teachers at the alternative school. This causes the youth at Hubert B. to receive teachers who Principal Patrick believes are substandard.

Principal Rae (Gladys C.) is in a similar situation, as she is principal of an alternative middle school and is also responsible for 11 programs, including DJJ sites. She expects that she will not be as effective as she could be with her current responsibility load, even though, like Principal Patrick, she also has three assistant principals who provide support. She has found it difficult to staff this facility with highly qualified teachers.

With the exception of Mae at Greta Olive, the math teachers believe they each went through many "trial and error" periods before coming up with a strategy to address teaching multiple levels of math during one class period. This was probably not a concern for Mae, because, as she shared, she spent years in facilities such as Greta Olive as a volunteer and teacher's aide, so she was able to learn effective strategies on how to go about teaching math effectively with this population. However, although Mary (Hubert B.), Vicki (Gladys C.), and Israel (Philip I.) have figured out a system that works for now, they expect that they will receive support to be more effective for teaching math to their incarcerated youth. If the math teachers in this setting are not well equipped, how are incarcerated youth truly expected to meet or exceed math standards?

Each setting is unique, even with expectations for lesson plans. Some are collected; some aren't. It's interesting to see how little writing is expected for the educators at Greta Olive, yet how many components are expected for the teachers to write at Gladys C. It's important to note that despite the long lesson plans written by the teachers at Gladys C., what I observed during the execution of the lessons were not indicated in the lesson plans. This finding emphasizes the importance of revisiting expectations, specifically the best approach and requirements for teachers and also the accountability structures that must be in place to maximize opportunities for planning components like lesson plans.

The educators at all four facilities expect the juvenile justice staff to be effective in their roles of maintaining order in the classrooms. The educators at Greta Olive and Philip I. believe that the juvenile justice staff do a good job, overall, maintaining order. David (Greta Olive) shared that he feels that the juvenile justice staff are too demanding and negative toward the students; but his example also demonstrated that they attempt to maintain order so that all students have an opportunity to learn. Although James cited some past negative experiences with some of the juvenile justice workers at Philip I., both he and Israel shared their contentment with the current juvenile justice staff, who maintain order, allowing teachers to teach.

Donna (Gladys C.) and Susan (Hubert B.) shared that they believe that the juvenile justice staff are too lenient with the students. This becomes problematic when teachers are trying to maintain order in the classroom so that they can teach. During my classroom observations, the juvenile justice staff at Gladys C. appeared to be more diligent and clearer about their roles of support and what was expected than the juvenile justice staff at Hubert B. There were still a significant amount of disruptions that occurred in both learning environments—an average of 1 disruption occurred every 52.8 seconds at Hubert B. and every 67 seconds at Gladys C.

It was very interesting to note that each facility had at least one educator who believes that it doesn't take much to be a highly effective teacher. David at Greta Olive, Principal Patrick at Hubert B., Principal Rae and Donna at Gladys C., and James at Philip I. each shared that all they or teachers need are the basics: a few books, paper, pencils, and a chalkboard, to teach effectively. Principal Patrick and James, however, included another element that they believe is imperative—the ability to motivate the youth. Most people involved with education would agree with the importance of motivating students, but agreeing on the items needed to be an effective teacher would perhaps generate a greater dichotomy. The fact that they believe not much is needed yet again emphasizes the all-too-common push for more money and more funding for schools without a guarantee for high student achievement.

The ability to motivate the youth through use of explicit instructions and incentives was evident during my observations at Gladys C. and Philip I. At Gladys C., Vicki used the computers to incentivize the youth. After students completed their math assignment, they were able to go to the computer to play solitaire, pinball, and other non-academic games. Although the youth looked forward to being on the computer, almost 55 minutes of potential instructional time were lost. Vicki sees the need to incentivize students, but incentives should not hinder learners from missing much-needed instruction. Additionally, the math class with the highest level of participation—100%, or 7 out of 7 students—began by the juvenile justice staff member reminding the students of the classroom expectations and having the youth read the chart to themselves as he pointed to the words.

The educators at Philip I. also believe in the importance of motivating their youth. Fortunately, they use strategies that do not cause their youth to lose out on valuable instructional time. Two key expectations they have are that the students will keep their heads up at all times and complete their work. The possible rewards students can earn each month for following these expectations are also posted in the classrooms. The teachers believe that the way they deliver their instruction and the resources they provide for the youth also serve as motivators. The two computers in Juanita's classroom were used each lesson for youth who were either advanced or struggling with corresponding computer software to challenge and support their learning. The youth were also able to self-select their texts. In the math classroom, Israel allowed two students to come to the board and work through problems that were causing them difficulty. In both classes, with 18 and 19 students, up to 100% of the youth were on task during the reading and math lessons. Their students lived up to the established expectations.

Unfortunately, at Hubert B., the educators believe that their students have too many issues to be forced or expected to participate in class and nothing was used to motivate or incentivize the youth. The highest amount of students on task during any part of a lesson was 50%, or 4 out of 8 students, in Karen's reading class, and 63%, or 5 out of 8 students, in Mary's math class.

Resources Cross-Case Discussion

The proper resources and support are essential for the school leaders, educators and students to progress. According to Lynch, "Allocating and developing resources to support improvement in teaching and learning are fundamental leadership challenges."[3] With this challenge, he further emphasizes the importance of looking at all factors that affect learning outcomes for youth. "An abundance of money and time, for example, without the knowledge, motivation, and expertise of teachers (human capital) does little to maximize desired learning opportunities created for students."[4] More students were on task and less disruptions occurred in the facilities where the school districts provided ample resources for the juvenile justice school leader, educators, and students and placed an emphasis on support structures such as professional development, technology, knowledgeable and caring educators, and juvenile justice support. There are tremendous implications for this finding. I'm reminded about Neila A. Connor's book, *If You Don't Feed the Teachers They Eat the Students!* When people feel supported, they can in turn serve as a resource and support.

Both Principal Alexander (Greta Olive) and Principal Richard (Philip I.) believe there are ample resources and support structures in place. They are able to take advantage of professional development opportunities and they feel supported overall, by their school districts. Additionally, their experience and knowledge working with this population proves resourceful. Principal Richard believes he was effectively groomed and mentored for this position, while he served as the assistant principal. In the same manner in which they feel supported, they want to ensure the necessary support structures are also in place for their teachers and students.

Unfortunately, this is not the case for Principal Patrick (Hubert B.) or Principal Rae (Gladys C.). Principal Patrick acknowledges that the district provides the funding, particularly because of the quality assurance reviews, but he believes he works in isolation and does not have effective resources or support as he attempts to adequately oversee his alternative middle/high school and the other DJJ facilities and programs for which he is responsible. Although Principal Rae believes she receives some support, particularly in the area of marketing and being able to hire certified candidates when the district is in a hiring freeze, she feels as if she works in isolation. When she presents her problems at the district level, it is evident that they do not understand the incredible challenges she faces, and she is left to feel as if she is on her own.

Professional development opportunities, staff meetings, and lunch and common planning times are all potential resources and support mechanisms for the teachers at all four facilities. At Hubert B. and Gladys C., professional development topics are selected for the teachers and are general topics, not specific to the unique population they teach. At Greta Olive, specific DJJ professional development topics are provided. And, at Philip I., the teachers completed a survey and identified the topics they felt would be critical for them to learn more about, including gender-based instruction, right/left-brain learning, and gang awareness. Furthermore, Philip I. teachers who are aspiring administrators take the lead on reaching out to and bringing in some of the facilitators for the professional development sessions. Completing the survey, helping coordinate the professional development topics, and receiving the requested trainings help the educators at Philip I. feel empowered. Overall, the students at Philip I. displayed a sense of accomplishment.

Three of the facilities (all except Greta Olive) have early release days for professional development. The only facility that had a scheduled early release professional development session while I was visiting was Gladys C. With Donna, the reading substitute teacher who had been there for five weeks, and Vicki, the math teacher in her second year at the facility, I was certain there would be myriad professional development opportunities planned for their professional growth. Unfortunately, however, there were none. Although Principal Rae decided to launch a new online reading program for the youth at this facility and offer training for the teachers at the sites where this program would be implemented, Donna was not asked to participate in the training because she is a substitute teacher. This was a missed opportunity for growth as it's an early release day and she would still be within her contracted time. Moreover, Vicki informed me that neither she nor the print shop teacher would be heading to the alternative school for training. She said they received word on the morning of the early release professional development session that training was only scheduled for teachers who would be implementing the new online reading program and for teachers who were in their first year of teaching—another missed opportunity for development.

While the educators at Greta Olive and Philip I. believe they were well prepared to teach in these facilities, the educators at Hubert B. and Gladys C. wished they had received some type of training prior to teaching at their respective sites. Aside from the experiences some may have brought with them to the facility, overall, the educators indicated that they received no prior training for working with incarcerated youth. And much of what they learned was only a result of what they experienced

firsthand with the youth in this setting. The participants indicated trainings that would have been most helpful before beginning their roles as
teachers in this environment. Specific requested professional development topics included how to work collaboratively with the juvenile justice staff, how to motivate and engage disenfranchised youth, and how
to teach multiple content areas and ages within the same classroom.

In addition to professional development, Principal Alexander (Greta
Olive) and Principal Rae (Gladys C.) also purchased books as resources
for their teachers. It's interesting, however, how they felt these would
serve as resources. Principal Alexander shared that he would use his as
a book study. This would allow for rich discourse to potentially further
promote camaraderie and improve teachers' practices. Principal Rae
explained that she thought it was a good match for their new evaluation tool, so she bought each teacher a copy. Through this approach, she
presumes the teachers will be motivated to find the time and have the
desire to read the book on their own. While it is a potential resource, if
it's not presented in the appropriate format, it could end up untouched,
like the SMART boards that are still in boxes in the Gladys C. classrooms.

While Principal Patrick believes he is providing additional resources
and support for his teachers and students at Hubert B. with the three
ancillary support staff, most often, when I asked the teachers what the
support staff's roles were, they replied, "I don't know." That indicates a
high probability that they haven't received the types of resources Principal Patrick intended for them to receive. This finding also magnifies the
need for camaraderie and accountability.

There were a variety of educational courses and programs at the facilities that provided resources for the incarcerated youth—options that
may help the youth be successful once they transition back to their
communities. Students at Greta Olive have been able to participate in
an educational program that includes their core courses, an employability class and a vocational class. Kyle worked hard over the past couple of
years to implement the NCCER vocational program to ensure students
who take and pass the vocational course receive their NCCER card, a
national certification to work on any construction or industrial site. At
Gladys C., Principal Rae believed students needed something in addition to their core courses and the print shop elective and introduced
the NCCER vocational program to the youth this year. Principal Richard (Philip I.) was eager to share the unique programs they offer their
students. In addition to the Home Builders program that the juvenile
justice facility helped to establish, they offer a computer mentoring program, a dog training program, and, for the first time, physical education

214 Educating Incarcerated Youth

and driver's education for their youth. Unfortunately, Principal Patrick (Hubert B.) does not believe he is providing the adequate resources for the youth at this facility. He believes, ideally, he should be able to provide vocational or career-technical classes, in addition to their course courses. Despite this desire, and the abundance of funding, Principal Patrick feels as if his hands are tied and believes that without the appropriate relationship with the facility leader, the students will continue to not be afforded the resources they need to be successful.

Kyle, at Greta Olive, Mary at Hubert B., and Donna at Gladys C. discussed how much their students like to draw, yet there is no formal art class provided for these youth. Based on what they've shared, an ideal resource would be an art class or art program for the incarcerated youth. In traditional school settings, when budgets are tight, art is one of the first programs to get cut. These educators expressed that many of these disenfranchised youth are artistically inclined and would thrive with such programs in place.

The computers were being used as an academic resource in only one of the three sites I observed. While computers have the potential to serve as a tremendous resource for students, some educators choose to use them; others do not fully use this technology. At Philip I., Juanita uses the two computers in her classroom each day to provide the youth with programs that both challenge and support their learning. At Gladys C., Vicki shared her frustration, that although she has enough computers for a one-to-one student to computer ratio, without consistent Internet access, she feels like she can't maximize the computers to differentiate students' learning. She instead uses the computers as incentives for the youth to complete their work and allows them to play non-academic games for the remaining duration of the class. During one of my classroom observations, students had more time to play on the computer than Vicki spent teaching the lesson and the students spent completing their assignments. Mary and Karen at Hubert B. don't believe they have the support they need from the juvenile justice staff to help with the monitoring of the computers, so they don't use the computers at all. Karen stated that she asked for the computers to be removed from her classroom. Again, resources are available yet are not always being fully utilized.

Mentors are provided for the youth at Greta Olive. Principal Alexander shared that he solicits their assistance and he also has community members come in and offer their help. He cited two powerful examples of how mentors can effectively work with the youth in this environment. It was interesting to hear the educators at Hubert B. and Gladys C. share their expectations that the incarcerated youth would benefit from having mentors from the community. They believe mentors would serve as invaluable resources for them, perhaps in the same way Principal Alexander and his students have already experienced.

The responsibilities differed significantly between the principals who oversee the educational services provided at Greta Olive and Philip I., the two superior-rated facilities, and the principals who oversee the educational services at Hubert B., rated satisfactory, and Gladys C., rated marginal satisfactory. Principal Patrick (Hubert B.) and Principal Rae (Gladys C.) who are responsible for overseeing alternative schools and more facilities than just juvenile justice programs, were perceived as providing less resources and support for their teachers and students than Principal Alexander (Greta Olive) or Principal Richard (Philip I.).

Upon closer examination of the data, the two school districts with the largest number of African American youth are Walter County Public Schools, where Gladys C. is located, with 45%; and Carmen County Public Schools, where Hubert B. is located, with 40%. More than 50% of the students in both of these school districts qualify for Free or Reduced Price Meals (FRPM). This means that one out of every two children in these school districts is considered a child in poverty, or one with a low socioeconomic status. Yet Principal Rae and Principal Patrick are given an inordinate amount of responsibilities as school leaders within their districts. Both are responsible for overseeing the educational services at alternative middle and/or high schools and 10 to 11 additional programs or facilities.

The stark contrast appears when you look at the data for the Milton County Public Schools and Joyce County Public Schools, where the percentage of African American students is much less. In Joyce County, more than 50% of their students qualify for Free or Reduced Price Meals (FRPM), but the African American student population is approximately 20%. Principal Richard is responsible for overseeing 11 sites that encompass juvenile justice or similar programs. Although the number of facilities he is responsible for is still significant, he is not given the added responsibility of running an alternative or traditional school. In Milton County, where the number of African American students is just above 10%, and just over 30% of the students qualify for Free or Reduced Price Meals (FRPM), Principal Alexander is responsible for the seven juvenile justice facilities—no additional programs, no additional schools.

This dichotomy between the leadership responsibilities provides yet another example of the opportunity gap that continues to persist. It also demonstrates the need for school districts to really look at the structures they have in place to determine if the expectations and the resources provided yield leader, teacher, and student success or failure. If failure, the appropriate organizational, structural changes must be made.

Accountability Cross-Case Discussion

According to Abelmann, Elmore, Even, Kenyon, and Marshall, "Accountability mechanisms are, literally, the variety of formal and informal ways by which people in schools *give an account* of their actions to someone in a position of formal authority, inside or outside the school."[5] There were accountability mechanisms identified within each of the four juvenile justice residential facilities and outside the facilities. The types of inside accountability included master schedules developed and posted, the administrator visiting classrooms to hold teachers accountable and teachers holding each other and their students accountable. Outside accountability measures included the Florida Department of Juvenile Justice requirements, the state's end-of-course exams, the Florida Comprehensive Achievement Test (FCAT), NCLB requirements, and the JJEEP Quality Assurance reviews.

The two superior-rated facilities featured in this study, Greta Olive and Philip I., both have explicit ways for holding stakeholders accountable. At Philip I., a facility with more than 100 youth, there is a master schedule provided to all the teachers that includes the times, locations, and courses taught for every teacher and in what classrooms the ESE support facilitators are located. This mechanism helps to ensure that the teachers are where they are supposed to be. Furthermore, at Greta Olive, the master schedule includes the teachers' teaching schedule, a list of the students' names by class and identifies students who are banned from using the computer. Measures like these are clear, result in less ambiguity, and allow people to be held accountable by stating who should be where teaching what. Furthermore, instead of all students' losing the use of the computers for one or a few students who have abused their technology privileges, only those names identified in red are banned.

At Hubert B., only the class periods were posted, which noted the Group A or Group B rotation. Teachers and students were not listed on the schedules that were posted. There was much less accountability at this facility as Susan, the ESE support facilitator, was allowed to create her own schedule. It wasn't until she arrived at a classroom that the teachers or students realized that she was there to give support. Moreover, she indicated that if a student needed her for the entire day, she would make herself available for him, even though this meant that the other 45 to 50 students would not receive any additional ESE support that day. Susan, however, believes that she is being held accountable, particularly by the ESE specialist who visits the site and asks students about the ESE support they receive. Additionally, instead of having an accountability mechanism in place similar to what Greta Olive has established, that identifies the youth who cannot be on the computers; at Hubert B., Mary and Karen decided they would not let any of their students use the computers and instead asked that the computers be removed from their classrooms.

Gladys C. provides a schedule with the classes and students' names. However, the reading and math teachers decide for themselves what days they would teach what subjects, even when this results in the students completing their assignments within the first 40–50 minutes of class, allowing them to go to the computers to play non-educational games for the remaining 55 minutes of class. Vicki has enough time to teach a 50-minute math and 50-minute science block to her students each day, and Donna has enough time for a 50-minute reading/English and 50-minute social studies period for each group of students each day. However, they opt to have a 105-minute period of math or science and a 105-minute period of reading/English or social studies. There is no accountability in place to make certain this decision is helping to ensure more youth are receiving a higher quality education.

Educators at three of the facilities discussed the new teacher evaluation tool and the new structure for merit pay to hold teachers accountable for being highly effective. Across the board, they wondered how this was going to work, particularly when their students come from all over the state of Florida and are only with them for an average of six months. One principal discussed a plan to give the teachers more points on their evaluation, with the notion that the expectations are unfair.

The No Child Left Behind Highly Qualified Teacher requirement is also an accountability structure designed to have a highly certified, highly qualified teacher in every classroom. Principal Alexander (Greta Olive) and Principal Richard (Philip I.) boasted all their teachers are both highly qualified and highly certified. Principal Rae (Gladys C.), however, shared her frustration with this requirement. She believes this is an unrealistic expectation in this environment and doesn't believe that she should be held accountable for maintaining the highly qualified teaching requirements at this facility.

The educators at Hubert B. and Gladys C. felt that it was difficult to hold their students accountable. If they didn't want to work, or if they wanted to act up, there were little or no consequences. Although Karen

(Hubert B.) shared how supportive the case managers were, she chose not to write up a student because she felt that the juvenile justice staff were in the classroom, observed what happened and still did nothing. She also stated she shouldn't bother going through the trouble, because nothing would be done to cause the youth to alter his behavior.

The Florida Department of Juvenile Justice holds each facility accountable for testing the youth when they enter the facility and before they exit the facility. Students are also held accountable for taking the state's end-of-course exams and the Florida Comprehensive Achievement Test (FCAT). Educators at Greta Olive and Philip I. welcome these assessment tools and shared their desires to help the youth pass these assessments, while educators at Hubert B. and Gladys C. believe that it is unreasonable to expect the youth to pass these assessments.

The JJEEP Quality Assurance process was in place from 1998 to 2010 to hold the juvenile justice educators accountable for the educational programs provided for the incarcerated youth. Uncertain about what the expectations are with this accountability mechanism, which is no longer provided, the principals talked about continuing to use these standards to ensure that they are providing the youth what the FLDOE and JJEEP deemed a high-quality educational program.

As evidenced in this cross-case analysis for the four sites, my findings suggest that incarcerated youth have a greater opportunity to be exposed to a high-quality education when there are strong relationships, high expectations, appropriate resources, and efficient accountability mechanisms. In addition to the four themes, my study also revealed the types of instructional practices that were used, the frequency students were brought late to class, the number of students on task at any given time during a lesson, and the frequency of classroom disruptions. Table 6 on page 219 provides a comparative chart of observed factors that affect the quality of instruction for the incarcerated youth at the three facilities where observations took place.

At Hubert B., where relationships were lacking, expectations were low, there was a lack of needed resources, and accountability was amiss, the educators employed direct instruction, round-robin reading, and one-on-one instruction. The students were brought to each class an average 14 minutes late. The highest percentage of students on task was 50%, or 4 out of 8 students, in reading and 63%, or 5 out of 8 students, in math. An average of 1 disruption occurred every 52.8 seconds during the youths' instructional time.

At Gladys C., where relationships were positive, expectations were divergent, some resources were provided—yet accountability was lacking—and

Table 6 Comparative chart of observed factors affecting the quality of education provided for the incarcerated youth at four Florida juvenile justice residential facilities

Facility	Four Themes	Positive/ Negative	Observed Factors Impacting the Quality of Education for Incarcerated Youth
Greta Olive Juvenile Justice Facility	Relationships	Positive (+)	Not Permitted to Observe
	Expectations	Positive (+)	
	Resources	Positive (+)	
	Accountability	Positive (+)	
Hubert B. Juvenile Justice Residential Facility	Relationships	Negative (−)	**Instructional Strategies** **Employed:** Direct instruction, round-robin reading, one-on-one
	Expectations	Negative (−)	**Students' Lateness:** Students were brought to each class an average 14 minutes late, causing students to miss 20% of their 75-minute learning time per class.
	Resources	Positive/ Negative (+/−)	**Students on Task:** The lowest percentage of students on task was 21%, or 3 out of 14 students, in reading and 40%, or 2 out of 5 students, in math. The highest percentage of students on task was 50%, or 4 out of 8 students, in reading and 63%, or 5 out of 8 students, in math.
	Accountability	Negative (−)	**Number of Disruptions:** During the instructional time, an average of 1 disruption occurred every 52.8 seconds.

(continued)

Table 6   (continued)

Facility	Four Themes	Positive/Negative	Observed Factors Impacting the Quality of Education for Incarcerated Youth
Gladys C. Juvenile Justice Academy	Relationships	Positive (+)	**Instructional Strategies** **Employed:** Direct instruction, round-robin reading, one-on-one
	Expectations	Positive/Negative (+/−)	**Students' Lateness:** Students were brought to each class an average 3.5 minutes late, causing students to miss 4% of their 105-minute learning time per class. **Students on Task:** The lowest percentage of students on task was 40%, or 2 out of 5 students, in reading and 16%, or 1 out of 6 students, in math. The highest percentage of students on task was 57%, or 4 out of 7 students, in reading and
	Resources	Positive/Negative (+/−)	100%, or 7 out of 7 students, in math. **Number of Disruptions:** During the instructional time, an average of 1 disruption occurred every 67 seconds.
	Accountability	Negative (−)	
Philip I. Juvenile Justice Residential Center	Relationships	Positive (+)	**Instructional Strategies** **Employed:** Direct instruction, guided practice, assessments (checking for understanding), self-selection of texts, two-on-one and one-on-one
	Expectations	Positive (+)	**Students' Lateness:** Students were brought to each class an average 5.8 minutes late, causing students to miss 8% of their 75-minute learning time per class. **Students on Task:** The lowest percentage of students on task was 84%, or 16 out of 19 students, in reading and 83%, or 15 out of 18 students, in math. The highest percentage of students on task was 100%, or 19 out of 19 students, in
	Resources	Positive (+)	reading and 100%, or 14 out of 14 and 18 out of 18 students, in math.
	Accountability	Positive (+)	**Number of disruptions:** During the instructional time, an average of 1 disruption occurred every 2 minutes and 50.52 seconds.

the educators employed direct instruction, round-robin reading, and one-on-one instruction. The students were brought to each class an average 3.5 minutes late. The highest percentage of students on task was 57%, or 4 out of 7 students, in reading and 100%, or 7 out of 7, students in math. An average of 1 disruption occurred every 67 seconds during the youths' instructional time.

At Philip I., where relationships were strong, expectations were explicit and high, adequate resources were provided, and effective accountability mechanisms were present, the educators employed direct instruction, guided practice, assessments (checking for understanding), self-selection of texts, and two-on-one and one-on-one instruction. The students were brought to each class an average of 5.8 minutes late. The highest percentage of students on task was 100%, or 19 out of 19 students, in reading and 100%, or 14 out of 14 and 18 out of 18 students, in math. An average of 1 disruption occurred every 2 minutes and 50.52 seconds during the youths' instructional time.

This data demonstrates that in this environment, there will be disruptions, but with positive relationships, high expectations, adequate resources and effective accountability, disruptions can be minimalized. This data also demonstrates that the lateness of youths being brought to class can be diminished and that even with a large class size of primarily disenfranchised youth, students can be engaged with their work, keep their heads up, and complete their class assignments. It may not be a perfect solution, but focusing on these four themes is certainly a good start.

8
Implications and Conclusion

Implications for Practice

This study provides several implications for practice. Juvenile justice educators need ongoing professional development specific to working with youth in a juvenile justice setting. Additionally, pre-service training is needed for educators who choose to teach incarcerated youth. Although a desire to work with these youth is optimal, passion alone will not ensure that educators are highly effective in this environment. Furthermore, joint training for juvenile justice providers/staff and the educational staff must be provided to ensure collaboration and a shared understanding to better serve the youth and provide them with the high-quality education to which they are entitled.

There must also be an effective and easily accessible venue for juvenile justice educators to learn more about effective teaching practices with this population of youth. Data warehouses, websites, conferences, and site visits should be among the resources in place for juvenile justice educators to learn more about the effective practices taking place within juvenile justice facilities both nationally and internationally.

Substitute teachers need training, too. Particularly when there are early release professional development days and substitutes are contracted for those days, substitute teachers should be expected and required to participate in professional development sessions to further assist them and to ensure that they are learning effective strategies for providing an optimal learning environment for their youth.

Teacher preparation programs should provide at least one course specifically dedicated for working with disenfranchised youth and the effective methods and strategies that can be used to reengage these youth in the learning process. Because of the high number of incarcerated youth with special needs, college special education courses could provide lessons that link effective teaching strategies when working with delinquent youth.

Juvenile justice leaders and teachers throughout our nation and internationally can use the four themes that emerged from this study as a guide to determine the areas they may need to augment to ensure that they are providing their youth with a high-quality education. If they determine that the four themes are positive, they can begin to think about and plan ways to further enhance these aspects of their educational programs. Necessary conversations, strategic plans, and training can be in place to address, as needed, any of the four themes that may not be as positive so that the incarcerated youth can be consistently exposed to a high-quality education.

Last, parents should be made aware of the educational programs afforded to their adjudicated children before the youths' incarceration. This will serve as an additional means to hold juvenile justice facilities accountable. Parents can ask informed questions during the treatment team meetings and ensure that their children are receiving the high-quality education to which all incarcerated youth should be entitled.

Implications for Policies

This research study provides several policy implications. Only 65% of our nation's juvenile justice facilities offer an educational program for all its incarcerated youth.[1] Just as there are state compulsory school attendance laws, there must be policies enacted to ensure that all juvenile justice facilities are also mandated to provide all incarcerated youth with an education. There must be high-quality educational programs for all incarcerated youth, and any youth who enter a juvenile facility without a GED should be required to attend classes. Youth who enter the facility with a GED should also be provided with an educational program, including college courses and hands-on training. If society expects incarcerated youth to be transformed when they return to their communities, these youth must be exposed to a high-quality education while they are incarcerated, in addition to the other resources provided by the juvenile justice facilities, such as counseling and therapy.

This study also provides evidence that there is a need for high-quality assurance measures to ensure that educators and students have what they need to provide a high-quality education. JJEEP began in 1998 to assist the Florida Department of Education with this task, but the state did not renew JJEEP's discretionary grant after the 2009–2010 school year. Facilities such as Gladys C. that had multiple corrective action plans, and Hubert B. that had multiple issues, as evidenced from this study, must be held accountable. Therefore, our nation, states, and the world need policies that will hold our juvenile justice facilities accountable for ensuring that their incarcerated youth are being provided with a high-quality education. This must extend beyond NCLB requirements. There is a need for high-quality assurance site visits to truly assess the quality of the facilities' educational programs.

At the local level, policies must be established where the partnerships between juvenile justice programs and the educational service providers are mandated to communicate and collaborate. Expectations, resources, and an accountability structure will be required from each state or region to ensure that its facilities are working collaboratively with the individuals who are responsible for providing the youth with academic support.

There should be policies for facilities that are awarded contracts. There should be a minimum requirement for the layout and size—including square footage per youth, classroom space, accommodations, bathroom locations, and cleanliness. And youth should not be permitted to clean their dorm or unit, or any part of the facility, during their instructional day.

Implications for Research

Future research is needed to determine whether, on a larger scale, in other states and countries, a similar study of juvenile justice education would yield the same four themes that emerged in this study—and, if this occurs, what the implications are for educating incarcerated youth. A similar study could also be conducted in traditional or alternative school settings with similar student demographic data to determine whether the same themes would emerge and how this data might inform the educators' practices for providing their youth with a high-quality education.

Research is also needed to determine how support structures differ or are similar when juvenile justice facilities are supported by urban, suburban, or rural school districts. An analysis of the varying support structures could explain the disparate outcomes for youth in these settings.

Consistent data sets of incarcerated youth are critical to truly compare demographic data and analyze the resources provided within our juvenile justice facilities. We must find a way to have consistent data comparisons of our incarcerated youth, regardless of the type of facility in which they are housed.

There is also a desperate need for math research to be conducted in juvenile facilities. As of 2005, no math studies have been conducted.[2] The math teachers who participated in this study were left to "figure things out" for themselves, including what they thought was the best way to teach multiple students different levels of math while youth aged 13–19 were in the same classroom. Perhaps, as the teachers in this study shared, there are universal topics, and although I am not advocating for more textbooks, researchers need to begin to identify practices that have shown positive student achievement while teaching multiple levels of math.

Research should also be conducted to identify the ideal credentials and characteristics of special needs teachers in a juvenile justice setting. Similar to the teachers at Greta Olive and the special needs teacher at Philip I., should all the teachers be certified in the content they teach and have special education certification? Researchers should seek to explore whether teachers certified in special education and their content provide better support and a higher quality of instruction for their incarcerated students compared to teachers who are only certified in their content or special needs teachers who are only certified as special needs teachers yet have no content specific training or certification.

Research should be conducted on effective technology tools that can be used in this environment. Knowing the challenges of using technology with this population, research must be conducted and appropriate technology developed to further enhance incarcerated students' learning.

Finally, the ideal educational leadership model yielding optimal effectiveness must also be investigated. My research indicates that the principals who are responsible for overseeing an alternative school in addition to juvenile justice facilities and other programs are perceived as providing fewer resources and support for their teachers and students. At Greta Olive, where Principal Alexander is only responsible for the juvenile justice programs, he is able to expend all his energies at these facilities to ensure that the youth there receive the high-quality education to which they are entitled. Research should be conducted on the responsibilities of juvenile justice leaders, including the number, types, and quality of facilities they oversee.

Conclusion

Teaching incarcerated youth is not for the faint or weary. It is an arduous task. This study focuses on four Florida juvenile justice residential facilities. Similar to school effectiveness studies conducted in traditional school settings (highlighted in this book's preface), my research suggests that there are very clear indicators of what should be in place for incarcerated youth to receive a high-quality education. Based on my study, the four components that matter most in a juvenile justice setting are **relationships**, particularly between the educational staff and the juvenile justice staff, but equally important among the educators themselves, between the educators and the students, and between the educators and their local school district and outside entities. **Expectations** are also important—teachers must be highly qualified, be certified in their areas of teaching, want to be there, be able to motivate their students, and have clear expectations for their students. One of the most important expectations posted was at the Philip I. Juvenile Justice Residential Center, where students were required to keep their heads up at all time and complete their work. **Resources** are also critical for all stakeholders, and particularly for school leaders, teachers, and students. Principal Alexander and Principal Richard feel supported and are thus able to impart the level of support they receive to their teachers, which further extends to the students. Adequate resources and support are imperative for the teachers to be well equipped and for the students to receive the quality resources they deserve. Finally, **accountability** measures are important, both within and outside the facility, to ensure that juvenile justice educators are providing their students with a high-quality education.

Fortunately for the incarcerated youth in the state of Florida, accountability for the juvenile justice education programs came in the form of the quality assurance visits. Unfortunately, however, the state of Florida chose to no longer fund the work provided by the Juvenile Justice Educational Enhancement Program (JJEEP), and although the juvenile justice facilities within this study continue to use the old quality assurance standards to measure their own effectiveness, they are unsure what this change in accountability structure means for them and their students. As of 2012, no quality assurance akin to the site visits (interviews, observations, and review of documentation) conducted earlier by JJEEP exists.

In addition to the four themes, my study also revealed the types of instructional practices that were used, the extent to which students were brought late to class, the number of students on task at any given time during a lesson, and the frequency of classroom disruptions. My findings suggest that incarcerated youth have a greater opportunity to be exposed to a high-quality education when there are strong relationships,

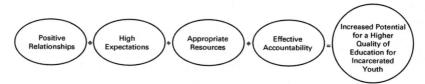

Figure 1   Four major themes that affect the quality of education provided for incarcerated youth in four Florida juvenile justice residential facilities

high expectations, appropriate resources, and effective accountability mechanisms. As indicated in Figure 1 on page 226, the more positive these collective themes are, the greater the potential for the incarcerated youth to be exposed to a high-quality education.

It is my hope that this study will serve as a catalyst to ensure that all incarcerated youth are exposed to a high-quality educational program each day and that juvenile justice educators have the vital relationships, expectations, resources, and accountability to provide all incarcerated youth with a high-quality juvenile justice education.

Notes

Preface

1 O'Cummings, M., Bardack, S., & Gonsoulin, S. (2010). Issue brief: The importance of literacy for youth involved in the juvenile justice system. The National Evaluation and Technical Assistance Center. Retrieved on January 21, 2011 from http://www.neglected-delinquent.org/nd/docs/literacy_brief_20100120.pdf.
2 Read, N. W., & O'Cummings, M. (2011). Fact sheet: Juvenile justice education. The National Evaluation and Technical Assistance Center. Retrieved on February 3, 2012 from http://www.neglected-delinquent.org/nd/docs/NDFactSheet.pdf.
3 Payne, C. M. (2008). *So Much Reform, So Little Change: The Persistence of Failure in Urban Schools*. Cambridge, MA: Harvard Education Press.
4 Schultz, B. D. (2008). Spectacular Things Happen Along the Way: Lessons from an Urban Classroom. New York, NY: Teachers College Press.

Chapter 1

1 Platt, J. S., Casey, R. E., & Faessel, R. T. (2006). The need for a paradigmatic change in juvenile correctional education. *Preventing School Failure, 51*(1), 31–38 (pg. 31).
2 Black, S. (2005). Learning behind bars. *American School Board Journal*, September, 50–52.
3 Cannon, A., & Beiser, V. (2004). Juvenile injustice. *U.S. News and World Report, 137*(4), 28–32.
4 Leone, P. E., Krezmien, M., Mason, L., & Meisel, S. M. (2005). Organizing and delivering empirically based literacy instruction to incarcerated youth. *Exceptionality, 13*(2), 89–102.
5 Foley, R. M., & Gao, J. (2002). Correctional education programs serving incarcerated juveniles: A status report. *Journal of Correctional Education, 53*(4), 131–138. Houchins, D. E., Puckett-Patterson, D., Crosby, S., Shippen, M. E., & Jolivette, K. (2009). Barriers and facilitators to providing incarcerated youth with a quality education. *Preventing School Failure, 53*(3), 159–166.
6 Wilder, S. (2004). Educating youthful offenders in a youth development center. *Journal of Addictions and Offender Counseling, 24*, 82–91.
7 Foley, R. M. (2001). Academic characteristics of incarcerated youth and correctional educational programs: A literature review. *Journal of Emotional and Behavioral Disorders, 9*(4), 248–259 (pg. 259).
8 Juvenile Justice Educational Enhancement Program (2005). 2005 Annual Report to the Florida Department of Education, *Chapter 5: Teacher Retention and Qualifications*, 81–98 (pg. 96).

9 Houchins, D. E., Puckett-Patterson, D., Crosby, S., Shippen, M. E., & Jolivette, K. (2009). Barriers and facilitators to providing incarcerated youth with a quality education. *Preventing School Failure, 53*(3), 159–166.

10 Foley, R. M., & Gao, J. (2002). Correctional education programs serving incarcerated juveniles: A status report. *Journal of Correctional Education, 53*(4), 131–138.

11 Wilder, S. (2004). Educating youthful offenders in a youth development center. *Journal of Addictions and Offender Counseling, 24*, 82–91.

12 Wilder, S. (2004). Educating youthful offenders in a youth development center. *Journal of Addictions and Offender Counseling, 24*, 82–91 (pg. 84).

13 Special education teachers are referred to as Exceptional Student Education Support Facilitators in Florida.

14 Maxwell, Joseph A. (2005). *Qualitative research design: An interactive approach.* California: Sage Publications (pg. 22).

15 Boyatzis, R. E. (1998). *Transforming qualitative research: Thematic analysis and code development.* Thousand Oaks, CA: Sage Publications.

16 Yin, R. K. (2009). *Case study research: Design and methods.* Thousand Oaks, CA: Sage Publications.

17 Office of Program Policy Analysis and Government Accountability, an office of the Florida Legislature. (2010). Youth entering the state's juvenile justice programs have substantial educational deficits; Available data is insufficient to assess learning gains of students, 1–16. www.oppaga.state.fl.us/Monitor-Docs/Reports/pdf/1007rpt.pdf.

18 Juvenile Justice Educational Enhancement Program (2009). 2008–2009 Quality Assurance Report (Final). www.criminologycenter.fsu.edu/jjeep/qa-educational-reports-2008-2009.php.

19 Boyatzis, R. E. (1998). *Transforming qualitative research: Thematic analysis and code development.* Thousand Oaks, CA: Sage Publications. Creswell, J. W. (2009). *Research design: Qualitative, quantitative, and mixed methods approaches,* 3rd ed. Thousand Oaks, CA: Sage.

20 Juvenile Justice Educational Enhancement Program (2009). 2008–2009 Annual Report to the Florida Department of Education. www.criminologycenter.fsu.edu/jjeep/pdf/2008-09_JJEEP_Annual_Report.pdf.

21 Malmgren, K. W., & Leone, P. E. (2000). Effects of a short-term auxiliary reading program on the reading skills of incarcerated youth. *Education and Treatment of Children, 23*(3), 239–247. Black, S. (2005). Learning behind bars. *American School Board Journal,* September, 50–52. Leone, P. E., Krezmien, M., Mason, L., & Meisel, S. M. (2005). Organizing and delivering empirically based literacy instruction to incarcerated youth. *Exceptionality, 13*(2), 89–102.

22 Baltodano, H. M., Harris, P. J., & Rutherford, R. B. (2005). Academic achievement in juvenile corrections: Examining the impact of age, ethnicity, and disability. *Education and Treatment of Children, 28*(4), 361–379; Juvenile Justice Educational Enhancement Program (2005). 2005 Annual Report to the Florida Department of Education, *Chapter 6: Incarcerated Delinquent Youths: Educational Deficiencies and Related Best Practices,* 99–116. Harris, P. J., Baltodano, H. M., Artiles, A. J., & Rutherford, R. B. (2006). Integration of culture in reading studies for youth in corrections: A literature review. *Education and Treatment of Children, 29*(4), 749–778. Zhang, D., Barrett, D. E., Katsiyannis,

A., & Yoon, M. (2011). Juvenile offenders with and without disabilities: Risks and patterns of recidivism. *Learning and Individual Differences, 21,* 12–18.

23 Rabionet, S. E. (2011). How I learned to design and conduct semi-structured interviews: An ongoing and continuous journey. *The Qualitative Report, 16*(2), 563–566.

24 Wolfinger, N. H. (2002). On writing fieldnotes: Collection strategies and background expectancies. *Qualitative Research, 2*(1), 85–95.

25 Fyfe, N. R. (1992). Observations on observations. *Journal of Geography in Higher Education, 16*(2).

26 Seidman, Irving. (2006). *Interviewing as qualitative research: A guide for researchers in education and the social sciences.* New York: Teachers College Press.

27 Seidman, Irving. (2006). *Interviewing as qualitative research: A guide for researchers in education and the social sciences.* New York: Teachers College Press.

28 Maxwell, Joseph A. (2005). *Qualitative research design: An interactive approach.* Thousand Oaks, CA: Sage Publications.

29 Boyatzis, R. E. (1998). *Transforming qualitative research: Thematic analysis and code development.* Thousand Oaks, CA: Sage Publications.

30 Chester, D. R., Tracy, J. A., Earp, E., & Chauhan, R. (2002). Correlates of quality educational programs. *Evaluation Review, 26*(3), 272–300. Florida Department of Juvenile Justice. (2010–2011). Fiscal Year 2010–2011 Annual Report. www.djj.state.fl.us/docs/about-us/djj-annual-report.pdf.

31 Read, N. W., & O'Cummings, M. (2010). Fact sheet: Juvenile justice facilities. The National Evaluation and Technical Assistance Center. www.neglected-delinquent.org/nd/docs/factSheet_facilities.pdf.

Chapter 2

1 Puzzanchera, C., Adams, B., & Hockenberry, S. (2012). Juvenile court statistics 2009. National Center for Juvenile Justice, Pittsburgh, PA. www.ojjdp.gov/pubs/239114.pdf.

2 Sickmund, M., Sladky, T. J., Kang, W., & Puzzanchera, C. (2013) Easy access to the census of juveniles in residential placement. www.ojjdp.gov/ojstatbb/ezacjrp/.

3 Brookins, G. K., & Hirsch, J. A. (2002). Innocence lost: Case studies of children in the juvenile justice system. *Journal of Negro Education, 71*(3), 205–217.

4 Morrison, H. R., & Epps, B. D. (2002). Warehousing or rehabilitation? Public schooling in the juvenile justice system. *Journal of Negro Education, 71*(3), 218–232. Quinn, M. M., Rutherford, R. B., Leone, P. E., Osher, D. M., & Poirier, J. M. (2005). Youth with disabilities in juvenile corrections: A national survey. *Exceptional Children, 71*(3), 339–345. Harris, P. J., Baltodano, H. M., Bal, A., Jolivette, K., & Malcahy, C. (2009). Reading achievement of incarcerated youth in three regions. *Journal of Correctional Education, 60*(2), 120–145.

5 Foley, R. M., & Gao, J. (2002). Correctional education programs serving incarcerated juveniles: A status report. *Journal of Correctional Education, 53*(4), 131–138.

6 Morrison, H. R., & Epps, B. D. (2002). Warehousing or rehabilitation? Public schooling in the juvenile justice system. *Journal of Negro Education, 71*(3),

218–232. Leone, P. E., Krezmien, M., Mason, L., & Meisel, S. M. (2005). Organizing and delivering empirically based literacy instruction to incarcerated youth. *Exceptionality, 13*(2), 89–102. Quinn, M. M., Rutherford, R. B., Leone, P. E., Osher, D. M., & Poirier, J. M. (2005). Youth with disabilities in juvenile corrections: A national survey. *Exceptional Children, 71*(3), 339–345.

7 Jenson, J. M., & Howard, M. O. (1998). Youth crime, public policy, and practice in the juvenile justice system: Recent trends and needed reforms. *Social Work, 43*(4), 324–334. Brookins, G. K., & Hirsch, J. A. (2002). Innocence lost: Case studies of children in the juvenile justice system. *Journal of Negro Education, 71*(3), 205–217. Abrams, L. S., Kim, K., & Anderson-Nathe, B. (2005). Paradoxes of treatment in juvenile corrections. *Child and Youth Care Forum, 34*(1), 7–25; Puzzanchera, C., Adams, B., & Hockenberry, S. (2012). Juvenile court statistics 2009. National Center for Juvenile Justice, Pittsburgh, PA. www.ojjdp.gov/pubs/239114.pdf.

8 Morrison, H. R., & Epps, B. D. (2002). Warehousing or rehabilitation? Public schooling in the juvenile justice system. *Journal of Negro Education, 71*(3), 218–232 (pg. 220).

9 Feld, B. C. (2000). The juvenile court: Changes and challenges—where has the juvenile justice system been, and where is it going? *Update on Law-Related Education, 23*(2), 10–14.

10 Foley, R. M., & Gao, J. (2002). Correctional education programs serving incarcerated juveniles: A status report. *Journal of Correctional Education, 53*(4), 131–138. Mendel, R. A. (2011). No place for kids: The case for reducing juvenile incarceration. The Annie E. Casey Foundation, Baltimore, MD.

11 Arum, R., & Beattie, I. R. (1999). High school experience and the risk of adult incarceration. *Criminology, 37*(3), 515–540 (pg. 526).

12 Baltodano, H. M., Harris, P. J., & Rutherford, R. B. (2005). Academic achievement in juvenile corrections: Examining the impact of age, ethnicity, and disability. *Education and Treatment of Children, 28*(4), 361–379 (pg. 362).

13 Wilhite, K., & Cessna, K. K. (1996). Safeguarding the education of incarcerated juvenile offenders: The critical role of state departments of education. *Preventing School Failure, 40*(2), 56–59. Hellriegel, K. L., & Yates, J. R. (1997). *Collaboration between correctional and public school systems for juvenile offenders: A case study.* Chicago: American Educational Research Association. Baltodano, H. M., Harris, P. J., & Rutherford, R. B. (2005). Academic achievement in juvenile corrections: Examining the impact of age, ethnicity, and disability. *Education and Treatment of Children, 28*(4), 361–379. Juvenile Justice Educational Enhancement Program. (2005). 2005 Annual Report to the Florida Department of Education, *Chapter 6: Incarcerated Delinquent Youths: Educational Deficiencies and Related Best Practices*, 99–116. Quinn, M. M., Rutherford, R. B., Leone, P. E., Osher, D. M., & Poirier, J. M. (2005). Youth with disabilities in juvenile corrections: A national survey. *Exceptional Children, 71*(3), 339–345. Harris, P. J., Baltodano, H. M., Artiles, A. J., & Rutherford, R. B. (2006). Integration of culture in reading studies for youth in corrections: A literature review. *Education and Treatment of Children, 29*(4), 749–778; Platt, J. S., Casey, R. E., & Faessel, R. T. (2006). The need for a paradigmatic change in juvenile correctional education. *Preventing School Failure, 51*(1), 31–38. Zhang, D., Barrett, D. E., Katsiyannis, A., & Yoon, M. (2011). Juvenile offenders with and

without disabilities: Risks and patterns of recidivism. *Learning and Individual Differences, 21,* 12–18.

14 Leone, P. E., Krezmien, M., Mason, L., & Meisel, S. M. (2005). Organizing and delivering empirically based literacy instruction to incarcerated youth. *Exceptionality, 13*(2), 89–102.

15 Wolford, B. I. (2000). *Juvenile justice education: "Who is educating the youth?"* Council for Educators of At-Risk and Delinquent Youth. www.edjj.org/Publications/educating_youth.pdf.

16 Quinn, M. M., Rutherford, R. B., Leone, P. E., Osher, D. M., & Poirier, J. M. (2005). Youth with disabilities in juvenile corrections: A national survey. *Exceptional Children, 71*(3), 339–345.

17 Jenkins, H. D. (1994). Mandatory education. *Journal of Correctional Education, 45*(1), 26–29. Tonry, M. (1999). Why are U.S. incarceration rates so high? *Crime and Delinquency, 45*(4), 419–437. Keith, J. M., & McCray, A. D. (2002). Juvenile offenders with special needs: Critical issues and bleak outcomes. *Qualitative Studies in Education, 15*(6), 691–710. Juvenile Justice Educational Enhancement Program. (2005). 2005 Annual Report to the Florida Department of Education, *Chapter 6: Incarcerated Delinquent Youths: Educational Deficiencies and Related Best Practices,* 99–116. Sheridan, M. J., & Steele-Dadzie, T. E. (2005). Structure of intellect and learning style of incarcerated youth assessment: A means to providing a continuum of educational service in juvenile justice. *Journal of Correctional Education, 56*(4), 347–371. Vacca, J. S. (2008). Crime can be prevented if schools teach juvenile offenders to read. *Children and Youth Services Review, 30,* 1055–1062.

18 Morrison, H. R., & Epps, B. D. (2002). Warehousing or rehabilitation? Public schooling in the juvenile justice system. *Journal of Negro Education, 71*(3), 218–232. Harris, P. J., Baltodano, H. M., Bal, A., Jolivette, K., & Malcahy, C. (2009). Reading achievement of incarcerated youth in three regions. *Journal of Correctional Education, 60*(2), 120–145.

19 O'Rourke, T. (2003). Improving the odds for incarcerated youths. *Corrections Today,* February, 83–87. Baltodano, H. M., Harris, P. J., & Rutherford, R. B. (2005). Academic achievement in juvenile corrections: Examining the impact of age, ethnicity, and disability. *Education and Treatment of Children, 28*(4), 361–379. Hardy, L. (2007). Children at risk. *American School Board Journal,* April, 35–41. Zabel, R., & Nigro, F. (2007). Occupational interests and aptitudes of juvenile offenders: Influence of special education and gender. *Journal of Correctional Education, 58*(4), 337–355.

20 Morrison, H. R., & Epps, B. D. (2002). Warehousing or rehabilitation? Public schooling in the juvenile justice system. *Journal of Negro Education, 71*(3), 218–232. Leone, P. E., Krezmien, M., Mason, L., & Meisel, S. M. (2005). Organizing and delivering empirically based literacy instruction to incarcerated youth. *Exceptionality, 13*(2), 89–102. Quinn, M. M., Rutherford, R. B., Leone, P. E., Osher, D. M., & Poirier, J. M. (2005). Youth with disabilities in juvenile corrections: A national survey. *Exceptional Children, 71*(3), 339–345.

21 Hellriegel, K. L., & Yates, J. R. (1997). *Collaboration between correctional and public school systems for juvenile offenders: A case study.* Chicago: American Educational Research Association.

22 Arum, R., & Beattie, I. R. (1999). High school experience and the risk of adult incarceration. *Criminology, 37*(3), 515–540.

23 Keith, J. M., & McCray, A. D. (2002). Juvenile offenders with special needs: Critical issues and bleak outcomes. *Qualitative Studies in Education, 15*(6), 691–710. Black, S. (2005). Learning behind bars. *American School Board Journal,* September, 50–52. Hardy, L. (2007). Children at risk. *American School Board Journal,* April, 35–41. Harris, P. J., Baltodano, H. M., Bal, A., Jolivette, K., & Malcahy, C. (2009). Reading achievement of incarcerated youth in three regions. *Journal of Correctional Education, 60*(2), 120–145.

24 Malmgren, K. W., & Leone, P. E. (2000). Effects of a short-term auxiliary reading program on the reading skills of incarcerated youth. *Education and Treatment of Children, 23*(3), 239–247.

25 Leone, P. E., Krezmien, M., Mason, L., & Meisel, S. M. (2005). Organizing and delivering empirically based literacy instruction to incarcerated youth. *Exceptionality, 13*(2), 89–102.

26 American Correctional Association. (1977). Project READ (Reading Efficiency and Delinquency), Annual Report 1976-1977. https://www.ncjrs.gov/pdffiles1/Digitization/40594NCJRS.pdf.

27 Black, S. (2005). Learning behind bars. *American School Board Journal,* September, 50–52.

28 Baltodano, H. M., Harris, P. J., & Rutherford, R. B. (2005). Academic achievement in juvenile corrections: Examining the impact of age, ethnicity, and disability. *Education and Treatment of Children, 28*(4), 361–379.

29 Zabel, R., & Nigro, F. (2007). Occupational interests and aptitudes of juvenile offenders: Influence of special education and gender. *Journal of Correctional Education, 58*(4), 337–355.

30 Heckel, R. V., & Mandell, E. (1981). A factor analytic study of the demographic characteristics of incarcerated male and female juvenile offenders. *Journal of Clinical Psychology, 37*(2), 426–429.

31 Risler, E., & O'Rourke, T. (2009). Thinking exit at entry: Exploring outcomes of Georgia's juvenile justice educational programs. *Journal of Correctional Education, 60*(3), 225–239.

32 Alltucker, K. W., Bullis, M., Close, D., & Yovanoff, P. (2006). Different pathways to juvenile delinquency: Characteristics of early and late starters in a sample of previously incarcerated youth. *Journal of Child and Family Studies, 15*(4), 479–492. Zhang, D., Barrett, D. E., Katsiyannis, A., & Yoon, M. (2011). Juvenile offenders with and without disabilities: Risks and patterns of recidivism. *Learning and Individual Differences, 21*, 12–18.

33 Cannon, A., & Beiser, V. (2004). Juvenile injustice. *U.S. News and World Report, 137*(4), 28–32. Platt, J. S., Casey, R. E., & Faessel, R. T. (2006). The need for a paradigmatic change in juvenile correctional education. *Preventing School Failure, 51*(1), 31–38.

34 Small, M. A. (1997). Juvenile justice: Comments and trends. *Behavioral Sciences and the Law, 15*, 119–124, Feld, B. C. (2000). The juvenile court: Changes and challenges—where has the juvenile justice system been, and where is it going? *Update on Law-Related Education, 23*(2), 10–14. Cannon, A., & Beiser, V. (2004). Juvenile injustice. *U.S. News and World Report, 137*(4), 28–32.

35 Keeley, J. H. (2004). The metamorphosis of juvenile correctional education: Incidental conception to intentional inclusion. *Journal of Correctional Education, 55*(4), 277–295. Mazzotti, V. L., & Higgins, K. (2006). Public schools and

the juvenile justice system: Facilitating relationships. *Intervention in School and Clinic, 41*(5), 295–301.

36 Feld, B. C. (2000). The juvenile court: Changes and challenges—where has the juvenile justice system been, and where is it going? *Update on Law-Related Education, 23*(2), 10–14.

37 Small, M. A. (1997). Juvenile justice: Comments and trends. *Behavioral Sciences and the Law, 15,* 119–124.

38 Whitebread, C., & Heilman, J. (1988). An overview of the law of juvenile delinquency. *Behavioral Sciences and the Law, 6*(3), 285–305.

39 Feld, B. C. (2000). The juvenile court: Changes and challenges—where has the juvenile justice system been, and where is it going? *Update on Law-Related Education, 23*(2), 10–14.

40 Small, M. A. (1997). Juvenile justice: Comments and trends. *Behavioral Sciences and the Law, 15,* 119–124. Jenson, J. M., & Howard, M. O. (1998). Youth crime, public policy, and practice in the juvenile justice system: Recent trends and needed reforms. *Social Work, 43*(4), 324–334. Mazzotti, V. L., & Higgins, K. (2006). Public schools and the juvenile justice system: Facilitating relationships. *Intervention in School and Clinic, 41*(5), 295–301.

41 Whitebread, C., & Heilman, J. (1988). An overview of the law of juvenile delinquency. *Behavioral Sciences and the Law, 6*(3), 285–305.

42 Small, M. A. (1997). Juvenile justice: Comments and trends. *Behavioral Sciences and the Law, 15,* 119–124.

43 Whitebread, C., & Heilman, J. (1988). An overview of the law of juvenile delinquency. *Behavioral Sciences and the Law, 6*(3), 285–305. Small, M. A. (1997). Juvenile justice: Comments and trends. *Behavioral Sciences and the Law, 15,* 119–124. Feld, B. C. (2000). The juvenile court: Changes and challenges— where has the juvenile justice system been, and where is it going? *Update on Law-Related Education, 23*(2), 10–14. American Bar Association Division for Public Education. The history of juvenile justice. www.americanbar.org/content/dam/aba/migrated/publiced/features/DYJpart1.authcheckdam.pdf.

44 Small, M. A. (1997). Juvenile justice: Comments and trends. *Behavioral Sciences and the Law, 15,* 119–124 (pg. 122).

45 Jenson, J. M., & Howard, M. O. (1998). Youth crime, public policy, and practice in the juvenile justice system: Recent trends and needed reforms. *Social Work, 43*(4), 324–334.

46 Brookins, G. K., & Hirsch, J. A. (2002). Innocence lost: Case studies of children in the juvenile justice system. *Journal of Negro Education, 71*(3), 205–217.

47 Frazier, C. E., Bishop, D. M., & Lanza-Kaduce, L. (1999). Get-tough juvenile justice reforms: The Florida experience. *Annals of the American Academy,* July, 167–184. Cannon, A., & Beiser, V. (2004). Juvenile injustice. *U.S. News and World Report, 137*(4), 28–32. Rutherford, R. B., & Nelson, C. M. (2005). Disability and involvement with the juvenile delinquency system: Knowing versus doing. *Exceptionality, 13*(2), 65–67. Mincey, B., Maldonado, N., Lacey, C. H., & Thompson, S. D. (2008). Perceptions of successful graduates of juvenile residential programs: Reflections and suggestions for success. *Journal of Correctional Education, 59*(1), 8–31.

48 Keeley, J. H. (2004). The metamorphosis of juvenile correctional education: Incidental conception to intentional inclusion. *Journal of Correctional Education, 55*(4), 277–295.

49 Feld, B. C. (2000). The juvenile court: Changes and challenges—where has the juvenile justice system been, and where is it going? *Update on Law-Related Education, 23*(2), 10–14. Sheridan, M. J., & Steele-Dadzie, T. E. (2005). Structure of intellect and learning style of incarcerated youth assessment: A means to providing a continuum of educational service in juvenile justice. *Journal of Correctional Education, 56*(4), 347–371.

50 Abrams, L. S., Kim, K., & Anderson-Nathe, B. (2005). Paradoxes of treatment in juvenile corrections. *Child and Youth Care Forum, 34*(1), 7–25. Fagan, J. (2010). The contradictions of juvenile crime and punishment. *American Academy of Arts and Sciences,* summer, 43–61. Piquero, A. R., & Steinberg, L. (2010). Public preferences for rehabilitation versus incarceration of juvenile offenders. *Journal of Criminal Justice, 38,* 1–6.

51 Cannon, A., & Beiser, V. (2004). Juvenile injustice. *U.S. News and World Report, 137*(4), 28–32 (pg. 21).

52 Quinn, M. M., Rutherford, R. B., Leone, P. E., Osher, D. M., & Poirier, J. M. (2005). Youth with disabilities in juvenile corrections: A national survey. *Exceptional Children, 71*(3), 339–345. Platt, J. S., Casey, R. E., & Faessel, R. T. (2006). The need for a paradigmatic change in juvenile correctional education. *Preventing School Failure, 51*(1), 31–38. Houchins, D. E., Puckett-Patterson, D., Crosby, S., Shippen, M. E., & Jolivette, K. (2009). Barriers and facilitators to providing incarcerated youth with a quality education. *Preventing School Failure, 53*(3), 159–166.

53 Houchins, D. E., Puckett-Patterson, D., Crosby, S., Shippen, M. E., & Jolivette, K. (2009). Barriers and facilitators to providing incarcerated youth with a quality education. *Preventing School Failure, 53*(3), 159–166.

54 Cannon, A., & Beiser, V. (2004). Juvenile injustice. *U.S. News and World Report, 137*(4), 28–32.

55 Read, N. W., & O'Cummings, M. (2010). Fact sheet: Juvenile justice facilities. The National Evaluation and Technical Assistance Center. www.neglecteddelinquent.org/nd/docs/factSheet_facilities.pdf.

56 Read, N. W., & O'Cummings, M. (2010). Fact sheet: Juvenile justice facilities. The National Evaluation and Technical Assistance Center. www.neglecteddelinquent.org/nd/docs/factSheet_facilities.pdf.

57 Read, N. W., & O'Cummings, M. (2010). Fact sheet: Juvenile justice facilities. The National Evaluation and Technical Assistance Center. www.neglecteddelinquent.org/nd/docs/factSheet_facilities.pdf.

58 Black, S. (2005). Learning behind bars. *American School Board Journal,* September, 50–52 (pg. 50).

59 Read, N. W., & O'Cummings, M. (2011). Fact sheet: Juvenile justice education. The National Evaluation and Technical Assistance Center. www.neglected-delinquent.org/nd/docs/NDFactSheet.pdf.

60 Brooks, C. C. (2008). The challenge of following education legislation in confinement education programs. *Corrections Today,* February, 28–30, 46.

61 Gehring, J. (2005). NCLB's mandates on delinquent youths get attention. *Education Week, 24*(43).

62 Linton, J. (2005). United States Department of Education Update. *Journal of Correctional Education, 56*(2), 90–95.

63 Wolford, B. I. (2000). *Juvenile justice education: "Who is educating the youth?"* Council for Educators of At-Risk and Delinquent Youth. www.edjj.org/Publications/educating_youth.pdf.

64 Wolford, B. I. (2000). *Juvenile justice education: "Who is educating the youth?"* Council for Educators of At-Risk and Delinquent Youth. www.edjj.org/Publications/educating_youth.pdf.

65 Wolford, B. I. (2000). *Juvenile justice education: "Who is educating the youth?"* Council for Educators of At-Risk and Delinquent Youth. www.edjj.org/Publications/educating_youth.pdf.

66 Zabel, R., & Nigro, F. (2007). Occupational interests and aptitudes of juvenile offenders: Influence of special education and gender. *Journal of Correctional Education, 58*(4), 337–355 (pg. 352).

67 Read, N. W., & O'Cummings, M. (2011). Fact sheet: Juvenile justice education. The National Evaluation and Technical Assistance Center. www.neglected-delinquent.org/nd/docs/NDFactSheet.pdf.

68 Blomberg, T. G., & Waldo, G. P. (2001). Implementing research-based best practices in juvenile justice education. *Corrections Today,* December, 144–147.

69 Leone, P. E., Krezmien, M., Mason, L., & Meisel, S. M. (2005). Organizing and delivering empirically based literacy instruction to incarcerated youth. *Exceptionality, 13*(2), 89–102.

70 Platt, J. S., Casey, R. E., & Faessel, R. T. (2006). The need for a paradigmatic change in juvenile correctional education. *Preventing School Failure, 51*(1), 31–38.

71 Sheridan, M. J., & Steele-Dadzie, T. E. (2005). Structure of intellect and learning style of incarcerated youth assessment: A means to providing a continuum of educational service in juvenile justice. *Journal of Correctional Education, 56*(4), 347–371.

72 Zabel, R., & Nigro, F. (2007). Occupational interests and aptitudes of juvenile offenders: Influence of special education and gender. *Journal of Correctional Education, 58*(4), 337–355.

73 Foley, R. M., & Gao, J. (2002). Correctional education programs serving incarcerated juveniles: A status report. *Journal of Correctional Education, 53*(4), 131–138.

74 Kadish, T. E., Glaser, B. A., Calhoun, G. B., & Ginter, E. J. (2001). Identifying the developmental strengths of juvenile offenders: Assessing four life-skills dimensions. *Journal of Addictions and Offender Counseling,* April, 85–95.

75 Black, S. (2005). Learning behind bars. *American School Board Journal,* September, 50–52.

76 Killian, E., Brown, R., & Evans, W. (2002). What incarcerated youth say would help them succeed: Can extension play a role? *Journal of Extension, 40*(4).

77 Cole, B. G. (2002). Rehabilitation through education. *Journal of Correctional Education, 53*(1), 20–22.

78 Harris, P. J., Baltodano, H. M., Bal, A., Jolivette, K., & Malcahy, C. (2009). Reading achievement of incarcerated youth in three regions. *Journal of Correctional Education, 60*(2), 120–145.

79 Rutherford, R. B., & Nelson, C. M. (2005). Disability and involvement with the juvenile delinquency system: Knowing versus doing. *Exceptionality, 13*(2), 65–67.

80 Platt, J. S., Casey, R. E., & Faessel, R. T. (2006). The need for a paradigmatic change in juvenile correctional education. *Preventing School Failure, 51*(1), 31–38.

81 Morrison, H. R., & Epps, B. D. (2002). Warehousing or rehabilitation? Public schooling in the juvenile justice system. *Journal of Negro Education, 71*(3), 218–232.

82 Moody, B., Kruse, G., Nagel, J., & Conlon, B. (2008). Career development project for incarcerated youth: Preparing for the future. *Journal of Correctional Education, 59*(3), 231–243.

83 Harris, P. J., Baltodano, H. M., Artiles, A. J., & Rutherford, R. B. (2006). Integration of culture in reading studies for youth in corrections: A literature review. *Education and Treatment of Children, 29*(4), 749–778.

84 Platt, J. S., Casey, R. E., & Faessel, R. T. (2006). The need for a paradigmatic change in juvenile correctional education. *Preventing School Failure, 51*(1), 31–38.

85 Pasternack, R., & Martinez, K. (1996). Resiliency: What is it and how can correctional educational practices encourage its development? *Preventing School Failure, 40*(2), 63–66.

86 Oesterreich, H. A., & McNie Flores, S. (2009). Learning to c: Visual arts education as strengths based practice in juvenile correctional facilities. *Journal of Correctional Education, 60*(2), 146–162.

87 Sheridan, M. J., & Steele-Dadzie, T. E. (2005). Structure of intellect and learning style of incarcerated youth assessment: A means to providing a continuum of educational service in juvenile justice. *Journal of Correctional Education, 56*(4), 347–371. Moreno, P. (2008). Incarcerated youths get a second chance with CTE. *Techniques,* February, 18–21.

88 Pasternack, R., & Martinez, K. (1996). Resiliency: What is it and how can correctional educational practices encourage its development? *Preventing School Failure, 40*(2), 63–66.

89 Blomberg, T. G., & Waldo, G. P. (2001). Implementing research-based best practices in juvenile justice education. *Corrections Today,* December, 144–147.

90 Malmgren, K. W., & Leone, P. E. (2000). Effects of a short-term auxiliary reading program on the reading skills of incarcerated youth. *Education and Treatment of Children, 23*(3), 239–247.

91 Leone, P. E., Krezmien, M., Mason, L., & Meisel, S. M. (2005). Organizing and delivering empirically based literacy instruction to incarcerated youth. *Exceptionality, 13*(2), 89–102.

92 Pasternack, R., & Martinez, K. (1996). Resiliency: What is it and how can correctional educational practices encourage its development? *Preventing School Failure, 40*(2), 63–66. Keith, J. M., & McCray, A. D. (2002). Juvenile offenders with special needs: Critical issues and bleak outcomes. *Qualitative Studies in Education, 15*(6), 691–710.

93 Hellriegel, K. L., & Yates, J. R. (1997). *Collaboration between correctional and public school systems for juvenile offenders: A case study.* Chicago: American Educational Research Association.

94 American Correctional Association. (1977). Project READ (Reading Efficiency and Delinquency), Annual Report 1976–1977. https://www.ncjrs.gov/pdffiles1/Digitization/40594NCJRS.pdf.
Sheridan, M. J., & Steele-Dadzie, T. E. (2005). Structure of intellect and learning style of incarcerated youth assessment: A means to providing a continuum of educational service in juvenile justice. *Journal of Correctional Education, 56*(4), 347–371.

95 Bewley, R. J. (1999). The use of multimedia and hypermedia presentation for instruction of juvenile offenders. *Journal of Correctional Education, 50*(4), 130–139.

96   Keeley, J. H. (2004). The metamorphosis of juvenile correctional education: Incidental conception to intentional inclusion. *Journal of Correctional Education, 55*(4), 277–295.

97   Juvenile Justice Educational Enhancement Program. (2009). 2008–2009 Annual Report to the Florida Department of Education. www.criminologycenter.fsu.edu/jjeep/pdf/2008-09_JJEEP_Annual_Report.pdf.

98   Wilson, J. J. (1994). Developing a partnership with juvenile corrections. *Corrections Today, 56*(2), 74–76. Roush, D. W., & Jones, M. A. (1996). Juvenile detention training: A status report. *Federal Probation, 60*(2), 54–61. Blomberg, T. G., & Waldo, G. P. (2001). Implementing research-based best practices in juvenile justice education. *Corrections Today*, December, 144–147. Mathur, S. R., Griller Clark, H., & Schoenfeld, N. A. (2009). Professional development: A capacity-building model for juvenile correctional education systems. *Journal of Correctional Education, 60*(2), 164–185.

99   Wilhite, K., & Cessna, K. K. (1996). Safeguarding the education of incarcerated juvenile offenders: The critical role of state departments of education. *Preventing School Failure, 40*(2), 56–59. Blomberg, T. G., & Waldo, G. P. (2001). Implementing research-based best practices in juvenile justice education. *Corrections Today*, December, 144–147. Zhang, D., Barrett, D. E., Katsiyannis, A., & Yoon, M. (2011). Juvenile offenders with and without disabilities: Risks and patterns of recidivism. *Learning and Individual Differences, 21*, 12–18.

100 O'Cummings, M., Bardack, S., & Gonsoulin, S. (2010). Issue brief: The importance of literacy for youth involved in the juvenile justice system. The National Evaluation and Technical Assistance Center. www.neglecteddelinquent.org/nd/docs/literacy_brief_20100120.pdf.

101 College Board Advocacy & Policy Center. *Trends in College Pricing 2011.* http://trends.collegeboard.org/downloads/College_Pricing_2011.pdf.

102 Wolford, B. I. (2000). *Juvenile justice education: "Who is educating the youth?"* Council for Educators of At-Risk and Delinquent Youth. www.edjj.org/Publications/educating_youth.pdf.

103 Wolford, B. I. (2000). *Juvenile justice education: "Who is educating the youth?"* Council for Educators of At-Risk and Delinquent Youth. www.edjj.org/Publications/educating_youth.pdf.

104 Blomberg, T. G., Pesta, G., & Valentine, C. (2008). The juvenile justice No Child Left Behind collaboration project: A national effort to improve education for incarcerated youth. Florida State University College of Criminology and Criminal Justice. www.criminologycenter.fsu.edu/p/nationalDataClearinghouse/Publications%20Reports/JJ_NCLB_Final_Report_2008.pdf (pg. 27).

105 Keeley, J. H. (2004). The metamorphosis of juvenile correctional education: Incidental conception to intentional inclusion. *Journal of Correctional Education, 55*(4), 277–295.

106 Wolford, B. I. (2000). *Juvenile justice education: "Who is educating the youth?"* Council for Educators of At-Risk and Delinquent Youth. www.edjj.org/Publications/educating_youth.pdf.
     Risler, E., & O'Rourke, T. (2009). Thinking exit at entry: Exploring outcomes of Georgia's juvenile justice educational programs. *Journal of Correctional Education, 60*(3), 225–239.

107   American Correctional Association. (1977). Project READ (Reading Efficiency and Delinquency), Annual Report 1976–1977. https://www.ncjrs. gov/pdffiles1/Digitization/40594NCJRS.pdf.

108   Malmgren, K. W., & Leone, P. E. (2000). Effects of a short-term auxiliary reading program on the reading skills of incarcerated youth. *Education and Treatment of Children, 23*(3), 239–247.

109   Holsinger, K., & Crowther, A. (2005). College course participation for incarcerated youth: Bringing restorative justice to life. *Journal of Criminal Justice Education, 16*(2), 328–339.

110   Mendel, R. A. (2001). Less cost, more safety: Guiding lights for reform in juvenile justice. American Youth Policy Forum, Washington, DC. Black, S. (2005). Learning behind bars. *American School Board Journal*, September, 50–52.

111   Moody, B., Kruse, G., Nagel, J., & Conlon, B. (2008). Career development project for incarcerated youth: Preparing for the future. *Journal of Correctional Education, 59*(3), 231–243.

112   Wolford, B. I. (2000). *Juvenile justice education: "Who is educating the youth?"* Council for Educators of At-Risk and Delinquent Youth. www.edjj.org/Publications/educating_youth.pdf.
       Chester, D. R., Tracy, J. A., Earp, E., & Chauhan, R. (2002). Correlates of quality educational programs. *Evaluation Review, 26*(3), 272–300. Florida Department of Juvenile Justice. (2010–2011). Fiscal Year 2010–2011 Annual Report. www.djj.state.fl.us/docs/about-us/djj-annual-report.pdf.

113   Florida Department of Juvenile Justice. (2009). A four year strategic plan for 2008–09 through 2011–12. www.djj.state.fl.us/docs/about-us/2008-09-strategic-plan.pdf?sfvrsn=2

114   Florida Department of Juvenile Justice. (2009). A four year strategic plan for 2008–09 through 2011–12. www.djj.state.fl.us/docs/about-us/2008-09-strategic-plan.pdf?sfvrsn=2. Read, N. W. (2006) A look at legislation: Common pre-post assessments. The National Evaluation and Technical Assistance Center. www.neglected-delinquent.org/nd/resources/spotlight/spotlight200604b.asp. Florida Statute 1003.52. www.leg.state.fl.us/statutes/index.cfm?App_mode=Display_Statute&Search_String=&URL=1000-1099/1003/Sections/1003.52.html.

115   Florida Department of Education, Bureau of Exceptional Education and Student Services. (2005). No Child Left Behind in Juvenile Justice Education—Report to the Legislature. www.fldoe.org/ese/pdf/djj-all.pdf.

116   Office of Program Policy Analysis and Government Accountability, an office of the Florida Legislature. (2010). Youth entering the state's juvenile justice programs have substantial educational deficits; Available data is insufficient to assess learning gains of students, 1–16. www.oppaga.state.fl.us/MonitorDocs/Reports/pdf/1007rpt.pdf.

117   Blomberg, T. G., & Waldo, G. P. (2002). Implementing an evaluation research and accountability-driven system for juvenile justice education in Florida. *Evaluation Review, 26*(3), 239–240. Blomberg, T. G., & Waldo, G. P. (2002). Integrating research, policy, and practice in juvenile justice education. *Evaluation Review, 26*(3), 241–250.

118   Blomberg, T. G., & Waldo, G. P. (2002). Implementing an evaluation research and accountability-driven system for juvenile justice education in Florida. *Evaluation Review, 26*(3), 239–240.

119 Blomberg, T. G., & Waldo, G. P. (2002). Implementing an evaluation research and accountability-driven system for juvenile justice education in Florida. *Evaluation Review, 26*(3), 239–240.

120 Krisberg, B. & Patino, V. (2004). Juvenile justice in Florida: What kind of future? National Council on Crime and Delinquency.

121 Bohac, P., Evans, B., & Ritchie, B. (1996). Juvenile justice and the Florida legislature: Lessons, problems, and a possible template. *Preventing School Failure, 40*(2), 53–55.

122 Blomberg, T. G., & Waldo, G. P. (2002). Implementing an evaluation research and accountability-driven system for juvenile justice education in Florida. *Evaluation Review, 26*(3), 239–240.

123 Blomberg, T. G., & Waldo, G. P. (2002). Implementing an evaluation research and accountability-driven system for juvenile justice education in Florida. *Evaluation Review, 26*(3), 239–240.

124 Juvenile Justice Educational Enhancement Program. (2005). 2005 Annual Report to the Florida Department of Education, *Chapter 6: Incarcerated Delinquent Youths: Educational Deficiencies and Related Best Practices,* 99–116.

125 Read, N. W. (2006) A look at legislation: Common pre-post assessments. The National Evaluation and Technical Assistance Center. www.neglected-delinquent.org/nd/resources/spotlight/spotlight200604b.asp.

126 Wolford, B. I. (2000). *Juvenile justice education: "Who is educating the youth?"* Council for Educators of At-Risk and Delinquent Youth. www.edjj.org/Publications/educating_youth.pdf.
     Juvenile Justice Educational Enhancement Program. (2005). 2005 Annual Report to the Florida Department of Education, *Chapter 5: Teacher Retention and Qualifications,* 81–98.

127 Blomberg, T. G., & Waldo, G. P. (2002). Implementing an evaluation research and accountability-driven system for juvenile justice education in Florida. *Evaluation Review, 26*(3), 239–240.

128 Juvenile Justice Educational Enhancement Program. (2009). 2008–2009 Annual Report to the Florida Department of Education. www.criminologycenter.fsu.edu/jjeep/pdf/2008-09_JJEEP_Annual_Report.pdf.

129 Juvenile Justice Educational Enhancement Program. (2009). 2008–2009 Annual Report to the Florida Department of Education. www.criminologycenter.fsu.edu/jjeep/pdf/2008-09_JJEEP_Annual_Report.pdf.

130 Read, N. W. (2006) A look at legislation: Common pre-post assessments. The National Evaluation and Technical Assistance Center. www.neglected-delinquent.org/nd/resources/spotlight/spotlight200604b.asp.

131 Read, N. W. (2006) A look at legislation: Common pre-post assessments. The National Evaluation and Technical Assistance Center. www.neglected-delinquent.org/nd/resources/spotlight/spotlight200604b.asp.
     Office of Program Policy Analysis and Government Accountability, an office of the Florida Legislature. (2010). Youth entering the state's juvenile justice programs have substantial educational deficits; Available data is insufficient to assess learning gains of students, 1–16. www.oppaga.state.fl.us/MonitorDocs/Reports/pdf/1007rpt.pdf.

132 Juvenile Justice Educational Enhancement Program. (2010). 2009–2010 Annual Report to the Florida Department of Education. http//criminology.

fsu.edu/center/jjeep/pdf/JJEEP%202009-10%20Annual%20Report.pdf (pg. 7).

133 Florida Department of Juvenile Justice. (2010–2011). Fiscal Year 2010–2011 Annual Report. www.djj.state.fl.us/docs/about-us/djj-annual-report.pdf.
134 Chester, D. R., Tracy, J. A., Earp, E., & Chauhan, R. (2002). Correlates of quality educational programs. *Evaluation Review, 26*(3), 272–300.
135 Chester, D. R., Tracy, J. A., Earp, E., & Chauhan, R. (2002). Correlates of quality educational programs. *Evaluation Review, 26*(3), 272–300. Major, A. K., Chester, D. R., McEntire, R., Waldo, G. P., & Blomberg, T. G. (2002). Pre-, post-, and longitudinal evaluation of juvenile justice education. *Evaluation Review, 26*(3), 301–321. Florida Department of Juvenile Justice. (2010–2011). Fiscal Year 2010–2011 Annual Report. http://www.djj.state.fl.us/docs/about-us/djj-annual-report.pdf.
136 Florida Department of Education, Bureau of Exceptional Education and Student Services. (2005). No Child Left Behind in Juvenile Justice Education—Report to the Legislature. www.fldoe.org/ese/pdf/djj-all.pdf.
   Florida Department of Juvenile Justice. (2010–2011). Fiscal Year 2010–2011 Annual Report. www.djj.state.fl.us/docs/about-us/djj-annual-report.pdf.
137 Chester, D. R., Tracy, J. A., Earp, E., & Chauhan, R. (2002). Correlates of quality educational programs. *Evaluation Review, 26*(3), 272–300. Hardy, L. (2007). Children at risk. *American School Board Journal*, April, 35–41.
138 Florida Department of Juvenile Justice. (2012). DJJ transitions residential programs to private operation. www.djj.state.fl.us/news/press-releases/press-release-detail/2012/10/15/djj-transitions-residential-programs-to-private-operation.
139 Florida Department of Juvenile Justice. (2010). Program Accountability Measures—2009–10 Comprehensive Accountability Report.
140 Florida Department of Juvenile Justice. (2005). Department of Juvenile Justice's Program Accountability Measures: The 2006 PAM Report—A Two-Year Analysis. www.criminologycenter.fsu.edu/p/nationalDataClearinghouse/State%20Documents/Florida/Florida%20-%202006%20%20PAM%20Report.pdf.
141 U.S. Census Bureau. (2010). *Public Education Finances 2010*. http://www2.census.gov/govs/school/10f33pub.pdf.
142 Chester, D. R., Tracy, J. A., Earp, E., & Chauhan, R. (2002). Correlates of quality educational programs. *Evaluation Review, 26*(3), 272–300.
143 Juvenile Justice Educational Enhancement Program. (2009). 2008–2009 Annual Report to the Florida Department of Education. www.criminologycenter.fsu.edu/jjeep/pdf/2008-09_JJEEP_Annual_Report.pdf. Office of Program Policy Analysis and Government Accountability, an office of the Florida Legislature. (2010). Youth entering the state's juvenile justice programs have substantial educational deficits; Available data is insufficient to assess learning gains of students, 1–16. www.oppaga.state.fl.us/MonitorDocs/Reports/pdf/1007rpt.pdf.

Chapter 3

1 Pseudonyms are provided for the facility, the school district, and the participants.

2 Argyris, C., & Schon, D. A. (1978). *Organizational learning: A theory of action perspective*. Reading, MA: Addison Wesley Publishing.

Chapter 4

1 Pseudonyms are provided for the facility, the school district, and the participants.

Chapter 5

1 Pseudonyms are provided for the facility, the school district, and the participants.

Chapter 6

1 Pseudonyms are provided for the facility, the school district, and the participants.

Chapter 7

1 Witmer, M. M. (2005). The fourth R in education—relationships. *The Clearing House*, May/June, 224–228 (pg. 227).
2 Rubie-Davies, C. M., Peterson, E., Irving, E., Widdowson, D., & Dixon, R. (2010). Expectations of achievement: Student, teacher and parent perceptions. *Research in Education*, May (83), 36–53.
3 Lynch, M. (2012). Strategically allocating resources to support teaching and learning. *American Association of School Administrators Journal of Scholarship and Practice*, 9(1), 57–66 (pg. 58).
4 Lynch, M. (2012). Strategically allocating resources to support teaching and learning. *American Association of School Administrators Journal of Scholarship and Practice*, 9(1), 57–66 (pg. 58).
5 Abelmann, C., Elmore, R., Even, J., Kenyon, S., & Marshall, J. (1999). When accountability knocks, will anyone answer? *Consortium for Policy Research in Education* (pg. 4).

Chapter 8

1 Read, N. W., & O'Cummings, M. (2011). Fact sheet: Juvenile justice education. The National Evaluation and Technical Assistance Center. www.neglected-delinquent.org/nd/docs/NDFactSheet.pdf.
2 Leone, P. E., Krezmien, M., Mason, L., & Meisel, S. M. (2005). Organizing and delivering empirically based literacy instruction to incarcerated youth. *Exceptionality, 13*(2), 89–102.

Bibliography

Abelmann, C., Elmore, R., Even, J., Kenyon, S., & Marshall, J. (1999). When accountability knocks, will anyone answer? *Consortium for Policy Research in Education*.

Abrams, L. S., Shannon, S. K.S., & Sangalang, C. (2008). Transition services for incarcerated youth: A mixed methods evaluation study. *Children and Youth Services Review, 30*, 522–535.

Abrams, L. S., Kim, K., & Anderson-Nathe, B. (2005). Paradoxes of treatment in juvenile corrections. *Child and Youth Care Forum, 34*(1), 7–25.

Abramsky, S. (2004). Incarceration, Inc. Private prisons thrive on cheap labor and the hunger of job-starved towns. *The Nation*, July 19/26, 22–25.

Alltucker, K. W., Bullis, M., Close, D., & Yovanoff, P. (2006). Different pathways to juvenile delinquency: Characteristics of early and late starters in a sample of previously incarcerated youth. *Journal of Child and Family Studies, 15*(4), 479–492.

American Bar Association Division for Public Education. The history of juvenile justice. www.americanbar.org/content/dam/aba/migrated/publiced/features/DYJpart1.authcheckdam.pdf

American Correctional Association. (1977). Project READ (Reading Efficiency and Delinquency), Annual Report 1976–1977.

Argyris, C. & Schon, D.A. (1978). *Organizational learning: A theory of action perspective*. Reading, MA: Addison Wesley Publishing.

Armstrong, G. S. & MacKenzie, D. L. (2003). Private versus public juvenile correctional facilities: Do differences in environmental quality exist? *Crime and Delinquency, 49*(4), 542–563.

Arteaga, J. A. (2002). Juvenile (In)Justice: Congressional attempts to abrogate the procedural rights of juvenile defendants. *Columbia Law Review, 102*(4), 1051–1088.

Arum, R. & Beattie, I. R. (1999). High school experience and the risk of adult incarceration. *Criminology, 37*(3), 515–540.

Ashkar, P. J. & Kenny, D. T. (2008). Views from the inside: Young offenders' subjective experiences of incarceration. *International Journal of Offender Therapy and Comparative Criminology, 52*(5), 584–597.

Baltodano, H. M., Harris, P. J., & Rutherford, R. B. (2005). Academic achievement in juvenile corrections: Examining the impact of age, ethnicity, and disability. *Education and Treatment of Children, 28*(4), 361–379.

Bayer, P. & Pozen, D. E. (2005). The effectiveness of juvenile correctional facilities: Public versus private management. *Journal of Law and Economics, 48*, 549–589.

Bewley, R. J. (1999). The use of multimedia and hypermedia presentation for instruction of juvenile offenders. *Journal of Correctional Education, 50*(4), 130–139.

Bickerstaff, S., Hardner Leon, S., & Hudson, J. G. (1997). Preserving the opportunity for education: Texas' alternative education programs for disruptive youth. *Journal of Law and Education, 26*(4), 1–39.

Black, S. (2005). Learning behind bars. *American School Board Journal*, September, 50–52.

Blomberg, T. G. & Waldo, G. P. (2002). Integrating research, policy, and practice in juvenile justice education. *Evaluation Review, 26*(3), 241–250.

Blomberg, T. G. & Waldo, G. P. (2002). Implementing an evaluation research and accountability-driven system for juvenile justice education in Florida. *Evaluation Review, 26*(3), 239–240.

Blomberg, T. G. & Waldo, G. P. (2001). Implementing research-based best practices in juvenile justice education. *Corrections Today*, December, 144–147.

Bohac, P., Evans, B., & Ritchie, B. (1996). Juvenile justice and the Florida legislature: Lessons, problems, and a possible template. *Preventing School Failure, 40*(2), 53–55.

Bobby M. v. Chiles, 907 F.Supp. 368 (N.D.Fla. 1995)

Boyatzis, R. E. (1998). *Transforming qualitative research: Thematic analysis and code development.* California: Sage Publications.

Briscoe, R. V. & Doyle, J. P. (1996). Aftercare service in juvenile justice: Approaches for providing services for high-risk youth. *Preventing School Failure, 40*, 73–76.

Brookins, G. K. & Hirsch, J. A. (2002). Innocence lost: Case studies of children in the juvenile justice system. *Journal of Negro Education, 71*(3), 205–217.

Brooks, C. C. (2008). The challenge of following education legislation in confinement education programs. *Corrections Today*, February, 28–30, 46.

Brunner, M. S. (1993). National survey of reading programs for incarcerated juvenile offenders. Office of Juvenile Justice and Delinquency Prevention.

Bryan, K., Freer, J., & Furlong, C. (2007). Language and communication difficulties in juvenile offenders. *International Journal of Language and Communication Disorders, 42*(5), 505–520.

Bullis, M. & Yovanoff, P. (2006). Idle hands: Community employment experiences of incarcerated youth. *Journal of Emotional and Behavioral Disorders, 14*(2), 71–85.

Bullis, M., Yovanoff, P., & Havel, E. (2004). The importance of getting started right: Further examination of the facility-to-community transition of formerly incarcerated youth. *Journal of Special Education, 38*(2), 80–94.

Cannon, A. & Beiser, V. (2004). Juvenile injustice. *U.S. News and World Report, 137*(4), 28–32.

Chester, D. R., Tracy, J. A., Earp, E., & Chauhan, R. (2002). Correlates of quality educational programs. *Evaluation Review, 26*(3), 272–300.

Cole, B. G. (2002). Rehabilitation through education. *Journal of Correctional Education, 53*(1), 20–22.

College Board Advocacy & Policy Center. *Trends in College Pricing 2011.* http://trends.collegeboard.org/downloads/College_Pricing_2011.pdf

Creswell, J. W. (2009). *Research design: Qualitative, quantitative, and mixed methods approaches*, 3rd edition. Thousand Oaks, CA: Sage.

DelliCarpini, M. (2010). Building a better life: Implementing a career and technical education program for incarcerated youth. *Journal of Correctional Education, 61*(4), 283–295.

Diamond, J.B. (2007). Where the rubber meets the road: Rethinking the connection between high-stakes testing policy and classroom instruction. *Sociology of Education, 80*, 285–313.

Fagan, J. (2010). The contradictions of juvenile crime and punishment. *American Academy of Arts and Sciences,* Summer, 43–61.

Feierman, J., Levick, M. & Mody, A. (2009/10). The school-to-prison pipeline . . . and back: Obstacles and remedies for the re-enrollment of adjudicated youth. *New York School Law Review, 54*, 1115–1129.

Feld, B. C. (2000). The juvenile court: Changes and challenges—Where has the juvenile justice system been, and where is it going? *Update on Law-Related Education, 23*(2), 10–14.

Florida Department of Education, Bureau of Exceptional Education and Student Services. (2005). No Child Left Behind in Juvenile Justice Education—Report to the Legislature.

Florida Department of Education, Bureau of Exceptional Education and Student Services, Division of Public Schools, (2009). 2009–2010 Educational Quality Assurance Standards for Residential Juvenile Justice Commitment Programs.

Florida Department of Juvenile Justice. (2005). Department of Juvenile Justice's Program Accountability Measures: The 2006 PAM Report—A Two-Year Analysis.

Florida Department of Juvenile Justice. (2009). A four year strategic plan for 2008–09 through 2011–12.

Florida Department of Juvenile Justice. (2010). Program Accountability Measures—2009–10 Comprehensive Accountability Report.

Florida Department of Juvenile Justice. (2010-2011). Fiscal Year 2010–2011 Annual Report. www.djj.state.fl.us/docs/about-us/djj-annual-report.p

Florida Department of Juvenile Justice (2012). DJJ transitions residential programs to private operation. www.djj.state.fl.us/news/press-releases/press-release-detail/2012/10/15/djj-transitions-residential-programs-to-private-operation

Florida State Legislature, Tallahassee. Office of Program Policy Analysis and Government Accountability. (1998). Review of Education Services in Juvenile Justice Residential Facilities.

Florida State University College of Criminology and Criminal Justice. (2008). The Juvenile Justice No Child Left Behind Collaboration Project: A National Effort to Improve Education for Incarcerated Youth.

Foley, R. M. & Gao, J. (2002). Correctional education programs serving incarcerated juveniles: A status report. *Journal of Correctional Education, 53*(4), 131–138.

Foley, R. M. (2001). Academic characteristics of incarcerated youth and correctional educational programs: A Literature Review. *Journal of Emotional and Behavioral Disorders, 9*(4), 248–259.

Frazier, C. E., Bishop, D. M., & Lanza-Kaduce, L. (1999). Get-tough juvenile justice reforms: The Florida experience. *Annals of the American Academy,* July, 167–184.

Fyfe, N. R. (1992). Observations on observations. *Journal of Geography in Higher Education, 16*(2).

Gehring, J. (2005). NCLB's mandates on delinquent youths get attention. *Education Week, 24*(43).

Gemignani, R. J. (1994). Juvenile correctional education: A time for change. Office of Juvenile Justice and Delinquency Prevention.

Gondles Jr., J. A. (2006). ACA speaks up for correctional staff and inmates alike. *Corrections Today,* August, 6.

Grietens, H. & Hellinckx, W. (2004). Evaluating effects of residential treatment for juvenile offenders by statistical metaanalysis: A review. *Aggression and Violent Behavior, 9*, 401–415.

Guttman, J. (2007). Reading to freedom. *California School Library Association Journal, 31*(1), 25–26.

Hardy, L. (2007). Children at risk. *American School Board Journal*, April, 35–41.

Harr, D. (1999). A plea from behind bars: Take a chance on education. *Social Policy*, 50–54.

Harris, P. J., Baltodano, H. M., Bal, A., Jolivette, K., & Malcahy, C. (2009). Reading achievement of incarcerated youth in three regions. *Journal of Correctional Education, 60*(2), 120–145.

Harris, P. J., Baltodano, H. M., Artiles, A. J., & Rutherford, R. B. (2006). Integration of culture in reading studies for youth in corrections: A literature review. *Education and Treatment of Children, 29*(4), 749–778.

Heckel, R. V. & Mandell, E. (1981). A factor analytic study of the demographic characteristics of incarcerated male and female juvenile offenders. *Journal of Clinical Psychology, 37*(2), 426–429.

Hellriegel, K. L. & Yates, J. R. (1997). *Collaboration between correctional and public school systems for juvenile offenders: A case study.* Chicago: American Educational Research Association.

Houchins, D. E., Puckett-Patterson, D., Crosby, S., Shippen, M. E., & Jolivette, K. (2009). Barriers and facilitators to providing incarcerated youth with a quality education. *Preventing School Failure, 53*(3), 159–166.

Holsinger, K. & Crowther, A. (2005). College course participation for incarcerated youth: Bringing restorative justice to life. *Journal of Criminal Justice Education, 16*(2), 328–339.

Jenkins, H. D. (1994). Mandatory education. *Journal of Correctional Education, 45*(1), 26–29.

Jenson, J. M. & Howard, M. O. (1998). Youth crime, public policy, and practice in the juvenile justice system: Recent trends and needed reforms. *Social Work, 43*(4), 324–334.

Juvenile Justice Educational Enhancement Program (2009). 2008–2009 Quality Assurance Report (Final).

Juvenile Justice Educational Enhancement Program (2009). 2008–2009 Annual Report to the Florida Department of Education.

Juvenile Justice Educational Enhancement Program (2005). 2005 Annual Report to the Florida Department of Education, *Chapter 5: Teacher Retention and Qualifications*, 81–98.

Juvenile Justice Educational Enhancement Program (2005). 2005 Annual Report to the Florida Department of Education, *Chapter 6: Incarcerated Delinquent Youths: Educational Deficiencies and Related Best Practices*, 99–116.

Kadish, T. E., Glaser, B. A., Calhoun, G. B., & Ginter, E. J. (2001). Identifying the developmental strengths of juvenile offenders: Assessing four life-skills dimensions. *Journal of Addictions and Offender Counseling*, April, 85–95.

Keeley, J. H. (2004). The metamorphosis of juvenile correctional education: Incidental conception to intentional inclusion. *Journal of Correctional Education, 55*(4), 277–295.

Keith, J. M. & McCray, A. D. (2002). Juvenile offenders with special needs: Critical issues and bleak outcomes. *Qualitative Studies in Education, 15*(6), 691–710.

Killian, E., Brown, R., & Evans, W. (2002). What incarcerated youth say would help them succeed: Can extension play a role? *Journal of Extension, 40*(4).

Krezmien, M. P. & Mulcahy, C. A. (2008). Literacy and delinquency: Current status of reading interventions with detained and incarcerated youth. *Reading and Writing Quarterly, 24,* 219–238.

Krisberg, B. & Patino, V. (2004). Juvenile justice in Florida: What kind of future? National Council on Crime and Delinquency.

Leone, P. E., Krezmien, M., Mason, L., & Meisel, S. M. (2005). Organizing and delivering empirically based literacy instruction to incarcerated youth. *Exceptionality, 13*(2), 89–102.

Linton, J. (2005). United States Department of Education Update. *Journal of Correctional Education, 56*(2), 90–95.

Leve, L. D. & Chamberlain, P. (2005). Association with delinquent peers: Intervention effects for youth in the juvenile justice system. *Journal of Abnormal Child Psychology, 33*(3), 339–347.

Lynch, M. (2012). Strategically allocating resources to support teaching and learning. *American Association of School Administrators Journal of Scholarship and Practice, 9*(1), 57–66.

Major, A. K., Chester, D. R., McEntire, R., Waldo, G. P., & Blomberg, T. G. (2002). Pre-, post-, and longitudinal evaluation of juvenile justice education. *Evaluation Review, 26*(3), 301–321.

Malmgren, K. W. & Leone, P. E. (2000). Effects of a short-term auxiliary reading program on the reading skills of incarcerated youth. *Education and Treatment of Children, 23*(3), 239–247.

Mathur, S. R., Griller Clark, H., & Schoenfeld, N. A. (2009). Professional development: A capacity-building model for juvenile correctional education systems. *Journal of Correctional Education, 60*(2), 164–185.

Maxwell, Joseph A. (2005). *Qualitative research design: An interactive approach.* California: Sage Publications.

Mazzotti, V. L. & Higgins, K. (2006). Public schools and the juvenile justice system: Facilitating relationships. *Intervention in School and Clinic, 41*(5), 295–301.

Mears, D. P. & Butts, J. A. (2008). Using performance monitoring to improve the accountability, operations, and effectiveness of juvenile justice. *Criminal Justice Policy Review, 19*(3), 264–284.

Mendel, R. A. (2001). Less cost, more safety: Guiding lights for reform in juvenile justice. American Youth Policy Forum, Washington, DC.

Mendel, R.A. (2011). No place for kids: The case for reducing juvenile incarceration. The Annie E. Casey Foundation, Baltimore, MD.

Mental Health Weekly. (2004). Florida judges incarcerating juveniles to gain access to needed MH services, *14*(3), 3–5.

Mincey, B., Maldonado, N., Lacey, C. H., & Thompson, S. D. (2008). Perceptions of successful graduates of juvenile residential programs: Reflections and suggestions for success. *Journal of Correctional Education, 59*(1), 8–31.

Moody, B., Kruse, G., Nagel, J., & Conlon, B. (2008). Career development project for incarcerated youth: Preparing for the future. *Journal of Correctional Education, 59*(3), 231–243.

Moreno, P. (2008). Incarcerated youths get a second chance with CTE. *Techniques,* February, 18–21.

Morrison, H. R. & Epps, B. D. (2002). Warehousing or rehabilitation? Public schooling in the juvenile justice system. *Journal of Negro Education, 71*(3), 218–232.

Norrbin, S. C., Rasmussen, D. W., & Von-Frank, D. M. (2004). Using civil representation to reduce delinquency among troubled youth. *Evaluation Review, 28*(3), 201–217.

Oesterreich, H. A. & McNie Flores, S. (2009). Learning to c: Visual arts education as strengths based practice in juvenile correctional facilities. *Journal of Correctional Education, 60*(2), 146–162.

O'Cummings, M., Bardack, S., & Gonsoulin, S. (2010). Issue brief: The importance of literacy for youth involved in the juvenile justice system. The national evaluation and technical assistance center. www.neglected-delinquent.org/nd/docs/literacy_brief_20100120.pdf

Office of Program Policy Analysis and Government Accountability, an office of the Florida Legislature. (2010). Youth entering the state's juvenile justice programs have substantial educational deficits; Available data is insufficient to assess learning gains of students, 1–16.

Ohio State Legislative Office of Education Oversight. (2002). Education Funding for Residential Facilities.

O'Rourke, T. (2003). Improving the odds for incarcerated youths. *Corrections Today*, February, 83–87.

Parsons Winokur, K., Li, S., & McEntire, R. (2002). Data integration in the evaluation of juvenile justice education. *Evaluation Review, 26*(3), 322–339.

Pasternack, R. & Martinez, K. (1996). Resiliency: What is it and how can correctional educational practices encourage its development? *Preventing School Failure, 40*(2), 63–66.

Piquero, A. R. & Steinberg, L. (2010). Public preferences for rehabilitation versus incarceration of juvenile offenders. *Journal of Criminal Justice, 38*, 1–6.

Platt, J. M. & Beech, M. (1994). The effectiveness of learning strategies in improving performance and increasing the independence of juvenile offenders with learning problems. *Journal of Correctional Education, 45*(1), 18–24.

Platt, J. S., Casey, R. E., & Faessel, R. T. (2006). The need for a paradigmatic change in juvenile correctional education. *Preventing School Failure, 51*(1), 31–38.

Portner, J. (1996). Jailed youths shortchanged on education. *Education Week*, October.

Portner, J. (1996). Supportive district, vigilant judge make for model. *Education Week*, October.

Puzzanchera, C., Adams, B., & Hockenberry, S. (2012). Juvenile court statistics 2009. National Center for Juvenile Justice, Pittsburgh, PA. www.ojjdp.gov/pubs/239114.pdf

Quinn, M. M., Rutherford, R. B., Leone, P. E., Osher, D. M., & Poirier, J. M. (2005). Youth with disabilities in juvenile corrections: A national survey. *Exceptional Children, 71*(3), 339–345.

Rabionet, S. E. (2011). How I learned to design and conduct semi-structured interviews: An ongoing and continuous journey. *The Qualitative Report, 16*(2), 563–566.

Read, N. W. (2006) A look at legislation: Common pre-post assessments. The National Evaluation and Technical Assistance Center. www.neglected-delinquent.org/nd/resources/spotlight/spotlight200604b.asp

Read, N. & O'Cummings, M. (2010). Fact sheet: Juvenile justice facilities. The National Evaluation and Technical Assistance Center. www.neglected-delinquent.org/nd/docs/factSheet_facilities.pdf

Read, N. W. & O'Cummings, M. (2011). Fact sheet: Juvenile justice education. The National Evaluation and Technical Assistance Center. www.neglecteddelinquent.org/nd/docs/NDFactSheet.pdf

Risler, E. & O'Rourke, T. (2009). Thinking exit at entry: Exploring outcomes of Georgia's juvenile justice educational programs. *Journal of Correctional Education, 60*(3), 225–239.

Rogers-Adkinson, D., Melloy, K., Stuart, S., Fletcher, L., & Rinaldi, C. (2008). Reading and written language competency of incarcerated youth. *Reading and Writing Quarterly, 24*, 197–218.

Roush, D. W. & Jones, M. A. (1996). Juvenile detention training: A status report. *Federal Probation, 60*(2), 54–61.

Roush, D. W. & Miesner, L. D. (2005). Good news about strategic planning in juvenile justice: The jurisdictional planning assistance. *Journal for Juvenile Justice Services, 20*(1), 25–32.

Roush, D. W. (1983). Counseling and juvenile justice education. *Personnel and Guidance Journal*, February, 368–369.

Rubie-Davies, C. M., Peterson, E., Irving, E., Widdowson, D., & Dixon, R. (2010). Expectations of achievement: Student, teacher and parent perceptions. *Research in Education*, May (83), 36–53.

Rutherford, R. B. & Nelson, C. M. (2005). Disability and involvement with the juvenile delinquency system: Knowing versus doing. *Exceptionality, 13*(2), 65–67.

Seidman, Irving. (2006). *Interviewing as qualitative research: A guide for researchers in education and the social sciences*. New York: Teachers College Press.

Sheridan, M. J. & Steele-Dadzie, T. E. (2005). Structure of intellect and learning style of incarcerated youth assessment: A means to providing a continuum of educational service in juvenile justice. *Journal of Correctional Education, 56*(4), 347–371.

Sickmund, M., Sladky, T. J., Kang, W., and Puzzanchera, C. (2013) Easy Access to the Census of Juveniles in Residential Placement. www.ojjdp.gov/ojstatbb/ezacjrp/

Small, M. A. (1997). Juvenile justice: Comments and trends. *Behavioral Sciences and the Law, 15*, 119–124.

Smith, K. B. (2004). The politics of punishment: Evaluating political explanations of incarceration rates. *Journal of Politics, 66*(3), 925–938.

Tam, K. Y., Heng, M. A., & Bullock, L. M. (2007). What provokes young people to get into trouble: Singapore stories. *Preventing School Failure, 51*(2), 13–17.

Todis, B., Bullis, M., Waintrup, M., Schultz, R., & D'Ambrosio, R. (2001). Overcoming the odds: Qualitative examination of resilience among formerly incarcerated adolescents. *Exceptional Children, 68*(1), 119–139.

Tonry, M. (1999). Why are U.S. incarceration rates so high? *Crime and Delinquency, 45*(4), 419–437.

Unruh, D., Povenmire-Kirk, T., & Yamamoto, S. (2009). Perceived barriers and protective factors of juvenile offenders on their developmental pathway to adulthood. *Journal of Correctional Education, 60*(3), 201–224.

U.S. Census Bureau. *Public Education Finances 2010.* http://www2.census.gov/govs/school/10f33pub.pdf

Vacca, J. S. (2008). Crime can be prevented if schools teach juvenile offenders to read. *Children and Youth Services Review, 30,* 1055–1062.

Ward, G. & Kupchik, A. (2005). Accountable to what? Professional orientation towards accountability-based juvenile justice. *Punishment and Society, 11*(1), 85–109.

White, C. (2002). Reclaiming incarcerated youths through education. *Corrections Today,* April, 174–178, 188.

Whitebread, C. & Heilman, J. (1988). An overview of the law of juvenile delinquency. *Behavioral Sciences and the Law, 6*(3), 285–305.

Wilder, S. (2004). Educating youthful offenders in a youth development center. *Journal of Addictions and Offender Counseling, 24,* 82–91.

Wilhite, K. & Cessna, K. K. (1996). Safeguarding the education of incarcerated juvenile offenders: The critical role of State Departments of Education. *Preventing School Failure, 40*(2), 56–59.

Wilson, J. J. (1994). Developing a partnership with juvenile corrections. *Corrections Today, 56*(2), 74–76.

Witmer, M. M. (2005). The fourth R in education—relationships. *The Clearing House,* May/June, 224–228.

Wolfinger, N. H. (2002). On writing fieldnotes: Collection strategies and background expectancies. *Qualitative Research, 2*(1), 85–95.

Wolford, B. I. (2000). Youth education in the juvenile justice system. *Corrections Today,* August, 128, 130.

Wolford, B. I. (2000). *Juvenile justice education: "Who is educating the youth?"* Richmond, KY: Eastern Kentucky University.

Yin, R. K. (2009). *Case study research: Design and methods.* Los Angeles, CA: Sage Publications.

Zabel, R. & Nigro, F. (2007). Occupational interests and aptitudes of juvenile offenders: Influence of special education and gender. *Journal of Correctional Education, 58*(4), 337–355.

Zehr, M. A. (2010). Academy engages incarcerated youths. *Education Week, 30*(11), 1–3.

Zhang, D., Barrett, D. E., Katsiyannis, A., & Yoon, M. (2011). Juvenile offenders with and without disabilities: Risks and patterns of recidivism. *Learning and Individual Differences, 21,* 12–18.

Index

CPSIA information can be obtained
at www.ICGtesting.com
Printed in the USA
LVOW10*0032080917
547996LV00013B/430/P